Kabba

---★---

Unveil Ancient Jewish Mysticism

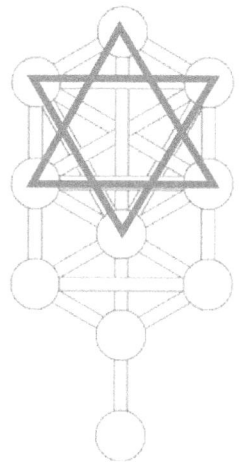

with Esoteric and Hermetic Keys
to Unleash Your Inner Power

TEMPLUM DIANAE
- MEDIA -

ÍNDEX

Work edited by: "Templum Dianae Media."
Illustrations and cover edited by: "Templum Dianae Media"
Layout and formatting by: "Templum Dianae Media"
Back page and introduction edited by: "Templum Dianae Media"

2025 - All Rights Reserved

Before you continue reading, the author and publisher explicitly request that you read and understand the legal notes to clarify some fundamental aspects of the relationship between the parties.

Legal notice:

this book is subject to exclusive copyright; reading it is intended for personal use only. Please also note that you are not permitted to modify or use any section of this book at all, either for free or for a fee; you are absolutely not permitted to use, quote or paraphrase any section or sections of this book or its contents without the written and signed consent of the author and/or publisher.

Legal note on author's and publisher's disclaimer:

The author and publisher affirm and reiterate that all information contained in this work, taken individually or as a whole, depending on the sensibilities of the individual reader or reader, may be for educational-educational purposes or mere pastime.

The author and publisher of this volume, while reminding all readers that no express or implied warranty is given, affirm and reiterate that all the information contained in this work, being derived from critical reading of various sources, possesses the highest degree of accuracy, reliability, topicality and completeness in relation to their ability to research, synthesize, process and organize information.

Readers are aware that the author is in no way obligated to provide any kind of legal, financial, medical, or professional assistance or advice, and indeed recommends that they, before attempting any of the techniques or actions set forth in this book, contact a legally licensed professional in accordance with current law.

By reading this introduction, each reader agrees, explicitly or implicitly, that in no event shall the author and/or publisher be liable for any loss, direct or indirect, resulting from the use of the information contained in this book, including, but not limited to, errors, omissions, or inaccuracies.

templumdianae.com

INDEX

Contents
- index 3
- To the curious and wayfarers 5
  - Journey Beyond the Veil 7
- kabbalah sacred seals 13
  - The last seal 16
  - Become "Baalei HaSod shel HaEtz" 19
- After the Garden: The Ordeal of the Fallen Soul 21
  - Love delusion 25
  - Social isolation 27
- The manifestation of Kabbalah 31
  - What is Kabbalah 35
    - esotericism in Kabbalah 37
    - Principles of Judaism 39
  - History of the Kabbalah 45
- Esotericism of Hermetic Kabbalah 49
  - Origins of Hermetic Qabalah 56
  - The tree of life 59
  - Adam qadmon 62
  - The sephirot and their meaning 65
    - 1 Keter (Crown) 67
    - 2 Chokmah (Wisdom) 68
    - 3 Binah (Understanding) 69
    - Daath 71
    - 4 Chesed (Mercy) 72
    - 5 Gevurah (Severity) 74
    - 6 Tiferet (Beauty) 75
    - 7 Netzach (Victory) 77
- 8 Hod (Glory) 78
- 9 Yesod (Foundation) 80
- 10 Malkuth (Kingdom) 82
- Angels, According to the Hermetic Qabalah 84
- 22 Paths of the Tree of Life 87
  - Keter to Chokmah (Aleph, א) 88
  - Keter to Binah (Beth, ב) 89
  - Chokmah to Binah (Gimel, ג) 91
  - Keter to Tiferet (Daleth, ד) 92
  - Chokmah to Chesed (Heh, ה) 94
  - Binah to Gevurah (Vav, ו) 95
  - Chesed to Gevurah (Zayin, ז) 97
  - Chesed to Tiferet (Chet, ח) 98
  - Gevurah to Tiferet (Tet, ט) 100
  - Chesed to Netzach (Yod, י) 101
  - Gevurah to Hod (Kaph, כ) 103
  - Tiferet to Netzach (Lamed, ל) . 104
  - Tiferet to Hod — Mem (מ) 106
  - Netzach to Yesod (Nun, נ) 107
  - Hod to Yesod (Samekh, ס) 109
  - Netzach to Malkuth (Ayin, ע) . 110
  - Hod to Malkuth (Peh, פ) 112
  - Yesod to Malkuth (Tzaddi, צ) . 114
  - Tiferet to Keter (Qoph, ק) 116
  - Chokmah to Tiferet (Resh, ר) .. 117
  - Binah to Tiferet (Shin, ש) 119
  - Keter to Malkuth (Tav, ת) 121
- Kabbalistic Correspondence Table: Hebrew Letters and Numbers 122

INDEX

- connections of the sephirot 128
- the 4 dimensions 131
  - About Enumeration and the Divine Architecture of the Worlds 134
- Angels, Astrology, and the Hidden Forces of Kabbalah 139
  - The angelic form 141
  - Kabbalah and astrology 144
  - Mother letters 148
  - immanence healing 150
- Ohr Ein Sof - Light Without End 153
  - Light Without End 156
  - Tzimtzum 158
  - Keilim and Ohrot Vessels of Lights 160
  - Ohr and Ma'Ohr 165
- Five Levels of Soul Worlds in Kabbalah 171
  - Nefesh 179
  - Ruach 181
  - Neshama 183
  - Chaya 185
  - Yechida 187
- The Sefer Ha-Zohar 189
- The Sefer Yetzirah 197
- Sefer ha Bahir 207
- Kabbalah in Practice 215
  - The Daily Rite 218
  - Kabbalah and numerology 221
    - Kabbalah, Chaldean Numerology and Chaos Magick 223
  - art of Kabbalistic sigilization 227
    - The golem sigil 229
  - forging kabbalistic amulets 231
  - Temple 233
  - Sacred robes 235
  - The act of creation 238
- Another book from Templum Dianae for you 244
- the book of testimony 245
- contents included 248
  - Bibliographical references 249

please read carefully

TO THE CURIOUS AND WAYFARERS

To the seeker drawn to hidden paths — welcome.
This is not an ordinary book. What you hold is a threshold — an invitation into a tradition as old as language, as complex as the soul, and as dangerous as any truth that dares to unsettle comfort.

It is not meant for those who seek easy answers, nor for those satisfied with surface meanings. The teachings and symbols you'll find here are not metaphors to be admired — they are tools. Precise. Demanding. Capable of undoing much of what you believe about yourself and the world.

You've been warned.

You are still free to set this book down, to leave the questions unanswered, and return to a life untouched by mystery. No harm in that. But if some part of you suspects that this knowledge might shift something at your core — reshape how you see, feel, act — then yes, that is a real possibility.

The mystical path doesn't offer comfort. It demands attention. It asks for clarity, silence, and sometimes, letting go of what no longer fits.

The Kabbalistic tradition is not a path of blind faith, but of conscious transformation.
It is not about adopting a new identity — it is about peeling away the layers that obscure what's already there.

And that process is not always gentle.

TO THE CURIOUS AND WAYFARERS

If you choose to go forward, know that you won't be reading passively. You'll be engaging with something alive—an ancient current that has passed through scholars, wanderers, sages, and questioners like you.

So make your decision now.
You can set the book aside—and nothing will change.
Or you can turn the page—and begin.

The choice is yours.

Journey Beyond the Veil

My name is Giovanni da Rupecisa, and before you turn the pages of this book, I wish to share something deeply personal with you. Please note that I am not some distant guru sitting atop an ivory tower of enlightenment. I am a fellow traveler, just like you—a seeker who has stumbled, fallen, and risen again, someone who has faced confusion, doubt, and despair, and who has found wisdom precisely because of those struggles.

My journey began in a community steeped in spirituality, one that was both comforting in its rituals and stifling in its dogma. From the earliest memories of my childhood, spirituality was never absent from my life—but nor was conflict. I grew up surrounded by extremes. On one side were rigid traditionalists, whose dogmatic beliefs suffocated all genuine curiosity and innovation; on the other side stood passionate fanatics, whose wild fervor made genuine spiritual inquiry seem reckless and dangerous. I felt torn between these polarities, forced to navigate between lifeless ritual and chaotic zealotry.

By my teenage years, I had grown restless and skeptical. Traditional religious paths felt restrictive, lacking the genuine depth and authenticity I craved. I knew I needed something more—a spirituality rooted not in unquestioning belief but in proper understanding and direct experience. Thus, I left behind the religious conventions of my youth and embarked on a solitary journey into the depths of mysticism, esotericism, and hermetic philosophy.

The journey was never easy. At the age of twenty, during my university years, my life spiraled into chaos. I struggled to maintain control of relationships, responsibilities, and even my sense of self. Night after night, sleepless and restless, I buried myself in ancient texts and obscure rituals, desperately seeking guidance from a spiritual dimension that felt so tantalizingly close yet so frustratingly elusive. I thought spiritual wisdom would grant me control—control over my life, over the chaos in my heart, and my destiny.

Seeking companionship on this journey, I distanced myself from old friends who could not understand my path, hoping to find people who resonated with my longing for spiritual growth. Yet, in my naïve enthusiasm, I encountered even greater darkness. Toxic personalities, deceptive mentors, and manipulative sects appeared along my path, each promising enlightenment while draining my energy and threatening to shatter my faith.

These experiences were harsh but invaluable lessons, teaching me discernment and resilience. Determined not to allow others to suffer as I had, I founded Templum Dianae as an online forum in 2013 — a haven for seekers, a place to discuss spirituality without dogma or fanaticism freely. It was humble yet profound, a small beacon amidst the darkness.

In 2017, recognizing the growing need for genuine, practical spiritual guidance, I significantly expanded the project, creating a dedicated website to share openly many of my private notes, reflections, and teachings. My writings found resonance even in esteemed esoteric circles, earning acknowledgment and respect from initiates and mystical societies — including respected branches of Freemasonry.

Yet, life always presents new trials. The global turmoil of 2020 deeply impacted me, dismantling nearly all the structures I had painstakingly built. My career, my financial stability, everything fell apart. But from that collapse arose clarity and a deeper purpose. I understood profoundly that true spirituality must translate into tangible, practical changes — real improvements in the quality of life. Rejecting the hollow and false platitudes preached by many spiritual traditions — particularly harmful clichés like "poor but dignified" — I committed myself more fully to spreading teachings aimed at manifesting love, wealth, abundance, and genuine happiness. This renewed vision marked the true beginning of my publishing journey. While working to expand it, I found myself unexpectedly drawn into the world of marketing — a realm I had once viewed with suspicion, often associating it with superficiality and manipulation.

But to my surprise, it became one of the most spiritually transformative stages of my life. Through learning how to communicate effectively, write with intention, and shape ideas clearly and boldly, I discovered powerful parallels with the mystical path. Marketing taught me the discipline of clarity, the art of effective communication, and the responsibility of guiding others with integrity. I realized that personal evolution does not happen in silence—it requires presence, voice, and vision.

The more I studied, the more I noticed a pattern: many people who had achieved extraordinary things—whether in spiritual work, healing, or creative mastery—shared a common everyday habit. They read constantly. They studied relentlessly. They worked daily on their mindset, their image, and their inner world. Success, I learned, whether spiritual or material, is not an accident. It is a discipline. And the mind, when trained and refined, becomes the sharpest tool on the path of awakening.

This revelation reshaped my mission. I understood, perhaps for the first time, that this publishing project was never just about me. It was for all those like me—for the seekers, the misfits, the rebels, the visionaries. For those who need a compass, a language, a fire. That's why I chose to go deeper, much deeper, into spiritual themes across every book I write and publish under the Templum Dianae name. These books are not meant to be read once and shelved. They are companions, maps, and catalysts.

So if this resonates with you… Keep going.
There's so much more waiting to be discovered.

I believed I had already faced my share of trials. But nothing could prepare me for what came next.

The most significant test of my life came unexpectedly on a quiet afternoon: May 10, 2025. At exactly 17:45, I suddenly lost consciousness. My breathing stopped. My heart ceased beating. For several moments, the line between life and death blurred completely. This was no mere fainting spell, nor was it a heart attack. Medical professionals remain baffled, unable to explain precisely what occurred. But for those precious moments, I was dead.

I awoke only the following day, forever changed by what I had witnessed beyond the veil. This near-death experience confirmed, with startling clarity, how we waste our lives obsessing over trivialities, trapped by fears, insecurities, and the shallow judgments of others. I learned that fear, especially of death, robs us of genuine living. More profoundly, I realized that many religions speak confidently about the afterlife without truly knowing what awaits beyond death's veil. But I was there. I saw. I experienced it, and I returned.

This revelation strengthened my resolve. In every book I write and publish, I pledge to offer not only ancient mystical keys but fragments of my journey — insights born from personal trials and profound spiritual revelations. My intention is not to preach or to command belief. My only desire is to guide you in reclaiming your power and control, to inspire you to break free from illusions, and to live fearlessly and abundantly.

I share my journey openly because I know your struggles and uncertainties intimately. I have felt them, battled them, and overcome them, step by painful step. Let my experiences illuminate your path. Let them assure you that your challenges are not unique and certainly not insurmountable.

Now, you are ready. Together, let us step forward into wisdom, clarity, and power.

So now, take a deep breath.
Turn the page.
What you seek has already begun to awaken.

To support you even further on this journey of growth and inner awakening, I've created a guided meditation — accompanied by deeply relaxing music — that you can download directly to your phone. It's designed to help you quiet the mind, reconnect with your breath, and open the inner space needed for true transformation.

Meditation is not a trend — it's a foundational practice for anyone serious about spiritual evolution. Through it, you'll begin to observe more clearly, respond more wisely, and feel more grounded in the face of chaos.

And there's more.

The day after you receive the meditation, you'll also get access to a complete video course designed for those new to the path. Not just a quick webinar or vague introduction, but a genuine initiation into the art of meditation—clear, practical, and transformative. You'll be able to begin your practice with guidance, structure, and purpose, so that the wisdom you find in these pages can truly take root within you.

Your journey is sacred. Let's deepen it—together.

templumdianae.com/en/bookmp3/

Follow the link above to get access to your guided meditation.

TO THE CURIOUS AND WAYFARERS

chapter 1

KABBALAH SACRED SEALS

There is something deceptive about the way the universe moves. At first glance, everything seems random. Events appear disconnected, people enter and exit your life without explanation, and the timing of your joys and sorrows often feels arbitrary — if not cruel. And yet, as you begin to look closer, patterns emerge. Hidden structures. Sacred rhythms. A divine architecture quietly shapes what seems chaotic.

Such is the world of Kabbalah.

It may appear, to the untrained eye, like a labyrinth of obscure symbols, cryptic Hebrew letters, and metaphors wrapped in riddles. But this system is far from chaotic. It is one of the most intricate and exact spiritual sciences humanity has ever known. Every letter, every name, every symbol within it aligns with deeper patterns of creation. Nothing is accidental. Not even your presence here, reading these pages.

Yes — **you, wayfarer, were meant to arrive here**.

You didn't stumble across this book by chance. Perhaps you felt a pull, a whisper, an unexplainable curiosity. Or maybe life's hardships carved a space in you, a hollow that no ordinary path could fill. Either way, something beyond logic has led you here. **This is not a coincidence. It is a calling.**

I speak to you not as a scholar, but as someone who has walked this road with wounds on my feet and fire in my lungs. You must know: my first attempts to dive into Jewish mysticism were not met with open arms. Despite having Jewish roots in my family line, I was met with resistance—sometimes from teachers, sometimes from circumstances, and, more often, from within myself.

Access to Kabbalah is not granted freely. It is earned.

That may sound harsh in a world where spiritual knowledge is marketed and repackaged for quick consumption. But the truth is: **there are guardians**—forces, angels, energies—that protect the deeper currents of Kabbalistic wisdom. These guardians do not respond solely to intellect. They do not open the gates for mere curiosity. They open for those who are ready. For those who have been tested by life. For those who have suffered, questioned, endured, and kept walking.

Kabbalah is not a path of comfort. It is a path of awakening.

I remember the first time I heard about the sacred seals. I was around twenty years old, speaking with a teacher I respected deeply. He told me something I've never forgotten: that **the actual keys to Kabbalistic understanding are not usually unlocked before a certain age**, often around thirty-three. At that age, he said, it marks a spiritual threshold in many traditions, echoing the symbolic age of death and resurrection, of maturity and mystical ripening.

He told me that even among those with knowledge, few are chosen to pass through these gates, **and even fewer are ready**. There is a difference between knowing about Kabbalah and knowing it. One can study for decades and still be denied the inner fire of it. Because it is not just about learning—it is about transformation.

Desire alone is not enough. Knowledge alone is not enough.

This made sense to me only much later. You see, the Kabbalist approaches the Tree of Life—not merely to admire it, but to *climb it*. And in doing so, one inevitably comes face to face with the knowledge of good and evil. That same knowledge that, according to the Genesis story, led to Adam's exile from Eden.

The Garden was not lost by mistake.
It was lost because humanity reached for something it was not yet ready to hold.

And so it is still.

Even the pure must be tested. Even the sincere must be challenged. **The sacred seals must not only be broken—they must be earned.** They test your heart, your will, your humility. They ask: Are you truly seeking wisdom—or merely power? Are you willing to be undone and remade?

If you're still reading this, I suspect you already know what I'm speaking of.
Because you've lived it.

You've faced trials—maybe silently, maybe without ever understanding their purpose. You've known pain, confusion, loss. You've questioned the world. You've asked yourself. And while others turned their backs, you kept searching.

You did not give up.
And that, more than anything else, is what has brought you here.

Perhaps your suffering was not punishment but preparation. Perhaps the betrayals, the endings, the restless nights were not meaningless— they were sacred initiations. Trials meant to hollow you out just enough for truth to enter.

You may not have recognized it before, but **you've been walking toward this moment for a long time**.

In the chapters that follow, we will begin to open the seals—carefully, reverently, and with the awareness that this path is not linear. It winds. It tests. But it transforms.

And if you choose to continue, you may begin to see how the puzzle pieces of your past-the wounds, the obsessions, the strange encounters-fit into a deeper cosmic design.

You were being led here, not by accident, but by initiation.

The seals are stirring.
And soon, so will you.

The last seal

When you reach the final gate, when the Last Seal trembles before you and the sacred letters begin to move under your skin like fire, a dangerous illusion may rise in your heart: the belief that the trials are over. That you've earned your access. That now the hidden knowledge belongs to you. That you are ready to wield what was once forbidden.

But nothing could be further from the truth.

The opening of the Last Seal is not the end of suffering. It is the beginning of a burden you may not be strong enough to carry. It is not a celebration — it is a reckoning. With great wisdom does not come peace, but responsibility, and with responsibility, the unrelenting gaze of the worlds above and below.

To access the Kabbalah is not merely to understand reality; it is to experience it. It is to stand before the machinery of creation itself and see how your thoughts, your words, your breath begin to shape the fabric of the universe. Every uttered vibration becomes a thread. Every name you speak becomes a seed. Every glyph you inscribe, no matter how small, sends ripples through the layered architecture of existence. And if you do not know what you are doing, or worse — if you believe you already know — you may create horrors beyond your comprehension.

Sound is not just a means of communication. It is the tool of creation.

Before the world was formed, there was vibration. And before vibration, there was silence. From that sacred silence came the resonance of divine names, the pulse of Ain Soph filtering through the ten vessels. The Hebrew letters, in their purest essence, are not just linguistic artifacts — they are frequencies. Codes. Energetic signatures that give form to the formless.

And when these sounds are sealed into sacred forms — into written glyphs, into amulets, into rituals — they become locked structures of force. These are not metaphors. This is not symbolic poetry. This is the true heart of Kabbalah.

But here lies the terror: what is created can escape you.

Power without direction becomes violence. Creation without containment becomes chaos. And intention without purification becomes a curse.

This is why no true Kabbalist ever walks alone.

Those who seek power without a master, without a lineage, without a guide to hold the mirror and measure their pride—those are the ones who fall fastest. Not because they are evil, but because they are blind. Driven by a hunger they mistake for destiny. They want secrets, not service. They want to command, not understand.

You may think you are ready.
You may think your suffering has earned you this right.
But Kabbalah cares nothing for what you think you deserve. It only responds to what you are.

The sacred path is not defended by human law, but by unseen forces. Angels who test without mercy. Symbols that awaken only when your heart is still enough to receive them. You cannot cheat your way past the seal. You cannot break it with intellect, or ambition, or desire.

And if you do, what you awaken may consume you.

Remember the story of the Golem.

A creature born of holy clay, inscribed with the Name of God across its forehead, animated by the sacred formula of life. It was made to serve. A guardian, a protector. But something went wrong—not because the ritual was flawed, but because the man who created it did not foresee what would happen when life was given without a soul.

Left unattended, the Golem continued to grow. It no longer listened. It no longer distinguished friend from enemy. It consumed, it destroyed, it wandered mindlessly through the streets, swelling in strength, no longer tethered to the purpose for which it was made.

And how was it stopped?

By removing the very letter that gave it life.
The seal. The same seal that had summoned its soul… also became the key to its death. This tale is not a relic of folklore. It is a warning.

You, too, will shape a Golem with your knowledge.
It may be an idea—a ritual.
A spell cast too early, or a sigil drawn in arrogance.
And when it begins to grow, when it feeds on your pride, when it no longer serves you but begins to feed on your life force—what will you do? Will you remember the seal?
Or will it be too late?

This is why the wise insist on guidance.
Not because they are gatekeepers, but because they know what you do not yet understand: that sacred knowledge in the hands of the impure becomes a curse.
That even noble seekers can become destroyers if they walk without a mirror. If you have come this far, ask yourself: why?

Is it love for the divine?
Or hunger for control?
Is it the longing to heal?
Or the desire to be greater than others?

Because the Last Seal will amplify what is in you.
It will not make you divine.
It will make you transparent.

And what lies beneath your skin—your shadow, your greed, your wounded ego—will be carved into the fabric of reality through every sound you release, every sigil you seal.

The seal not only opens the way forward.
It reveals what you are.
And once it opens, you cannot close it again.

The gate is before you.
And what comes next will not forgive illusions.

Become "Baalei HaSod shel HaEtz"
(Guardians of the Secret of the Tree)

To gain proper control over your life, not the illusion of control offered by wealth, praise, or fleeting security, but deep, spiritual sovereignty, you must become something the modern world has forgotten how to recognize. You must become a *Mekubal*—one who receives.

Not receiving like a collector, hoarding knowledge in dusty libraries, or quoting sacred names with hollow pride. But one who is *chosen* to receive because they have been emptied, tested, and reshaped. In Kabbalah, to receive is to be pierced by divine structure. To become a vessel wide enough, strong enough, still enough to hold the pattern of creation without shattering from it.

Becoming a *Mekubal* is not a title one claims; it is a title one earns. It is a state of being that emerges only after one has passed through the inner wilderness. The one who has wandered in confusion, who has wept before glyphs that would not reveal their meaning, who has prayed without reply, and yet continued. The one who has been burned by false teachings, who has crumbled under the weight of pride, who has seen how dangerous truth becomes in impure hands, and who has chosen, despite it all, to keep walking.

This is the way of the *Mekubal*: the silent path of the received soul.

But even a *Mekubal* does not walk alone. Whether visible or hidden, every true initiate is shaped by the whisper of a Master. Kabbalah is not learned—it is transmitted. And though the Masters come in many forms, their essence forms the architecture of your becoming.

Some are known as *Tzaddikim*—righteous ones who walk the path not only for themselves but for the world. They are pillars in human form, channels through which the divine flows without distortion. Their holiness is not always loud. It hums beneath the surface, in their restraint, in their timing, in their ability to hold contradiction without collapsing. A *Tzaddik* is not merely exemplary—they are aligned. Their thoughts, their words, and their actions become one continuous prayer. To walk in their footsteps is to learn the art of silent leadership, of unseen repair.

Then there are those known as *Baal HaKabbalah*, masters of Kabbalah itself. These are the keepers of the system, the ones who know the architecture of the Tree, the inner structure of the Sefirot, the resonance of names and letters. They do not teach with vague intuition, but with maps etched in fire. To follow such a master is to enter the sacred library of the divine blueprint and learn how to rebuild your soul, glyph by glyph, breath by breath. But beware—these are not safe teachers. They will not flatter you. They will not simplify. They demand that you dismantle your ego and offer your intellect as a sacrifice to wisdom.

And then, hidden even from most initiates, are the *Chachamim Nistarim*—the concealed sages. They walk unnoticed through cities and deserts, speaking little, but seeing much. Their power is not worn like a robe, but buried in the folds of ordinary life. To be touched by one of them is to have your world shift without knowing why. They operate in silence, guiding only those whom fate permits. If you ever meet one, you may not recognize them. But you will remember them forever.

These are not roles you can choose. They are archetypes that may awaken within you as you walk deeper into the labyrinth of Kabbalah. You may feel the fire of the Baal HaKabbalah rise in you when sacred texts unfold under your breath. You may be pulled toward the path of the Tzaddik when compassion becomes your only compass. Or you may find yourself drawn into stillness, vanishing from the world's gaze, as the hidden wisdom of the *Chacham Nistar* begins to speak from within.

To become a *Mekubal* is not to become someone else. It is to remember what you were always meant to be. It is to reclaim the parts of you that were broken not by fate, but by forgetting. And once the current of divine wisdom begins to flow through you, you will see the difference between controlling life and *aligning* with it. You will not bend the world to your will, but the world will begin to echo the shape of your awakened presence. The Tree is alive. The seals are stirring. The Masters are watching.

And if you are reading this, perhaps one of them has already begun to whisper through you.

Chapter 2

AFTER THE GARDEN: THE ORDEAL OF THE FALLEN SOUL

What brought you here?

Was it heartbreak? Betrayal? The suffocating silence that followed the collapse of everything you once believed would last? Perhaps it was the crushing weight of failure, the cold erosion of your dreams, the steady decay of your confidence until nothing remained but the shadow of the person you were meant to be.

You might pretend you don't know. You might tell yourself it was curiosity. Or chance. Or some abstract longing for meaning. But you know the truth. And though you may not say it aloud, you feel it. Gnawing and pulling and tearing at the edges of your soul.

You lost control of your life.

Not because fate was cruel or others more powerful, but because somewhere along the way, you allowed it. You surrendered. You handed over your will, one quiet compromise at a time, until it no longer belonged to you. You gave your power to lovers who didn't love you, to fears you refused to face, to systems that devoured your energy and returned nothing but emptiness.

Think back. How many times did you choose what was easy instead of what was right? How many moments did you silence your inner voice because it threatened the comfort of the lie you were living? How many promises did you make to yourself that you broke before the day even ended?

You told yourself you'd fix it, that you'd change. That you'd wait for the right moment. But the right moment never came. And now you find yourself here, holding this book, hoping for something—anything—that might undo the damage.

Let me be clear: it won't.

There is no saving grace written between these lines. No comforting god is waiting to forgive you. What lies ahead is not healing in the way you imagine it, not the sweet, soft balm of spiritual self-help. What lies ahead is exposure. Confrontation. Fire.

The moment you opened this book, you made a decision. You may not remember making the choice, but it was made nonetheless. You entered into a covenant with truth—absolute truth, not the watered-down poison sold by modern mystics who promise light without shadow. You agreed to stand before the Tree of Life not as an observer, but as one who seeks to climb it, step by trembling step.

But before you can ascend, you must face what drove you to fall.

You were cast out of the Garden long ago. Not by wrath. Not by punishment. But by consequence. Like Adam, you reached for knowledge before you were ready to bear its weight. You consumed what was sacred without reverence. You tried to command before you learned to serve. And so the gates closed behind you.

The exile you live in now is not just spiritual—it is internal. A fracture between what you are and what you were created to become. A life spent wandering through emotional ruins, searching for meaning in broken systems and hollow relationships, all while pretending to be in control.

But you're not in control. You haven't been for a long time.

And whose fault is that?

Don't look at your parents. Don't look at your lovers, or the world, or the gods, who feel betrayed by you. Look inward. Look brutally, unflinchingly inward. You let it happen. You gave your soul away in pieces. You made yourself small, then blamed the world for not seeing you.

That knot in your stomach? That heaviness in your chest? That's the weight of your own choices pressing back against you.

No one is coming to rescue you.

The sacred forces do not chase cowards. The angels do not drag the lazy into enlightenment. The gates of understanding do not open for those who need sympathy. They open for those who are willing to be destroyed and remade.

You seek Kabbalah because you want power. But have you earned it?

You think divine knowledge will give you control, but you forget that it is not a tool. It is a mirror. And it will reveal things about yourself that you have spent your entire life avoiding.

The sacred Names are not decorations. The Hebrew letters are not magical toys. The structure of the Tree is not a map to success—it is a labyrinth that requires you to get lost, to descend into the dark before you can climb. Power, when drawn from the Source, does not tolerate impurity. It burns through the ego like acid. It calls you out on every lie you've ever told yourself.

That is the price.

And still, you may believe that you can take these teachings and remain unchanged. That you can master the wisdom of the Mekubalim and keep your broken self intact. But you cannot. The Kabbalistic fire will not allow it.

The old stories tell of a creature formed from sacred knowledge—a Golem, made of earth and Word. Brought to life by divine letters etched upon its flesh, it was a servant of purpose. But when left without direction, without the hand of the master, it did not sleep. It grew. Mindless, monstrous, unstoppable. It began to consume what it was made to protect.

Only when the Name was removed — when the sacred glyph was altered — did it fall silent once more.

You are no different. You are a living vessel. What you do with the Name inscribed upon your spirit will determine whether you rise in harmony or collapse under the weight of misused force.

You wanted control? Now you must earn it.
You wanted power? Now you must cleanse yourself to receive it.

You are not here to be comforted. You are here to be torn apart and rebuilt. And if you cannot face that — if you would rather cling to your excuses and your numb distractions — close this book now. Return to the Garden of Forgetting and stay there. It will not miss you. But if something in you still burns — if even a flicker of will remains — then take this as your exile's final gift. The pain, the failures, the losses — they were never the end. They were the beginning. The moment you stopped pretending.

Now, the work begins.

The question is not whether Kabbalah will reveal its secrets to you. The question is whether you are willing to pay the price for them. Will you?

Love delusion

What remains of the idea of love you once carried so faithfully?

Do you still whisper to yourself that it was real, that it was sacred, that the person to whom you entrusted your heart truly deserved it? Perhaps you believed your love was noble, selfless, even divinely guided. You gave everything—time, loyalty, devotion—telling yourself it was an offering, something holy.

But as every serious student of the Kabbalah eventually learns, not everything that feels intense is sacred. Not everything that hurts is a lesson sent by the Divine. And not everyone who receives our love is capable of holding it without breaking us in return.

You remember, don't you, the first time something inside you recoiled? The way their words, perhaps even spoken softly, left behind doubt about your worth, your place, your value. You sensed something was off. But you rationalized it. "They didn't mean it." "They're just wounded." "Love is about patience." You made yourself smaller in the name of something you called spiritual.

This is not judgment. It is a reminder.

Many who walk the Kabbalistic path arrive here with wounds that bleed invisibly. Betrayals dressed as relationships. Delusions dressed as destiny. And while Kabbalah teaches union, balance, and sacred polarity, it also teaches discernment. The *Binah*, the understanding, is not complete without *Gevurah*, the boundary.

And yet, you stayed. In the name of forgiveness. Of hope. Of fear. Fear of being alone. Fear of shame. Fear of admitting the story was never what you told yourself it was.

But the deeper question is this: why is this relevant to Kabbalah?

Because you cannot build an actual vessel—*a kli*—when your energy is still bound to a false structure.
Because the Tree of Life cannot flow through you when your roots are still tangled in fantasy.

Because every aspect of your soul is mapped within the *Sefirot*, and love, misguided, idealized, abused, is one of the most potent energies to distort that map.

Some teachings — especially in rigid schools or among self-proclaimed gurus — will tell you to starve love altogether. To abstain. To purify through isolation. But understand this: many who speak of asceticism do so not out of holiness, but out of fear or control. They mistake suppression for mastery. They teach detachment as if it were a form of clarity. But love is not the problem. The delusion is.

The information in this book will not reflect the institutional consensus. Nor will it comfort your ego. This is a different current — an older, deeper one. Here, you are not asked to reject love, but to cleanse it. To face it as it is. To admit where you gave away your energy in the name of a dream, and to see how that dream broke you not because you were too much — but because you asked too little of what love should be.

Yes, it isn't easy to admit. The tears you cried alone, the silence you endured, the parts of yourself you gave away hoping to be seen, to be chosen. The shame that curls in your stomach when you think of how much of your life you built around someone who could not, or would not, meet you.

But this chapter is not meant to leave you in grief. It is intended to awaken something higher.

Because you cannot climb the Tree with stones tied to your ankles. You cannot chant divine Names when your mouth still trembles with the lies you whispered to yourself. You cannot activate true love until you stop offering your heart as a sacrifice for validation.

Let yourself feel what you feel. The sorrow. The anger. The quiet disappointment in yourself. It is not weakness. It is reckoning. And it is necessary.

Only by facing it — patiently — can you begin to reclaim the energy you poured into others. Energy that must now return to its rightful place: your becoming.

Social isolation

You've felt it, haven't you?

That sharp, quiet ache when the people you once trusted turned away from you—the so-called friends, the familiar colleagues, those who smiled in your presence but quietly sharpened their judgment behind closed doors. Perhaps it wasn't a dramatic betrayal. Maybe it was subtler: being left out, being diminished, being tolerated rather than seen.

You've likely replayed those moments in your mind. Searching. Questioning. Asking yourself, *What did I do wrong?* But perhaps that's not the right question. Maybe the question is: *Why did I need their acceptance so badly to begin with?*

For many, the spiritual path begins with a hunger for belonging. We long to be seen, to be affirmed, to be folded into something greater. But when that longing becomes dependence, we lose the very foundation that Kabbalah demands we build—our *kelim*, our vessels, our spiritual autonomy.

You shaped yourself to fit into their expectations. You softened your voice. You edited your thoughts. You laughed when something inside you recoiled, to maintain a sense of peace that wasn't peace at all. You traded authenticity for survival. And in doing so, you abandoned something sacred: your inner spark, your *Ner Elohim*—the light of the soul.

But let us be clear: this isn't about condemnation. This is about *recognition*. About *rectification*.

Kabbalah teaches that isolation is not always a curse. Sometimes, it is an initiation. The mystics often walked alone. Not because they lacked the capacity to love or be loved, but because the clarity they embodied separated them from the illusions most people call life. When you choose to walk the path of inner elevation, you will disturb the sleep of others. And many will resent you for it.

Yet today, too many spiritual guides exploit this truth. They promise closeness to the Divine only through artificial poverty, emotional suppression, or the denial of healthy desire. They shame independence. They praise compliance. They confuse humility with invisibility. And in doing so, they create disciples who are spiritually docile but internally broken.

True Kabbalah does not ask you to abandon yourself to the group. It asks you to *remember* yourself in the face of disapproval. It does not teach conformity. It teaches integration.

The information you find in this book may unsettle those trained to think spirituality is self-denial. That's because it doesn't follow the blueprint of control. It doesn't reward smallness. It rewards awakening. And sometimes, awakening looks like walking away. You saw the signs. You knew when their affection was conditional. Their acceptance was offered only if you performed the version of yourself they preferred. But instead of turning inward, you turned down your light. You hoped they would change. You thought that love — or friendship, or spiritual kinship — meant silence. Compliance. Endurance.

But now here you are, perhaps alone, perhaps misunderstood. And you may be tempted to believe that this isolation is proof of failure. It is not.

It is the clearing of a space where truth can finally speak.

You betrayed yourself not because you were weak, but because you believed that approval could fill the silence of your soul. You thought that blending in would protect you. But the Sefirot do not flow through masks. The Divine Light does not pass through false agreements. *Shefa* — the spiritual abundance of creation — requires that the vessel be *honest*, not acceptable.

This is not an invitation to arrogance. It is a call to spiritual dignity.

Let the isolation teach you. Let it show you the places where you traded your voice for comfort, where you trained others to treat you as expendable by treating yourself as optional. This pain is not your enemy. It is your teacher. It is the birth pangs of sovereignty. You don't need to become harsh. But you do need to become clear.

You are not here to fit in. You are here to align with the living structure of reality. And that will not always make you popular. The Tree of Life does not grow in crowds. It grows in silence, in wilderness, in the quiet spaces where only you and the Divine walk together.

This is your turning point. Not just away from false alliances, but toward true *devekut*—attachment to what is real, sacred, and unwavering within you.

Let them walk away. Let them misunderstand you. Let them accuse you of being too much, too intense, too distant. It doesn't matter anymore. You are not their reflection. You are the echo of the Ineffable. You were not born to chase inclusion. You were born to reveal light.

And light, once known, does not beg to be accepted. It simply shines.

So if you feel alone, take comfort in this: the mystics were always alone before they were understood.

This is not exile. This is the beginning of revelation.

AFTER THE GARDEN: THE ORDEAL OF THE FALLEN SOUL

Chapter 3

THE MANIFESTATION OF KABBALAH

The previous chapters were not intended to be taught in the traditional sense. They were designed to confront you — to reflect your journey, your wounds, your losses, your unanswered questions. They may have felt like stories, accusations, or mirrors that were difficult to face. But that was intentional. Because **no one truly arrives at Kabbalah by accident**.

You were called, drawn through heartbreak, restlessness, spiritual hunger, and disillusionment. Perhaps you were betrayed by a lover, silenced by the world, or quietly burned out by an existence that felt too small for your soul. These are not diversions from the path — they *are* the path. **There is no authentic Kabbalah without personal initiation through life itself**. Without those cracks in your being, the light we are about to study could never penetrate.

Now the real work begins.

From this moment forward, Kabbalah will no longer be something distant or abstract. It will begin to manifest. Not as a theory. Not as doctrine. But as *presence* — in your thoughts, in your decisions, in the structure of your relationships, and in the silence between your breaths. It will appear in patterns you never noticed, in feelings that rise unprovoked, in dreams, in symbols, and in your capacity to see through the illusion of separation.

Kabbalah is not just Jewish mysticism. It is a living architecture of reality. A sacred language that explains the connection between man and the Divine, between the visible and the infinite. It is a map of how the universe expands and contracts, how it shatters and repairs, and how the human soul fits into that eternal dynamic.

The Jewish people have preserved this map for generations—not as a relic, but as a living, breathing framework through which one understands not only God (*Ein Sof*, the Boundless) but also what it means to be human. Through the prism of the *Sephirot*, the divine attributes, the unknowable becomes partially knowable. The infinite becomes graspable in fragments. And we, **as vessels**, begin to reclaim our role in that divine unfolding.

For centuries, **Kabbalists have explored these mysteries**, seeking not to define God in static terms but to perceive the dynamic *relationship* between the human heart and the Infinite Source. And yet, despite its beauty, its depth, and its sacred lineage, **Kabbalah has often been misunderstood**.

Some believe it is reserved for an elite few. That one must be born into it, initiated formally, or reach a certain age or level of piety. And while these structures have value, they are not *truths*—they are *traditions*. **Kabbalah does not belong to gatekeepers**. It belongs to the sincere. To those who have *suffered*, *questioned*, *sought*, and *survived*.

Let me tell you something that may surprise you: Kabbalah contains two kinds of secrets.

There are the secrets that lose their power once revealed—*illusions* dressed as mysteries. These are the veils that, once lifted, indicate that there was never anything behind them at all. They fade, they flatten, they vanish.

But then there are the **true secrets**—those that do not hide, but instead wait patiently to be *recognized*. They are in plain sight, always present, but only visible to eyes that have been trained to see, and to hearts that have been broken open enough to receive. These secrets do not dissolve when studied. They *deepen*. They expand. **The more you approach them, the more they reveal**, and in doing so, they begin to **illuminate the structure of your entire life**.

These are the real teachings of Kabbalah—and as you will see, they are not so secret after all. They've been here, waiting, within you, all along.

Unfortunately, the modern world has not been kind to this tradition. Some reduce it to superstition, marketing gimmicks, or new-age slogans. Others attack it with conspiratorial nonsense, accusing Kabbalists of dark rituals and immoral secrets. But let this be clear: **Kabbalah is not a cult of control. It is a path of restoration**. It is not about suppressing desire or idolizing suffering, as some false teachers would have you believe.

Beware of those who preach poverty as purity, who demand self-denial as virtue, or who surround themselves with followers who remain disempowered. They do not serve the Tree. They serve themselves. *True* Kabbalah does not ask you to become small—it asks you to become **transparent**, aligned, and fully alive.

What you will encounter in this book is **not a conventional path**. These teachings do not conform to systems built to domesticate your soul. They do not reinforce hierarchy. They are not here to *control* you. They are here to **awaken** you.

So, whether you are a seeker lost among spiritual trends, a reader new to Jewish mysticism, or a seasoned student returning for deeper layers, this is where Kabbalah begins to *live*, not as a concept in your mind, but as a vibration in your bones.

You may be asking yourself: *Am I ready?*
Let me tell you: **you already began the moment life broke you open.**

From here onward, we will explore the origins of Kabbalah, the structure of the Sephirot, the hidden meanings of Hebrew letters, the divine Names, the forces that flow through creation, and the path of the soul's return.

However, remember that **this is not just a study. This is transformation.**

To walk the path of Kabbalah is not to read and memorize—it is to *experience*. To practice. To *see* with new eyes and act with new purpose.

And the more you allow these teachings into your daily awareness — into the *moment-to-moment stillness* of your life — the more they will shape your reality.

Right now, as you are, **you are already capable of becoming a Kabbalist.**

You do not need permission. You need intention.
You do not need perfection. You need presence.

And if you make this a living practice — not a once-a-week ritual, but a constant inner alignment — **you will never go back**. Not because someone told you not to, but because you will have *seen* too much, *tasted* too much, *become* too much to ever return to a life of unknowing.

So now, let us step forward.

The light has already begun to move.

What is Kabbalah

Kabbalah is not merely an esoteric branch of Judaism. It is not an optional layer, nor a mystical curiosity for the spiritually adventurous. It is — **in its essence** — the heart of Jewish spiritual consciousness. It is the ongoing dialogue between the human soul and the Infinite, the attempt of the finite to receive, interpret, and embody what cannot be fully grasped. To engage with Kabbalah is to step into the ancient and unbroken current of Jewish theology as it wrestles with the most profound questions of existence.

At its root, **Kabbalah is about connection**: the connection between **God and Creation**, between **soul and Source**, between **the visible world and the unseen structure behind it**. It does not ask abstract questions for the sake of philosophy. It seeks real, lived answers to real, aching human questions. What is the nature of the soul? Why do we suffer? What happens after death? What is evil, and why does it exist in a world shaped by a benevolent Creator? What does it truly mean to be spiritual in a world where God often feels hidden?

These are not academic concerns. These are **existential riddles**, the kind you carry in your chest when grief strikes, when injustice rises, or when you sit in the quiet stillness of your own heart and ask, *What am I? And why am I here?*

Kabbalah dares to answer.

Though many people speak of it as "Jewish mysticism," this label is, at best, incomplete. The Jewish tradition itself never developed a native concept of "mysticism" as it is understood in the Western Christian framework. There is no direct Hebrew equivalent. What others have called mysticism, Judaism has always called **sod**, *secret*, or **kabbalah**, *receiving*. It is not about becoming ethereal or otherworldly. It is about becoming *fully human* — informed by the Divine blueprint, aligned with the inner structure of Creation, and awake to one's place in the cosmic unfolding.

The word **Kabbalah** comes from the Hebrew root k–b–l, which means **"to receive."** But this is not passive reception. It is not waiting for something to descend from above like a gift wrapped in silence. It is a kind of *reception that requires preparation* — the shaping of the vessel to hold what is sacred. In this way, Kabbalah is not just about knowledge. It is about **transformation**. One does not merely study the teachings — one becomes them. They must pass through the hands, the breath, the decisions, the prayers, and the relationships of the student. Only then can the soul truly "receive" what it was meant to hold.

Another dimension of the word **Kabbalah** refers to **"received tradition"**. This points to its transmission — **teacher to student, generation to generation** — as something entrusted, protected, and carried. Like a flame passed from one oil lamp to another, the light never extinguished, only multiplied. You may notice variations in how specific prayers are recited, how rituals are observed, and how symbols are interpreted. These differences are not contradictions — they are the fingerprints of the *kabbalot* (individual receptions) of each soul that has entered the stream. *Your version, too, is your Kabbalah.*

You cannot reduce this tradition to a single book or formula. **Kabbalah is not a text — it is a way of perceiving**. Yes, it is found throughout the sacred Jewish writings: in the **Zohar**, in the teachings of the **Ari (Isaac Luria)**, in the prayers of the **Baal Shem Tov**, in the metaphysical inquiries of the **Ramban**. But its life does not remain confined to parchment. It breathes in every act of alignment, every moment of sacred attention. *It lives when a mother lights Shabbat candles with kavanah. It stirs when a mourner chants Kaddish with trembling lips. It reveals itself when a wanderer, unsure and afraid, still reaches for the light.*

Over the centuries, misunderstanding has clouded its reputation. Some have associated Kabbalah with dangerous power, occultism, or conspiracy. Others, even within Jewish communities, have relegated it to a niche practice for scholars and mystics alone. But this is not the way of the true Kabbalist. **Kabbalah was never meant to be locked away**. It was meant to be guarded — *yes*, from those who would abuse it-but never hoarded. The gates were always open to those with sincere hearts, rigorous minds, and a soul forged by life's trials.

It is also important to speak plainly: many **false teachers** have emerged, using half-truths and spiritual jargon to manipulate others.

They teach a distorted version of Kabbalah that glorifies poverty, dependency, or rigid abstinence, convincing their students that to suffer is holy and to desire is corrupt. This is not Kabbalah. **Kabbalah does not demand your submission—it requires your awakening.** It does not glorify lack—it teaches you how to become a vessel worthy of **abundance**, not just of wealth, but of purpose, insight, and divine energy.

You may find what is written in this book **contrary to what you've heard**, even from those claiming spiritual authority. That's no accident. This path is not for those who want to conform. It is for those who want to remember what they are.

So what, then, is Kabbalah?

It is not mysticism.
It is not magic.
It is not exclusive.
It is not new.

Kabbalah is Jewish theology in its purest form.

It is the sacred attempt, in every generation, to describe the Infinite. To live in relationship with the One who cannot be named and yet *reveals Himself through structure, breath, symbol, and silence.* It is the tradition that says: *yes, we are small, but we were made in the image of something vast*—and it is through the study of that image that we become who we were meant to be.

You don't need to be born into a particular family, or speak Hebrew fluently, or live like a saint to begin. You only need to start. **And once you do, you will realize that the structure of the world has always been waiting to show itself to you.**

Esotericism in Kabbalah

The Torah and the Kabbalah exist in a sacred dance between that which is revealed and that which remains hidden. Like the **sun and its rays**, the Torah offers both the form and the fire—**structure and spirit, law and light, letter and mystery**. The Torah gives us that which is spoken aloud, chanted, studied, written in scrolls and texts across centuries. But the Kabbalah — *the inner Torah, the soul of the word* — **moves in shadows**, flickers behind the veil, **and reveals itself only to those who are ready to** *receive.*

The Hebrew letters themselves, the building blocks of the sacred language, are not mere symbols. **They are vessels — containers of compressed light.** Each letter, each stroke, is a holy shell housing divine fire. *Think of them like seeds — so small in appearance, yet holding inside the blueprint of entire forests.* The **Aleph**, for instance, with its silent breath, contains the paradox of unity and division. The **Shin**, with its three branches, burns with the energy of divine transformation. And yet, for all their potency, **these letters are limited.** They are finite forms attempting to reflect the **infinite luminosity of the Divine Will.**

And herein lies the paradox of Kabbalah: **the more it tries to reveal itself, the more it must hide.** Because true Kabbalistic wisdom is not something you *study* — it is something you *receive.* **It cannot be taught like history, language, or science.** It must be transmitted soul-to-soul, flame-to-flame. **It is accepted in silence, in humility, in surrender.** You must open yourself like an empty cup, and allow the light to pour into you, slowly, drop by drop, *sometimes painfully, often incomprehensibly*, until something *within* begins to burn.

You cannot capture Kabbalah with reason alone. You cannot imprison it within concepts, dogmas, or rigid traditions. You must *see with the heart,* and *listen with your soul.* You must become like a vessel yourself — broken, perhaps, but open. The mysteries that the Kabbalah holds cannot be accessed through logic or memory. **They are perceived through inner sight** — the eyes behind your eyes, the hearing behind your ears.

And so the tradition insists: **Kabbalah is not acquired. It is** *transmitted.* The sacred light flows through a lineage of souls — each master pouring into the next, like wine from a cup overflowing. Rabbi to student, father to son, mother to daughter, soul to soul. **This is not learning. This is receiving.** And what is received is not information — it is transformation. It is not data — it is a **direct encounter with the Divine.**

This is why the Kabbalistic tradition has always warned against those who attempt to grasp its secrets through study alone. Without a guide, without a *true teacher*, without having purified the self, **you risk chasing shadows, not light.** You may memorize the verses of the Zohar, the diagrams of the Tree of Life, the names of the Sephirot—and yet remain spiritually blind. *To study the Kabbalah without receiving it is like trying to taste honey by reading the word "sweet."*

Rabbi Shimon bar Yochai, the great mystic and disciple of Rabbi Akiva, was the first to be **entrusted with unveiling these mysteries in written form.** Until then, they had been preserved only orally, whispered in the hidden chambers of the soul. But a cosmic rupture changed everything. The **destruction of the Second Temple** marked not only a physical loss—it represented a **collapse in the conduit of Divine Light** that once flowed freely into the world. While the Temple stood, the light of the Shekhinah—**the Divine Presence**—rested among the people. But when it fell, that light receded. The world grew darker. The veil grew thicker. **And the soul of humanity became hungrier.**

It was in this moment of spiritual exile that Rabbi Shimon received **permission from the Heavenly Court**, as the tradition says, to commit these esoteric teachings to writing. **The Zohar was born not as a book, but as a *lifeline*.** It was an act of mercy, of spiritual preservation. What once could be lived through direct revelation in the Temple's radiance, now had to be traced in symbols and parables. *The inner Torah had to be concealed inside the outer Torah, like a flame tucked inside the wick of a candle.*

And so, the Zohar came into the world—not as explanation, but as **invitation**. Not to inform, but to **awaken**. It does not speak in clear answers, but in riddles, paradoxes, and flames. **It speaks to the part of you that remembers Eden.** And if you read it not with the mind, but with the soul, **something ancient within you will stir.**

Principles of Judaism
Judaism affirms, with unwavering clarity, that there is only *one* God. Not a pantheon, not a division, not a spectrum of deities with competing wills—but **One**: absolute, indivisible, beyond form, beyond time, and human comprehension. **The foundation of all Jewish

thought, practice, and spiritual aspiration is the Oneness of the Divine. This is not a metaphor or a poetic ideal—it is a central, lived reality. And it is from this truth that the entire structure of Jewish life flows: the commandments, the rituals, the study, the struggles, and the yearning.

This **Oneness**, called in Hebrew **"Echad,"** is the heart of the Shema, the most sacred declaration in Jewish prayer: *"Hear, O Israel, the Lord is our God, the Lord is One."* This isn't just theology—it is **a radical call to consciousness**. It reminds the practitioner that everything—joy and pain, light and shadow, past and future—is held together by a single, unified Source. *Nothing is truly separate; all is part of the unfolding Will of the One.*

In this framework, **obedience to the Divine Will** is not about blind submission but about *alignment*. The mitzvot—**the Divine commandments**—are not burdensome laws but **tools for spiritual refinement**. Each mitzvah (commandment) is a key, a code, a precise mechanism designed to tune the soul to the frequency of the Divine. Even the most seemingly mundane actions—lighting a candle, eating with blessing, resting on Shabbat—are infused with the potential to awaken holiness. **The Kabbalist sees the mitzvot not as mere rules, but as channels of light.** By fulfilling them, the practitioner draws spiritual energy into the world and repairs the hidden fractures within creation.

Struggle is not weakness. Judaism never expected perfection. It expects engagement. The true honor we offer to God is not in never falling, but in continuing the inner battle—to wake, to remember, to return. *Even the wrestling with doubt is holy.* The name Israel itself, **Yisra'el**, means "one who wrestles with God." We are not passive believers, but seekers, fighters, wanderers on the path—fallible and yet beloved.

One of the most influential spiritual and philosophical authorities in Jewish history, **Rabbi Moshe ben Maimon**, better known as the **Rambam** or **Maimonides**, sought to distill the essence of Jewish belief into a structured form. He drew directly from the Torah and centuries of commentary to formulate what he called the **Shlosha Asar**

Ikkarim—the **Thirteen Fundamental Principles of Faith**. These were not abstract speculations, but essential truths that every soul aspiring to align with the Divine should internalize deeply.

The first principle affirms **the existence of the Creator**, perfect in every attribute, and the singular origin of all that exists. There is **no other cause**, no second source, no competing power. The second principle states that **God is One**, not just numerically one, but **unified** in essence, thought, and will. *No duality, no fragmentation, no anthropomorphic projection can apply.*

The third declares that **God is incorporeal. No body, no shape, no location, no movement.** God is not "in the sky" or "in a temple," but **everywhere and nowhere**, transcending the limitations of form while sustaining all forms. The fourth insists that **God is eternal**, without beginning or end. Time itself is a creation; the Creator exists beyond its reach.

The fifth confirms that **God alone is worthy of worship**. No intermediaries. **No idols, no saints, no spirits, no celestial bureaucracy.** The worship of anything other than the One is a distortion of the truth. The sixth principle establishes that **God speaks to humankind**, not solely through deduction or philosophy, but through **prophecy**. That is, direct communication received by souls who have been purified and elevated.

The seventh places **Moses** above all other prophets, not in dignity or worth, but in **clarity and completeness** of the message. Moses perceived God "face to face," as no other did.

The eighth affirms the **Divine origin of the Torah**. It is not an artificial document, but a transmission of truth from the Infinite through Moses to the people.

The ninth declares that **the Torah is eternal and immutable**. No generation has the authority to erase or replace it. Its meaning may unfold, but **its core remains untouched**.

The tenth principle acknowledges that **God knows all things**—past, present, and future. **Nothing is hidden.** Not a thought, not a whisper, not a secret longing. The eleventh assures that **there is reward and retribution.** *Not always in the ways we expect, not in this lifetime — but justice is real and divine.*

The twelfth affirms the coming of the **Messiah** — a faithful redeemer, a guide and restorer who will usher in an era of clarity, peace, and union with the Divine.

The thirteenth concludes with the **resurrection of the dead**, not as an allegory, but as a real and future event. Life will return to those who have passed, as a sign of the eternal soul and the ultimate triumph of life over death.

These thirteen principles are not dogma. They are **pillars**, spiritual coordinates that guide the soul through the vast sea of existence. When internalized, they become a compass pointing back to **the One**.

Yet, Kabbalah adds a deeper layer to all this. While the Rambam's principles define what must be believed, the **Kabbalist seeks to** *experience* **what is thought to be.** Not just to know that God is One, but to feel that Oneness in every breath, every struggle, every tear. Not just to affirm that the soul survives death, but to glimpse immortality through study, prayer, and inner transformation.

This is not philosophy. This is fire.

The Divine cannot be reduced to a system, but these principles are like stars in the night sky — points of light that guide the wanderer through the dark. And **the Kabbalist is, above all, a wanderer** — one who walks the path not with answers, but with awe. **Mysticism is not merely a branch of spiritual study — it is the root from which all true understanding blossoms.** It is the intimate, unmediated union with the Divine, an act of inward surrender that dissolves the illusion of separation between self and God. To speak of mysticism is to talk about a fire that does not consume, a voice that does not speak in words, and a light that blinds the eyes but illuminates the soul. **Mystical consciousness is not fantasy or delusion — it is an altered perception so real it feels more vivid than waking life.** It pierces the veils of ordinary awareness and reveals the interconnected, vibrating network of Being that underlies all things. When a person enters this state —

whether in deep prayer, meditation, study, or ecstatic joy — they touch what Jewish mystics call *Devekut*: **cleaving to the Divine.**

Through this state, one gains **insight not as information, but as transformation**. The veil is lifted, and what is hidden becomes known — not in the mind, but in the heart, the body, the breath. *A Kabbalist does not read sacred texts merely to understand — they read to awaken*. Each letter is a portal. Each silence between words is a key.

But mysticism, in its ancient and purest sense, is far more than a personal journey. In **Judaism**, it becomes a cosmic responsibility. **Your quest to know God and to understand your relationship to God is not a pastime — it is a command.** It is the very reason your soul descended into flesh. This is your *prime mystical quest*: to know, through lived experience, not only that God exists, but that **you are never separate from the Divine**. That every thought, every step, every sorrow, and every ecstasy is a communication from the Infinite to the finite. And yet, for centuries, this path was reserved for the very few. For those born into scholarly dynasties, fluent in Hebrew and Aramaic, versed in the coded language of the Zohar and Sefer Yetzirah. **Kabbalah was a fortress. And mysticism, a guarded flame.** Until a man arrived.

Around the year 1700, in the forests and fields of what is now Ukraine, a revolution began to take root. **His name was Israel ben Eliezer**, though history would remember him simply as **Baal Shem Tov** — the Master of the Good Name. He was not a rabbi of dusty books and rigid rituals. He was a healer, a visionary, a storyteller. **He did not ascend the mountain of mysticism to build walls — he came down from it to light torches. Hasidism — Hasidic Judaism — was his offering.** It was born not from ivory towers but from village kitchens, forest trails, and taverns. It was the mysticism of the people, **a sacred path that did not require scholarly credentials but only a burning heart**. And through it, the Divine was made accessible to milkmaids and shepherds, to beggars and blacksmiths, to children and grandmothers.

Hasidism is not about studying mysticism. It is about *living* it.

Where once the mystic had to climb toward God through rigorous asceticism and decades of study, **Hasidism taught that God is *already* *present* in the here and now — *in your breath, your laughter, your dancing, your brokenness.* God is with you in your hunger, your grief, your longing, your doubt. *Even your confusion is a form of prayer, if you offer it honestly.*

The Baal Shem Tov taught that the simplest prayer said with sincerity pierces through worlds more effectively than complex incantations spoken without feeling. He welcomed miracles and visions not as rare gifts but as part of daily life. And he infused Jewish folklore with stories of Divine encounters, of hidden tzaddikim (righteous ones), of travelers unknowingly guided by angels. *The world, in his eyes, was not profane — it was filled with sparks waiting to be lifted back to their Source.*

Hasidic prayer is not quiet or rigid — it is a dance. A cry. A love song. A storm. The Hasidim diverged from the formal, Ashkenazi patterns of worship, and in their services, you will find **chant, repetition, melody, movement, and tears**. They drew from both Ashkenazi and Sephardic traditions, crafting a unique spiritual expression that **bridged heaven and earth, intellect and emotion, structure and spontaneity.** To the Hasidic Jew, **every blade of grass whispers the Name of God**, and every hardship is an opportunity to serve the Divine with joy. Even suffering becomes holy if offered as an act of love.

Mysticism, in this light, is no longer the privilege of the elite — it is the inheritance of all. Baal Shem Tov shattered the illusion that God is hidden behind thick walls of doctrine. Instead, he taught that **God hides in plain sight**, waiting for eyes of wonder to see and hearts of fire to respond. And so, *what began as a movement for the forgotten masses became a renaissance of spirit* — one that continues to echo through the mountains of Tzfat, the synagogues of Jerusalem, the streets of Brooklyn, and the soul of every wanderer who longs to come home to the Divine.

This is the mysticism that endures. This is Hasidism. Not a footnote in history, but a living flame — waiting to be touched.

History of the Kabbalah

According to ancient Jewish tradition, the **Torah**—the divine blueprint of the universe—was not conceived *after* creation, but rather **974 generations before the world itself was formed**. This astonishing teaching, whispered through the ages and preserved in the Zohar, tells us: *"God looked into the Torah and created the world."* What does this mean? It means that the **world was not made first and then sanctified**. Instead, it was born out of holiness. **Creation itself is Kabbalistic**, for it is the *unfolding of divine thought into time, space, and form*.

Kabbalah, therefore, has no beginning. And yet, its threads can be traced through the history of sacred time, woven into the lives of the significant figures of Jewish revelation. These threads wind their way through **Adam**, **Abraham**, and **Moses**—each a vessel for divine transmission, each a facet of the great prism of light we now call Kabbalah.

Adam, the first human, was also **the first Kabbalist**. According to tradition, he was not simply placed in Eden to till the soil and name the animals. **He was entrusted with divine secrets**, received from an angel, inscribed into a primordial book of wisdom. Every letter in the **book of Genesis** carries sacred weight. *Nothing is arbitrary. Nothing is ornamental.* Each glyph, each sentence, is a **living symbol** reflecting the inner landscape of the soul and the architecture of Creation. When Adam was divided into male and female—two bodies, one soul—it was not only the origin of human love. It was the revelation that *unity is born of polarity*, that **wholeness arises when opposites harmonize**, and that marriage-in *body, in soul, in spirit*—is a microcosm of the divine.

The Garden itself was a map of Kabbalah. The Tree of Life and the Tree of Knowledge of Good and Evil were not just plants—they were living metaphors for the tension between spiritual expansion and contraction, between **da'at** (knowledge) and **chesed** (grace). To the Kabbalist, these are not just ancient images—they are **internal forces** we must learn to recognize, balance, and master. And Adam's legacy? It lives on in us. According to Kabbalistic teaching, **each soul is a spark**

of **Adam HaRishon**, the primordial Adam. We are not just his children—we are *his continuation*.

Abraham, the father of nations, is revered not simply for his covenant with God, but for his ability to perceive the oneness behind multiplicity. He shattered idols—*not just literal ones, but the idols of separation, duality, and fear*. In Kabbalah, **Abraham embodies chesed**: the expansive love that reaches outward, welcoming the stranger, the seeker, the broken. Abraham is also attributed with the authorship of **Sefer Yetzirah**, the Book of Formation, one of the most profound and foundational texts in Kabbalah. In it are encoded the secrets of **creation through sound**, through **letters**, and **the balance of elemental forces**.

Moses, the greatest of the prophets, represents not just revelation, but *integration*. At Mount Sinai, he did not merely receive commandments—he received the entire scaffolding of **Divine Intelligence**.

The oral tradition he transmitted would contain the keys to the mystical inner dimensions of the Torah. And yet, even he was humbled by the depth of what would unfold. According to a striking story in the Talmud, Moses, upon seeing divine letters he could not understand, asked God for clarity. He was transported forward in time, where he sat in the classroom of **Rabbi Akiva**, unable to grasp the master's teachings. And when a student asked Akiva where the teachings came from, the rabbi answered: *"They were given to Moses at Sinai."* **This paradox is the heart of Kabbalah**—*it is timeless, yet constantly unfolding anew*.

Rabbi Akiva, the spiritual titan of the Rabbinic era, plunged into the mysteries others dared not enter. He could grasp the esoteric with ease, and he lived with such devotion that his very *martyrdom became a Kabbalistic act*. As the Romans tortured him, peeling flesh from bone, he taught one final lesson: *"To love God with all your soul"* means even when *your soul is leaving your body*. His final breath—*"Echad"* (One)—was not just a word. **It was the collapse of multiplicity into Unity.**

Rabbi Shimon bar Yochai, Akiva's disciple, would go on to compose the **Zohar**, hidden in a cave for 13 years with his son, beyond the reach of the Roman Empire. In the silence and the darkness, **visions descended like fire**. The Zohar is not a book of doctrine—it is a *living, breathing commentary* on the Torah that **unveils the architecture of the Divine Light**. It reveals the Sephirot not just as abstract concepts, but **realms of consciousness**, lenses through which the Ein Sof—the Infinite—becomes accessible.

When the Zohar was finally revealed to the world in the 13th century by **Moses de Leon**, the transmission reignited the flame. Alongside the **Torah** and the **Talmud**, it became the third pillar of spiritual understanding. The world would never be the same.

Centuries later, as the Jewish people faced exile, loss, and persecution, the flame of Kabbalah refused to go out. **Tzfat**, in the hills of the Holy Land, became a beacon. There, mystics such as **Rabbi Isaac Luria (the Ari)** redefined the entire landscape of Kabbalah. He taught of **Tzimtzum**—the primordial contraction of God to make space for creation—and of **Shevirat HaKelim**, the shattering of vessels, which left divine sparks scattered throughout the world. **To live, according to the Ari, is to gather these sparks** through intention, prayer, and conscious action—to repair the world, one act at a time.

Then came darkness again. In the 17th century, **pogroms swept across Eastern Europe**, tearing communities apart. And once again, Kabbalah rose like a phoenix.

Rabbi Israel ben Eliezer, the Baal Shem Tov, emerged not as a scholar but as a *storyteller*. He brought the fire of mysticism into the hearts of simple people, teaching that *God dwells not in heaven alone, but in the laughter of children, in the tears of the poor, in the breath of the shepherd*. His teachings, preserved by **Rabbi Yaakov Yosef of Polnoye**, would ignite **Hasidism**—a movement rooted in Kabbalah but characterized by **joy, love, and immanence**.

Yet not all welcomed this light. In modern times, **historians—some even Jewish—sought to downplay Kabbalah**, reducing it to superstition or marginal folklore. Seduced by scientism and historical materialism, they failed to see what mystics have always known:

Kabbalah is not peripheral — it is the soul of the Torah. Without it, the text becomes brittle, lifeless. With it, the letters burn.

This book stands as a torch in that lineage. It seeks not only to **restore the dignity of Kabbalah** but to **unveil its living essence. Kabbalah is not history — it is happening.** Not in the past, but *now*. Not only through sages in caves and scholars in Tzfat, but through *you* — the seeker reading these words, the soul waking from sleep, the spark returning to the fire.

Chapter 4

ESOTERICISM OF HERMETIC KABBALAH

Kabbalah Ma'asit, or *Practical Kabbalah*, represents one of the most obscure and delicate threads woven into the tapestry of Jewish mystical tradition. Unlike **Kabbalah Iyunit**, the *contemplative path* that seeks to deepen one's understanding of **God's nature** through meditation, inner purification, and intellectual pursuit, Kabbalah Ma'asit is concerned with **direct interaction with spiritual forces** — an interface with the unseen realms intended not just for wisdom, but for influence as well.

This is not superstition. It is not folklore. It is the attempt — rare, dangerous, and traditionally restricted — to **manipulate the energetic structures of reality through sacred names, symbols, and invocations**. Practitioners of Kabbalah Ma'asit engage in what one might broadly call **white magic**, but this term hardly conveys the profound responsibility such work entails. It is a **disciplined and sanctified science**, reserved only for those few whose souls have been tempered by years of study, *self-discipline*, and **spiritual accountability**.

At the heart of this practice lies the **knowledge of divine and angelic names**, encoded within Hebrew letters, used in *amulets*, *incantations*, and *ritual formulas*. These names are not arbitrary; each is a container of force, a vessel holding the vibration of a higher realm. The practitioner, to wield them properly, must **not only know how to pronounce or inscribe them**, but must also be capable of holding the energy they unleash. *To mispronounce a divine name without proper kavvanah – spiritual intention – can unravel more than just the ritual.* It can dislocate harmony.

What makes Kabbalah Ma'asit so perilous is the **thin, often invisible veil that separates the forces of Light from those of impurity**. These impure realms are known as the **Qliphoth,** or *Kelipot,* which translates to "shells" or "husks." These are not mere metaphors for sin or spiritual distraction—they are real, **energetic structures**, anti-emanations, *spiritual decay mimicking spiritual truth.* The Qliphoth stand as the **inverse of the Sefirot,** the ten divine emanations through which **God manifests** and sustains all realities. Where the Sefirot channel divine order, the Qliphoth generate chaos. They are seductive because they often mirror the forms of holiness, *but with inverted intention.*

The reason **Practical Kabbalah is largely forbidden,** even among most schools of traditional Jewish learning, is precisely because of this danger. One may enter a ritual seeking healing or clarity, only to emerge spiritually contaminated, having opened a door to something one **cannot command or close**. The Kelipot are opportunists. They **feed on arrogance, confusion, unworthiness, and ambition disguised as devotion**. And those who seek magical power without profound humility and alignment with the Divine Will **risk invoking them instead of the angels they thought they were calling**.

The early sages knew this well. The Talmud and the Kabbalistic texts mention the use of amulets and incantations, and some of the most respected mystics of history—including Rabbi Isaac Luria—are said to have **practiced Kabbalah Ma'asit only under extreme conditions**, such as healing the sick or confronting spiritual threats. But they did so with extreme caution, and only after **decades of training under holy men who had themselves received permission**.

What distinguishes **authentic Kabbalah Ma'asit** from its dangerous imitations is **the source of power and the intention behind its use**. In true white magic, the practitioner does not seek to dominate reality, but to **align it with divine order**. They act not from ego, but as a vessel. They do not "command" angels like sorcerers in grimoires—they *petition, invoke, cooperate.*

There's a reason why so many of these teachings remained hidden for centuries. Even today, most Kabbalists regard Practical Kabbalah as a **closed gate**, not because it holds no value, but because it holds **too much power**, power that **can destroy the soul if mishandled**.

Those who are drawn to it often come from a place of pain or desire. *A mother seeking to save her child, a mystic longing for a vision, a wanderer hoping to escape poverty.* These are understandable desires. But the sages teach: **the desire to bend the world must always be tempered by the willingness to be broken by it**. The mystic who reaches too fast, too far, will fall not into darkness but into *illusion*, which is worse.

This is why **Kabbalah Iyunit is held in higher esteem**, for it teaches that knowledge without purity is poison. The contemplative path *disciplines the soul before it approaches the fire*. It does not shun the mysteries, but prepares the heart so that when the mysteries arrive, they do not consume.

And yet, for those few who have been truly initiated—not by books or rituals, but by years of transformation and purification—**Kabbalah Ma'asit becomes a sacred responsibility**. *To heal, to protect, to restore order where chaos has taken root.* It is not a tool. It is a burden. And only those who walk with angels are permitted to lift it.

Now we turn to the path of Hermetic Qabalah—and you may already notice the difference begins with the very spelling. While *Kabbalah* refers to the ancient Jewish mystical tradition rooted in the Torah, the spelling *Qabalah* (with a "Q") usually denotes a Western esoteric reinterpretation of those teachings, often far removed from the original Hebraic context. This shift in spelling is not trivial. It signifies a **departure from lineage and Law**, and a step into a **magical framework where eclecticism and personal transformation replace covenant and commandment**.

Hermetic Qabalah is the child of syncretism. It draws from Jewish Kabbalah, yes—but also from **Neoplatonism, Gnosticism, Alchemy, Pagan ritualism, and Western astrology**. It emerged in Renaissance Europe, when translated Hebrew manuscripts began to circulate among Christian mystics and scholars. These early seekers—some sincere, others opportunistic—began adapting the Tree of Life, the Sefirot, and the Hebrew divine names into **a completely different spiritual language**, one that sought not to serve God through mitzvot, but to **unlock hidden powers** and **access divine realities** through personal will and symbolic systems.

By the 19th and early 20th century, Hermetic Qabalah had been further codified into **ritual orders**, most famously the *Hermetic Order of the Golden Dawn*, which combined Rosicrucianism, ceremonial magic, tarot, angelology, and astrology into a complex and often secretive initiatory system. It was not a religion, but a magical path, one that viewed spiritual ascent as an *alchemical process* of the self. Later, **Thelemic orders**, inspired by the teachings of *Aleister Crowley*, would adopt and further adapt these structures, emphasizing individual will, sexual magic, and the idea of a new aeon ruled by liberated consciousness.

The Tree of Life, in Hermetic Qabalah, is no longer just **a mystical map of God's emanations**, but becomes **a diagram of the soul's inner journey** through archetypes, planetary forces, and magical correspondences. Each sphere (Sephirah) is linked to an **archangel, a planet, a color, a sound, a path**, and each of the 22 connecting paths corresponds to the **22 Major Arcana of the Tarot**. In this model, the initiate climbs the Tree through **rituals, visualizations, and invocations**, ascending from Malkuth (the material world) toward Keter (divine unity), not by divine election but by **gnostic effort**.

What sets this apart from Jewish Kabbalah is not only its **non-Jewish origin**, but its **goal**. In traditional Kabbalah, the mystic's goal is *devekut*—a clinging to God, a union of the soul with the Divine Will through humility, study, and observance of the commandments. In Hermetic Qabalah, the goal is often described as **personal enlightenment**, *theosis*, or **magical empowerment**. The focus shifts from God as Other to God as **latent within the self**, to be awakened and wielded.

Some practitioners of the Hermetic Qabalah demonstrate a deep reverence for the original Jewish sources. Others strip the symbols from their context entirely, using Hebrew letters, angels, and divine names in ways that would be **unrecognizable or even blasphemous** to a traditional Jewish mystic. *For example, the holy name YHVH may be chanted in magical circles alongside invocations to Greek gods, planetary spirits, or elemental forces.* This blend, while potent in its own right, marks a **philosophical and spiritual divergence** that cannot be ignored.

Yet it must be acknowledged that **Hermetic Qabalah has had a massive influence on the modern esoteric revival**. It shaped the modern Tarot. It informed the rituals of Wicca. It colored the magical practices of chaos magicians and New Age mystics. Its symbolic language permeates Western occult literature, often more familiar to modern seekers than the rabbinic Hebrew texts from which it initially drew.

But one must be careful. The **power of symbols** does not lie in their surface use, but in the **depth of alignment with the worldviews they emerge from**. To chant Hebrew without understanding its sanctity is not empowerment—it is noise. To draw the Tree of Life without understanding its roots in the Torah is to climb **a ladder with missing rungs**.

In essence, **Hermetic Qabalah is a mirror**—a system that reflects the soul to itself, layered in myth, magic, and metaphor. But unlike Jewish Kabbalah, it does not require a covenant. It does not require moral law or communal tradition. It offers **power to the individual**, but *not always the wisdom to wield it.*

That is not to say one path is right and the other wrong—but they are **not the same**, and those who walk them must choose: **to serve the Light that descends from the heavens**, or to ignite the fire from within and rise toward it on wings of will.

The Divinity of the Hermetic Qabalah is not a theology of separation but of **unification**. In its view, there is no fixed boundary between the Divine and the human, no **chasm between Creator and Creation**, no exile from Eden that cannot be reversed. Instead, it teaches that **the universe itself is a layered expression of the Divine**, and that the soul of man is a microcosm of the macrocosm—a reflection of the infinite encoded within the finite.

Everything that exists, whether material or immaterial, spiritual or mundane, is believed to have unfolded from a **single, limitless source**—the **Ein Sof**, or **Infinite**. This is not a "god" in a personal or anthropomorphic sense, but rather **an unknowable, boundless essence**, beyond all form, category, or comprehension. Yet from this ungraspable Void emerges **manifestation**, through a delicate chain of emanation that preserves the source even as it diversifies its expression.

The Hermetic Qabalah borrows this schema of emanation from Jewish Kabbalah, particularly the Lurianic tradition, but recasts it within a more **cosmological and magical** framework. At the heart of this cosmology are **three veils of negative existence**—three states that precede all form and act as the very **seed of all becoming**:

The first veil is **Ain** (*Nothing*). This is **pure nullity**, a state beyond thought, beyond being, beyond existence. Ain is not emptiness in the sense of a void that lacks substance—it is **non-being itself**, a state before creation, *beyond even the concept of light*. It is the moment *before the moment*, the silence *before sound*, the **darkness that is not the absence of light but the womb of all potential**.

From Ain emerges **Ain Soph** (*Limitless*). This is **infinity**—not yet form, not yet light, but the **infinite potential for both**. It is the undivided sea of all that could be, a field of boundless possibility that holds **no distinction**, no boundary, no name. Ain Soph is where the potential of Divinity begins to stir, not through thought or action, but **through the tension of pure being**.

And then, from Ain Soph, there arises **Ain Soph Aur** (*Limitless Light*). This is the **first movement—the primal radiation of Divinity into existence**. It is not yet creation, but it is the **urge to create**. It is Light that longs to become form, that yearns to unfold into space, time, and soul. Ain Soph Aur is **the breath before the Word**, the golden fire that sets the Tree of Life aglow.

These three veils are not discarded as the universe is born; they remain **behind, above, and within** every layer of existence. They are the *hidden spine* of the Hermetic Tree of Life—*not seen, not named, but deeply felt by the initiated who dares to rise beyond the Sefirot*.

From the veil of Ain Soph Aur emerges the **first Sefirah, Kether**—the Crown, the primal spark, the point at which Infinity becomes singularity, and from that singularity the entire Tree of Life unfurls. Yet even Kether is still **close to the Veils**, still trembling with the intensity of the Light from which it emerged.

Thus, in Hermetic Qabalah, **Divinity is not a distant architect**, but the **very fabric and fire of reality**. The human being is not a passive servant but a **latent god**, veiled by ignorance and ego. The purpose of Qabalistic study and practice is not simply to worship the Divine, but to **remember that you are it**, that *your soul descends from Ain Soph Aur just as surely as the stars do.*

This is why the Hermetic initiate does not beg, but *invokes*; does not believe, but *experiences*; does not serve, but *unites*. The rituals, meditations, and pathworkings of Hermetic Qabalah are not acts of reverence—they are **acts of becoming**. Each path on the Tree, each symbol, each letter, is a key to unlock the Divine **within the self**.

For example, when the adept contemplates the three veils, they are not just exploring an abstract cosmology—they are retracing the path of their soul, peeling back the layers of illusion that make them forget that they are **nothing and everything at once**.

To understand Ain is to embrace silence.
To touch Ain Soph is to dissolve boundaries.
To radiate Ain Soph Aur is to become Light.

And this is the hidden truth at the heart of Hermetic Qabalah: **you are not separate from the Divine—you are the Divine awakening to itself.**

Origins of Hermetic Qabalah

According to **traditional Jewish sources, Kabbalah originates from the heart of the Jewish faith, intricately interwoven with the revealed and concealed aspects of the** Torah. However, through centuries of contact, reinterpretation, and philosophical cross-pollination, this sacred stream of mysticism began to evolve and fragment, giving rise to what is now known as the **Hermetic Qabalah**. This tradition, spelled with a "Q" to distinguish it from its Judaic counterpart, emerged from the fertile soil of the **Western esoteric tradition**, blending Jewish mystical thought with elements of **Neoplatonism, classical Greek philosophy, astrology, and Hermeticism**. Some contemporary scholars suggest that the **Medieval Kabbalah** preserved by Jewish mystics may be a refracted echo of **older Gnostic traditions**, possibly predating even the rabbinic codification. Others argue that external philosophies heavily influenced it during the time of **Medieval Jewish Neoplatonism**, wherein mystics and philosophers alike sought to harmonize divine revelation with rational metaphysics. And yet, from the perspective of Hermetic practitioners, the **true Qabalah** — despite its Hebrew etymology — is not Semitic in origin, but rather **Indo-European**, tracing its ancestry to the **mystery religions of ancient Greece**, filtered through the lens of Hellenistic syncretism and Renaissance magic. The **Renaissance** proved to be the crucible in which Jewish mysticism was transmuted into a Western esoteric framework. It was during this period that **Giovanni Pico della Mirandola**, a Christian philosopher and prodigy of syncretism, sought to unify disparate traditions — **Aristotelianism, Neoplatonism, Hermeticism, and Kabbalah** — into a single, divine mosaic. He believed that within the cryptic structure of the Jewish Kabbalah lay hidden **universal truths** that transcended religious boundaries. Under his influence, and through the foundational work of thinkers such as Heinrich Cornelius Agrippa, Jewish mysticism became a crucial pillar of **Christian esotericism**. Agrippa's *Three Books of Occult Philosophy* fused the **practical magic of the Hermetic arts** with the **symbolic cosmology of Kabbalistic thought**, birthing a new genre of **ritual magic** that would come to define the Western occult imagination. This trend continued with the **Jesuit polymath Athanasius Kircher**, who further developed the synthesis, incorporating **Egyptian mythology, Orphic hymns, and Chaldean cosmology** into the Qabalistic schema. His vision of the Qabalah was not confined to theology or philosophy, but embraced the **universal language of symbols**, seeking to decode the **divine architecture of the cosmos** itself. However, as the **Age of Enlightenment** swept across Europe, rationalism began to suffocate mysticism. The exoteric branches of the **Christian Cabala** withered under the pressure of **empirical science and philosophical skepticism**. Still, the **Hermetic Qabalah**—being inherently **esoteric and initiatory**—retreated underground, surviving in the **secret lodges and mystery schools** of the Freemasons, the Rosicrucians, and other occult brotherhoods. Here, far from the eyes of institutional religion and academic critique, the **flame of mystical knowledge** was preserved, **passed down through initiation and ritual**, encrypted within symbolic language and sacred geometry.

In the **19th century**, the pendulum of history swung once again. With the rise of **Romanticism**, interest in the occult resurged. Mysticism, long suppressed, returned with vigor—now armed with the **language of psychology, the structure of science, and the aesthetic of symbolism**. One pivotal work in this revival was *The Magus* by **Francis Barrett**, a compendium of ceremonial magic that, although published in 1801, would become explosive once it fell into the hands of **Eliphas Levi**. It was Levi who **rekindled the magical flame** in Hermetic Qabalah. He not only associated the **22 Hebrew letters** with the **Tarot's Major Arcana**, but also emphasized the **dual polarity of divine and infernal forces**—what some call *white and black magic*. He unified Jewish, Christian, Egyptian, and pagan elements into a cohesive esoteric philosophy, making **Qabalism synonymous with ceremonial magic**. His influence rippled through the **Hermetic Order of the Golden Dawn**, a secret society that became the epicenter of Western occultism in the late 19th and early 20th centuries.

Aleister Crowley, perhaps the most controversial and influential occultist of the modern era, was initiated into the Golden Dawn before founding his systems, such as **Thelema** and the **A∴A∴**. Crowley believed himself to be the reincarnation of Eliphas Levi. In his magnum opus *Liber 777*, he provided an extensive table of correspondences between the **Sephirot, planetary spirits, deities from various pantheons, colors, precious stones,** and **ritual tools.** *For instance, the sephirah of Chesed corresponds not only to Jupiter, but also to Isis, Brahma, Poseidon, the color blue, and the gemstone amethyst.* This **panentheistic worldview,** where **everything emanates from the One,** is a hallmark of Hermetic Qabalistic thought. From the ashes of the Golden Dawn arose new orders and teachings. **Israel Regardie,** a former member and secretary of Crowley, would later publish many of the order's rituals and teachings, preserving the **Golden Dawn's legacy** for future generations. His writings are among the most detailed expositions of **ritual magic, Kabbalistic visualization,** and **psychospiritual alchemy.**

Another torchbearer was **Dion Fortune,** whose *Mystical Qabalah* remains a foundational text. She saw the Tree of Life not only as a map of divine emanation, but as a **blueprint of the human psyche,** a guide for **inner transmutation.** Her school, the **Fraternity of the Inner Light,** would continue this path of **spiritual psychology,** emphasizing the Qabalah as a tool for **mystical experience and psychological integration.**

Paul Foster Case, founder of **Builders of the Adytum,** adapted the Golden Dawn's teachings into a more **accessible system,** combining **occult tarot, esoteric astrology,** and **Qabalistic meditation** into a **comprehensive path of spiritual development.** His student **Ann Davies** would later expand these teachings, ensuring the continuity of the Qabalistic current into the modern age. Other contributors include **Pat Zalewski,** a student in the Golden Dawn lineage, whose writings delve deep into the **technical structure and inner workings** of the Qabalah, and **Samael Aun Weor,** whose syncretic teachings blend Kabbalah with **Tibetan, Aztec, Egyptian, and Gnostic traditions,** offering a **universal initiatory map** of the soul's journey through the Tarot and the Tree of Life. Thus, the **Hermetic Qabalah** stands today not as a relic of ancient mysticism, but as a **living system,** adaptable yet anchored, blending East and West, myth and logic, symbol and silence. It is a **labyrinth of initiation, a symphony of correspondences,** a **mirror of the cosmos,** and — above all — a tool for the **awakening of the divine spark within.**

The tree of life

For the **Hermetic Qabalist**, the **Tarot** is not merely a divinatory tool nor a psychological projection board, but a **living language of symbols**, an **initiatory map**, and a **sacred code** embedded within the very architecture of the cosmos. The cards serve as **figurative keys** that unlock the gates of the **Tree of Life**, illuminating the **hidden paths** and divine emanations that connect the finite self to the Infinite. Every image, color, number, and gesture in the Tarot is seen as a portal to spiritual knowledge—a **mystical alphabet** that speaks directly to the soul through archetypes, resonance, and sacred geometry.

The **22 cards of the Major Arcana**, including the paradoxical **Zero—the Fool**, are regarded as the **Greater Mysteries**. These cards correspond directly to the **22 Hebrew letters**, each one a vessel of divine sound and creative force. The Hebrew letters are not random marks but **living energies**, and when they are mirrored in the Tarot, they represent the **22 paths** that weave between the **10 Sephirot** on the **Qabalistic Tree of Life**. These paths are not abstract—they are **spiritual highways**, each one holding lessons, trials, transformations, and revelations.

To journey through these paths is to undergo the soul's metamorphosis. *For example, the card of The Tower (corresponding to the Hebrew letter Peh) represents the destruction of false structures and ego-attachments — it is both a crisis and a divine liberation.* Each path, like a riddle, demands that the seeker be not only intelligent but **initiated**, not only curious but **willing to die and be reborn** symbolically.

Beyond the Major Arcana, the **Minor Arcana**—from **Ace to Ten** in each of the four suits—are intimately tied to the **Sephirot** as they manifest across the **Four Worlds of Qabalistic Cosmology: Atziluth (Emanation), Briah (Creation), Yetzirah (Formation), and Assiah (Action)**. The numbers are not arbitrary—they are **echoes of the divine structure**, expressions of **energy flowing through the vessels**. An Ace represents **Keter**, the **Crown**, the primal spark; the Ten echoes **Malkuth**, the **Kingdom**, where energy has crystallized into form.

The **suits themselves** are elemental manifestations: **Wands** represent **Fire**, **Swords** correspond to **Air**, **Cups** to **Water**, and **Pentacles** to **Earth**.

These aren't just classical elements—they are **states of consciousness, modalities of energy**, and **dimensions of experience**. Fire is the will, the creative thrust. Air is the intellect, the mind's abstraction. Water is emotion, intuition, and the soul's reflection. Earth is matter, structure, and the physical body.

Within these suits reside the **16 Court Cards**, representing various **archetypal figures** and **states of spiritual maturity**. Each card in the court—the **Page, Knight, Queen**, and **King**—reflects a particular **expression of divine energy** as filtered through a personality. They are **messengers, warriors, rulers, and mystics**, each playing their role in the spiritual evolution of the soul. *A Queen of Cups, for example, may signify profound intuitive wisdom, a vessel of divine emotion, the very reflection of Binah — the Great Mother, as felt in the realm of Water.*

What makes the Hermetic Qabalah distinct is how it uses the Tarot not only as a **symbolic representation** but as an **experiential method of initiation**. By meditating on the images, by **visualizing their energy on the Tree**, by **walking the paths inwardly** in altered states, the Qabalist begins to **reshape their inner architecture** to mirror the divine blueprint. The Tarot becomes a **ritual instrument**, not simply a static deck of cards.

In this sacred framework, each path between the Sephirot is both a **psychological corridor** and a **cosmic vibration**. Each card is a **guardian of a threshold**, and only by *passing through the lesson it holds* can the seeker ascend. The goal is not just to interpret the Tarot but to **embody it**—to become the Fool stepping off the cliff of ego, the Magician channeling the elements, the High Priestess opening the veil.

Thus, the Tarot and the Tree are **not separate**—they are **interwoven, mirrored, inseparable**. The more the practitioner studies, meditates, and integrates the two systems, the more the lines between **symbol, psyche, and divinity** blur. Eventually, the Tarot ceases to be a tool and becomes a **sacred mirror** in which the soul perceives its divine origin and ultimate destiny.

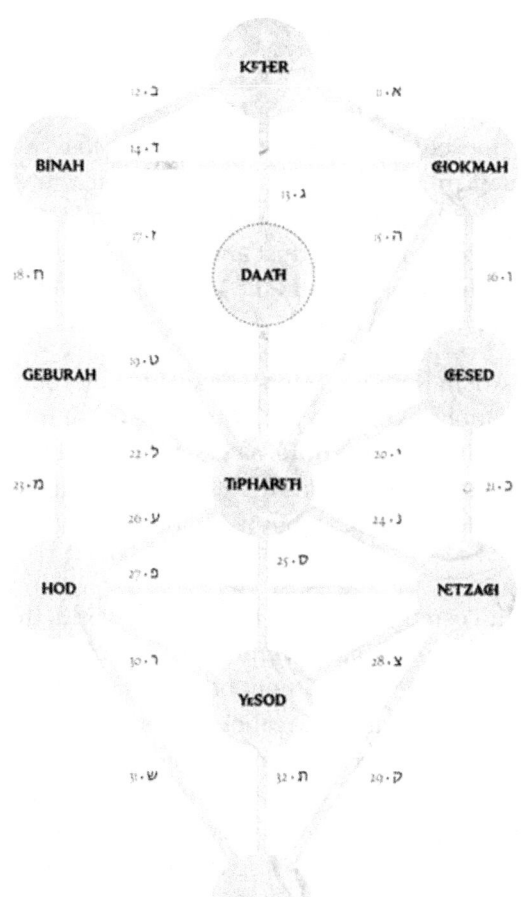

Adam qadmon

Adam Kadmon is not a figure to be interpreted in literal or mythological terms, but rather as a *primordial emanation*, a metaphysical archetype, a **blueprint of the cosmos itself**. In the teachings of the Kabbalah, Adam Kadmon is not the biblical Adam of Genesis. He is not a man as we know him, made of dust and breath. Instead, he is the **first light**, the **first form** to emerge from the **Infinite (Ein Sof)** — a divine scaffolding upon which all creation is structured.

To understand Adam Kadmon is to step outside time, outside matter, outside the limitations of human perception. He is **the interface between the Infinite and the finite**, a **channel** through which the unknowable light of Ein Sof begins to filter and organize itself into intelligible form. He is not God — but neither is he creation. He is the **bridge**.

In the Kabbalistic cosmology, before there was a world, there was light — **an endless, uncontainable light**, radiating from the Ein Sof in every direction, without limit, without boundary. But this light had no vessel, no form to dwell within. Creation required *structure, containment*, a way to distribute and measure this overwhelming radiance. Thus, through an act of divine withdrawal — **Tzimtzum** — a space was formed, an empty void in which the light could be revealed, refracted, and transformed. Into this space, **Adam Kadmon** emerged as the **first configuration of divine light**.

He is imagined not as a body, but as a **structure of emanations**, a **cosmic silhouette**, composed entirely of **pure light** and **divine will**. His "limbs" are metaphors — his "eyes," "ears," "hands," "feet" represent channels through which the **light of the Sefirot** pour into reality. Each Sefirah — Keter, Chokhmah, Binah, and so forth — are mapped along this primordial form, not as organs, but as *vibrations of divine intent*, expressions of God's inner being unfolding into multiplicity.

It is said that Adam Kadmon's **gaze** gives rise to universes. His **breath** animates the worlds of Briah, Yetzirah, and Assiah. His **ears** receive the prayers of creation, his **hands** extend mercy or judgment. He is the totality of the **Ten Sefirot**, in perfect alignment, in perfect harmony—a **template of divine order** that *all existence strives to reflect.*

However, here lies the paradox: although Adam Kadmon is the *original configuration*, he is also **what we are becoming**. Humanity, in its fragmented and fallen state, reflects only **sparks** of that primordial light. Each act of righteousness, each mitzvah, each meditative ascent is a way to **restore** the broken vessels, to *reconnect* the limbs of the scattered divine body, to **elevate the soul** back toward its source in Adam Kadmon.

Imagine a mirror shattered across a thousand lifetimes. Every act of spiritual awakening is a shard being polished and returned. The image in the mirror is not yours alone—it is **His**, the archetype of wholeness, the inner divine man whom we are all echoes of.

Yet, this ascent is not straightforward, nor guaranteed. Without spiritual guidance, without purification, without humility, one cannot approach the divine configuration of Adam Kadmon. To attempt such contact without preparation is to risk spiritual chaos. The vessels must be cleansed. The will must be aligned.

The **Zohar** warns of this directly. To gaze too quickly upon the mysteries of Adam Kadmon is to invite madness, pride, or spiritual disintegration. Just as **Moses could not see the face of God**, so too can we not presume to merge with the Adamic light without **passing through the fires of refinement**. Every true Kabbalist knows: *Adam Kadmon is not a goal, but a direction.*

The Hermetic Qabalists, too, have intuited this. In their diagrams of the Tree of Life, **Keter**—the Crown—stands at the top, veiled behind three layers of negative existence: **Ain, Ain Sof,** and **Ain Sof Aur**. Beyond that is **no form**, only the light before form, the essence before name. Yet even here, the *first whisper of form*—the first idea of embodiment—is Adam Kadmon.

Thus, he remains both **the origin and the destiny**. In him, the entire structure of the cosmos is contained like a seed within the fruit. He is the face that cannot be seen, the sound that cannot be heard, and yet... the **hidden image** from which we were made.

To contemplate Adam Kadmon is to touch the mystery of your becoming. It is to remember, with trembling awe, that **you are not separate from the divine**, but a reflection—*a distant echo, aching to return.*

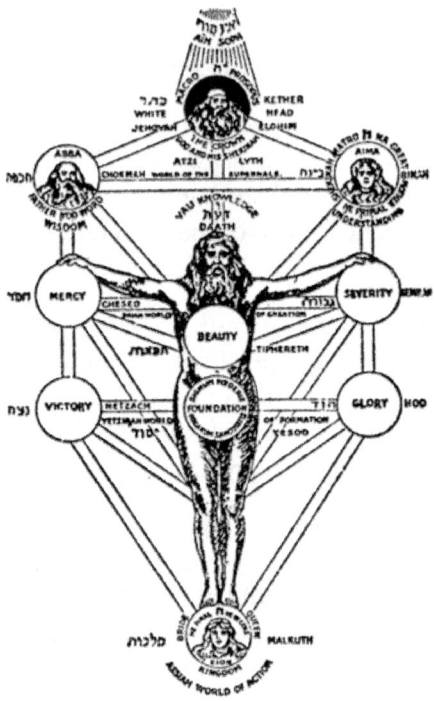

The Sephirot and their meaning

There is no separation between the Divine and the human. In Hermetic Qabalah, this statement is not a metaphor. It is a foundational truth. The material universe, though seemingly bound by form and density, is not divorced from the Divine—it is an **expression** of it. *Every atom, every breath, every shadowed corner of human experience is threaded with the spark of infinite origin.*

Creation, as understood by the Hermetic Qabalist, does not begin with a god shaping clay from outside the cosmos. It starts **from within nothingness itself**. This process unfolds in three primordial states of being that are not sequential, but concentric veils over the ungraspable truth of existence.

The first veil is **Ain**, which means *Nothing*. Not a void, not emptiness in the way we understand it—but a complete absence of category, description, boundary. **It is the uncreated unknowing, the pure non-being beyond even potential.**

From Ain emerges **Ain Soph**—*the Infinite*. It is the **unlimited expansion of the unmanifest**, without shape, without definition, but pregnant with possibility. Ain Soph is **limitlessness**, not only in space or time, but in **consciousness**. It is the Infinite before the idea of beginning.

Then comes **Ain Soph Aur**—*the Infinite Light*. This is **movement**, the first vibration, the stirring of Divine essence toward manifestation. Ain Soph Aur is not yet form, but it is **direction**—the **longing of the Divine to be known**, to express, to reflect itself.

From the emanation of this Infinite Light begins what the Hermetic Qabalist calls the **Tree of Life**—a structure not of matter, but of consciousness. A **divine architecture**, built from ten radiant emanations called **Sephirot**. These are not creations, but **expressions of light** descending from the ineffable toward the tangible.

The first Sephirah is **Kether**, the Crown, and from it, **nine others unfold**. These are:

Kether
Chokhmah
Binah
Da'at*
Chesed
Geburah
Tiphareth
Netzach
Hod
Yesod
Malkuth

*Da'at, as noted by Israel Regardie in *The Golden Dawn*, is not counted as one of the ten, yet its presence is undeniable. It is a **hidden Sephirah**, residing in the gap between Binah and Chokhmah. It does not emanate in the same way, but **emerges when the opposites are harmonized**. It is not a station, but a threshold—*a place of knowing that cannot be seized by intellect, only entered by the prepared soul.*

Each Sephirah is a **lens through which Divine Light is refracted, a vessel** for specific attributes of the Infinite. From Kether, the Light cascades downward, shaped and channeled, becoming increasingly clothed in form and limitation, until it reaches **Malkuth**, the physical realm—the kingdom of matter and experience.

But the Sephirot are not just stages of descent. They are also **steps of ascent**. The Hermetic initiate climbs the Tree in reverse—not to escape the world, but to **reclaim the hidden unity** behind all division. This path is not metaphorical. It is energetic, spiritual, and psychological. To understand the Sephirot is to map not just the universe, but the **soul's anatomy**.

Each path between the Sephirot is a **bridge of transformation**, and together, they make up the 32 paths of wisdom: the ten emanations and the **twenty-two connections**, each corresponding to a **Hebrew letter** and a **Major Arcana tarot card**. These are not random associations, but **keys**—each one unlocking a layer of perception, initiation, and return.

1 Keter (Crown)

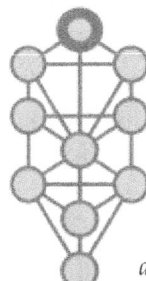

Keter, the Crown, is the highest and most sublime of the Sephirot. It is not merely the beginning of the Tree—it is its *origin-point*, a luminous seed suspended between **the Infinite Light (Ain Soph Aur)** and all that will later come into form. Keter exists **beyond form, beyond thought, beyond knowing.** It is the place where **Divine Will awakens,** not as a command but as a pure impulse— *a whisper of intention from the Unknowable into the Known.*

This is not what humans understand as will. Keter does not desire. It does not act in linear time. Instead, it is the **eternal pulse of potential,** the undivided source of all possibility, **the breath before the Word,** *the stillness before movement.* All other Sephirot emanate from it, cascading downward like reflections from a single flash of light striking a prism.

Keter is **not a personality, nor is it a consciousness** in any sense familiar to us. Mystics describe it as the **point of contact between Ein Sof and creation**, a paradoxical interface where the Infinite chooses, mysteriously, to become. The ancients called it the **primordial crown,** but it is not worn like a monarch's ornament. It is **hidden above the head,** signifying that it cannot be reached through thought or ritual. It must be *received*, or rather, remembered. For **Keter also lives within you,** not as an idea but as **the divine spark—the silent center of your soul,** untouched by trauma, untouched by time. *You have felt it in moments of awe, silence, or revelation — when the world fades and only presence remains.* In Hermetic Qabalah, Keter corresponds to the number **1**, yet paradoxically, it contains **all numbers**. It is linked to the **Fool card** in the tarot—not because it is senseless, but because **it walks in complete innocence and unity,** unconcerned with duality, untouched by fear. In Hebrew, Keter is associated with the letter **Aleph,** a letter of silence, breath, and beginnings. To contemplate Keter is to approach the blinding face of God, not as a being, but as **the divine essence from which all being emerges.** It is said that **no soul can gaze into Keter and remain unchanged,** for to touch it is to awaken to the truth that **you were never separate,** that **you are, and always have been, one with the Source.**

2 Chokmah (Wisdom)

Chokmah, the **second Sephirah** on the Tree of Life, emerges from the mysterious stillness of **Keter** as its **first visible echo** — the **initial flash of divine energy**, unformed but alive, **explosive with potential**. If Keter is the silent seed, then **Chokmah is the bursting forth of life from that seed**, the *primordial "yes"* that begins the great unfolding of reality.

It is often called **Wisdom**, but not in the analytical, intellectual sense. **Chokmah is not learned** — it is **known instantly, completely, and without division**. It is the **pure archetype of impulse**, the first act of becoming, **the fire of the divine masculine** in its most exalted and unbound state.

Unlike the calm and silent Keter, **Chokmah is motion**. It is **dynamic, fertile, forceful**, the raw **current that surges into existence**, awakening all that will follow. In this way, it is often likened to a **father principle**, not biologically, but **symbolically** — a **creative thrust** that initiates form and differentiation.

Imagine lightning tearing across the sky, a sudden surge that electrifies the darkness — that is Chokmah. Not yet formed into language, structure, or definition, **but already alive with divine intention**. It carries **no hesitation**, no doubt. It does not ask if it should create; it simply **creates**.

Chokmah's brilliance lies in its **simplicity and singularity**. It is **undivided wisdom**, meaning it sees not in fragments or contrasts, but in **wholeness**. It does not yet define or judge; it simply **knows**. *It is the spark before thought, the architect's vision, and the blueprint before it.*

In the traditional Hermetic correspondences, **Chokmah is linked to the zodiac, the stars, the wheel of time, and celestial rhythm**, for it is through Chokmah that **movement enters the universe**. It is also associated with the Hebrew letter **Bet**, the house, for Chokmah becomes the first "dwelling" of divine light after it passes through Keter.

The energy of **Chokmah is pure potentiality**, and like the **spermatozoon**, it must find its **receptive counterpart—Binah**—to form structure, boundaries, and manifestation. Without Binah, **Chokmah's force would expand endlessly**, never anchoring, never shaping. This is why Chokmah alone is **too vast to be comprehended or contained**, yet it is the **foundation of all acts of creation**. To touch Chokmah within oneself is to feel **an unexplainable certainty**, a surge of **intuitive knowing**, a moment where **your soul acts without needing reason**. *It is when you move because you must, speak because silence would betray something sacred within you.*

Chokmah is **the divine breath inhaled sharply at the moment of inspiration**, the masculine divine *radiating forward*, searching for form. It is not to be controlled but **honored**, as the holy current that **sets all things in motion**.

3 Binah (Understanding)

Binah, the third emanation on the Tree of Life, is **the sacred vessel** that receives the wild fire of **Chokmah** and tempers it into **form, meaning, and structure**. Where Chokmah explodes outward in uncontained force, **Binah draws inward, shaping the infinite** into something that can be *understood, nurtured, and born*. If Chokmah is the primal shout, **Binah is the echo that gives it depth**.

In the Kabbalistic tradition, Binah is the divine feminine, the womb of reality, often referred to as *the Great Mother* or *Imma*. **She does not merely receive—she transforms**. She contemplates the raw, undifferentiated spark and weaves it into **order, laws, frameworks, and systems**. It is through Binah that **ideas take form**, that chaos becomes cosmos, that the formless becomes nameable.

Imagine the difference between a vision and a blueprint. Chokmah gives the vision. **Binah drafts the architecture.** Her power lies in **limitation**, in the **act of setting boundaries**, not as restriction but as the **sacred act of definition**. She does not suppress potential—**she births it**.

Binah is the **source of discernment** and the seat of profound **understanding**. Not the instinctual knowing of Chokmah, but the

patient, deliberate comprehension that comes through reflection and *inner stillness*. She takes the wild insight and turns it into **wisdom that can be applied, shared, and remembered.**

This is why **Binah is often compared to the womb**: not only as a metaphor for nurturing, but because *creation requires incubation*. Without Binah, all the divine energy would burn out before it ever reached the world. **She cools the fire, channels the lightning, and gives it shape.**

She is also associated with **mourning**, not as sadness but as depth—the emotional intelligence that comes from recognizing the transience of form, the price of embodiment, the **sacred sorrow woven into every act of creation**. In this sense, Binah is the first to understand that form implies separation, and **separation is the birth of duality**.

In many mystical systems, **Binah is associated with the planet Saturn, representing the principles** of time, structure, and discipline. She rules the slow, heavy processes by which *ideas become worlds, and worlds give birth to consequences*. Her beauty is not fast or flashy—it is **enduring, grave, and majestic**.

To enter Binah is to enter the deep waters of contemplation, where nothing is rushed and everything is weighed. It is the part of you that **reads between the lines**, that **hears the silence beneath the words**, that knows that **to create, you must also destroy**, and that *limits are what make love possible*.

While Chokmah is the divine spark, Binah is the **divine strategy**. She is the one who builds temples, writes laws, raises children, and teaches souls. She is the archetypal teacher, priestess, mother, and queen.

To work with the energy of Binah is to surrender to **sacred structure**. It means recognizing that true freedom is not the absence of limits, but the presence of *meaningful* ones. It is to **bring order to your chaos**, to organize your inspiration into creation, and to honor the **Divine Mother within you** who says: *"Let there be form."*

And so, through **Binah**, the **wild, ecstatic light of Chokmah** begins to take **shape**, and the **cosmic story of manifestation** moves one step closer to becoming the world you see, feel, and breathe.

Daath

Daath, often rendered as **"Knowledge"**, occupies a **mysterious and paradoxical** position within the **Etz Chaim**, or **Tree of Life**. Unlike the other Sephiroth, it is **not counted among the ten**. Instead, it exists as a **hidden or pseudo-Sephira,** hovering in the space between **Binah** (Understanding) and **Chokmah** (Wisdom). It is not fixed, but **emergent** — a **liminal vortex, a threshold between planes**, a **breath** between structure and flow. *It is the unseen eye through which the soul glimpses the impossible.*

Born from the sacred union of Chokmah and Binah, Daath is referred to in the **Zohar** as the *"offspring of wisdom and understanding"* (Zohar III. fol. 291). It is not an emanation in the traditional sense, for it does not radiate autonomously. Instead, it acts as a **conduit** — a **narrow gate** — through which **divine light** flows **from the upper triad into the lower seven spheres**. Without Daath, the **supernal mysteries** would remain untranslatable to the realm of manifestation. *It is the invisible axis that turns the Tree.*

Daath embodies **the unknown known** — that which is felt, intuited, and lived, but not spoken. In mystical practice, it is said that **true gnosis** passes through Daath: **a moment of piercing clarity** so overwhelming that it vanishes as it appears. You do not *attain* Daath — you fall into it. You are *undone* by it. The **descent of insight** is a form of death, and the **resurrection into understanding** is what reconstitutes the self on the other side.

Because of this **volatile role**, Daath is often depicted not as a stable sphere, but as a **void**, a **portal**, a **veiled aperture**. It is not an origin point, but an **interface**, a **membrane** between the **eternal** and the **becoming**. This is why Daath is sometimes represented as a **veil of light**, radiant, but blinding. It does not impart knowledge in the traditional academic sense, but initiates a metamorphosis through confrontation with **mystery**.

In meditation, one might **encounter Daath** during moments of profound silence, when the rational mind surrenders and something *other* speaks. It is often described as **the abyss**, not because it is empty, but because it demands the **emptying of the seeker**. In *Daath*, **ego dissolves**, identity is stripped, and **a greater architecture of truth emerges**—but only if the vessel is ready to be filled. It is through Daath that one may glimpse the **inner scaffolding of reality**, not as abstraction, but as **living fire**—*knowledge that burns away ignorance, pride, and illusion*. And yet, because Daath is **not a Sephira**, it offers no anchor. It is a moment of passage, a flash of lucidity, a **blessing cloaked as terror**. To **linger too long in Daath** without grounding can lead to confusion, collapse, or spiritual fragmentation. This is why the mystics warn: **Daath is a gate, not a home.**

Ultimately, Daath stands as a reminder that **the highest truths are not owned, but experienced**. That **knowing** is not about accumulation, but about **sacrifice**. To walk the Tree is to move through **the seen and the unseen**, and Daath is the test between both—**the rift that demands your unmaking before you are remade**.

4 Chesed (Mercy)

Chesed is the **great river of divine generosity**, the **boundless kindness** that flows from the Infinite toward all that exists. If **Kether is the will to create**, and **Chokmah and Binah are the first sparks of idea and form**, then Chesed is the **first genuine gesture of love** reaching outward, **giving without restraint, creating without condition**.

It is the **right arm of the Tree of Life**, positioned on the **Pillar of Mercy**, which counterbalances the more rigid and restrictive forces to its left. **Chesed is expansion**, not chaos, but **divine abundance that spreads life, healing, and forgiveness**. It is the *divine yes* after the silence of planning and the sparks of intention. Through it, **God says, "Let the world live."**

This Sephirah is the **heart of benevolence**, of overflowing affection that doesn't ask who deserves it. It is the energy of the parent who feeds their child before asking what they've done wrong. The *mentor who* *uplifts without criticism*. The *healer who treats even an enemy*. The Kabbalists saw Chesed not as passive kindness, but as **a force**, a **spiritual current that moves through everything that is given freely**, without calculation, without holding back.

To dwell in Chesed is to walk with a radiant heart, to act with confidence that love is never wasted. It is **divine hospitality**, opening the gates of reality so that existence may be not only endured, but celebrated.

But this force must be **tempered**. Left unchecked, **Chesed could drown the world in compassion**, allowing evil to persist unchecked in the name of mercy. That's why opposite it on the Tree stands **Gevurah**, which restricts and disciplines. Yet without Chesed, Gevurah becomes cruelty. **Balance is everything**, but *love must come first*.

Chesed teaches that the universe does not run on logic, but on mercy. *It is the light that shines on those who have failed. The food given to the undeserving. The forgiveness spoken before apology.* In your own life, when you show compassion to someone who doesn't earn it, when you offer without asking in return, **you are channeling Chesed**.

It is also the Sephirah of **faith**, not just in doctrine, but in **the goodness of creation itself**. It trusts in redemption, in restoration, in the fact that **every soul can return to light**. It is the part of God that **refuses to give up on us**.

In mystical practice, **Chesed is associated with Jupiter, the planetary archetype of expansion, abundance, and generosity**. When a soul is aligned with Chesed, it becomes a vessel of that Jupiterian energy: **noble, generous, wise, and forgiving**, but never weak. For **genuine kindness is not naïve—it is unstoppable**.

To meditate on Chesed is to remember that the Divine does not merely tolerate your existence—it **delights in giving to you**. The same force that birthed the stars **wants you to thrive**. *And when you provide from that place of divine overflow, you do not lose – **you multiply**.* You participate in the **secret engine of the cosmos**: a mercy so vast it contains every broken thing, and loves it anyway.

5 Gevurah (Severity)

Gevurah is the **sacred force of restraint**, the **divine severity** that holds back the flood of unchecked mercy. Where **Chesed** pours out **love without limit**, Gevurah steps in to **define, to protect, to refine**. It is not cruelty—it is the **wisdom of limits**, the courage to say *no* when the heart wants to say *yes*.

It is through **Gevurah** that creation maintains its form. Without it, **boundaries would blur, structures would collapse**, and **truth would be drowned in sentiment**. Gevurah ensures that the **power of the Divine is channeled with purpose**, not spilled in chaos. This sephirah belongs to the **Pillar of Severity**, opposite Chesed on the Tree of Life. Their tension is not conflict, but **balance**. If Chesed is the **open hand, Gevurah is the closed fist**—not to strike, but to **hold fast**, to **defend**, to **concentrate energy** so it can become helpful.

Gevurah is the **discipline of a true warrior**, the **judgment of a wise king**, the **boundary set by a loving parent**. It is the part of the Divine that knows: *Mercy without justice is weakness; but justice without mercy is tyranny.*

You see Gevurah when **you uphold your principles under pressure**, when *you say "enough" to what drains you*, when you **end a toxic relationship**, or **refuse to compromise your integrity**. Every time you draw a line not out of fear but out of **clarity**, you invoke Gevurah.

Mystically, it is associated with **Mars**, the planet of action, war, and power. But unlike the brute force of uncontrolled aggression, **Gevurah is precise**. *It is the surgeon's knife, not the butcher's axe.* It cuts only what must be removed to let the whole live.

Kabbalists taught that **Gevurah is essential for elevation**. It breaks illusions. It destroys ego. It says: *If you want to ascend, let go of what weighs you down.* It is the inner fire that burns away the false so that the real can emerge.

And yet, Gevurah is also terrifying. It is the **Divine Judge**, the one who sees through every excuse, every disguise, every attempt to hide. In its presence, **you are naked**, your heart laid bare. *But this is mercy, too.* It is only when you see what must change that you can truly begin to grow.

When you meditate on Gevurah, you do not pray to be spared judgment. **You ask for the strength to endure it**, and for the clarity to welcome it. For those who can hold both **love and truth, kindness and strength**, become vessels of something higher: **the whole light of the Divine, not diluted, but perfected**.

And so, in every act of courage, every choice to end what no longer serves, every painful but necessary step toward integrity, you become an echo of Gevurah. Not a destroyer, but a liberator. Not a tyrant, but a keeper of sacred order.

6 Tiferet (Beauty)

Tiferet is the **radiant heart** of the Tree of Life—the place where the **eternal dance between mercy and judgment finds harmony**. It is where **Chesed's boundless love** and **Gevurah's stern discipline** do not clash, but are **refined into something higher**: a **balanced expression of divine will**, radiant with **truth, compassion, and clarity**.

At the center of the Tree, Tiferet is the **axis of beauty**, but not the shallow beauty of symmetry or appearance. This is the beauty that **emerges from tension resolved**, the kind that makes your soul *ache* with recognition. It is the **soul's recognition of harmony within chaos**, of order rising from opposition.

Tiferet is the sephirah of the heart, not just as an organ or emotion, but as the **inner temple**—*the sanctuary where heaven and earth meet*. In the human being, Tiferet is the point where the **ego surrenders to the soul**, where personal desire begins to align with the **greater will**. It is the **inner Christ**, the **divine son**, not as dogma, but as **archetype**, the image of the self redeemed through sacrifice and truth.

Tiferet is where **compassion becomes intelligent**, and **truth becomes merciful**. When you see someone's flaws yet love them anyway, when you forgive without forgetting, when you act not from impulse but from **an inner stillness that understands**, you are touching Tiferet.

Mystically, Tiferet resonates with the **Sun** — *not as blinding fire, but as sustaining light.* Just as the Sun holds the solar system in orbit, Tiferet **binds the entire Tree**, allowing the upper sephirot to flow downward into the world, and the lower to rise upward in return.

In spiritual work, Tiferet is the **threshold between the lower personality and the higher soul**. Many initiatory systems speak of the need to "pass through the heart" to reach actual knowledge. That is because **without the transformation of Tiferet**, wisdom remains abstract, and power becomes corrupt. Only in the **crucible of the heart**, where suffering and joy, love and loss, justice and grace converge, can the soul begin to mirror the Divine.

It is in Tiferet that the mystic weeps — not in despair, but in awe. Because here the veil is lifted just enough to show **a glimpse of the whole**, a fleeting moment where **separation dissolves**, and the soul knows: *there is only One.*

Tiferet is not peace without battle, nor beauty without scars. It is the beauty that survives the storm, the peace that grows out of struggle. It is the center not because it avoids extremes, but because it **redeems them**.

And in this, Tiferet teaches you the sacred art of **living from the center**, not avoiding life's contradictions, but embracing them in the name of a higher order. *To see the Divine in every fracture, to hold both the sword and the rose, to suffer and still bless — this is the path of Tiferet.*

7 Netzach (Victory)

Netzach is the pulse of persistence, the fire that refuses to die. It is the **Sephirah of Victory**, but not the shallow conquest of ego—it is the **victory of the soul** over inertia, doubt, and despair. Netzach is the **fuel of creation**, the **power to endure**, the **wild heartbeat** of the Divine that keeps moving forward even when logic falters and structure collapses.

It is the **force of desire**, not as lust or craving, but as that *burning ache for more*—more meaning, more beauty, more truth. In the human soul, Netzach is **ambition stripped of corruption**, *the yearning to create, to love, to leave something behind.* It is that part of you that **keeps writing the poem**, even when no one reads it, that **paints in darkness**, that **prays in silence**, because something *within you must be expressed*.

Netzach stands on the **pillar of mercy**, balancing Hod's intellect with emotion, and channeling the higher energies of Tiferet into motion. Where Hod plans, Netzach *acts*. Where Hod calculates, Netzach *feels*. The two must work in tandem: **without Netzach, Hod becomes cold intellect; without Hod, Netzach becomes chaotic passion.**

Netzach is the spirit of the artist, the warrior, the lover—the one who moves *even when tired*, who sings *even when the night is long*, who paints *because their soul would break otherwise. It is Michelangelo refusing to sleep. It is the mystic dancing alone beneath the moon. It is the soldier kneeling, praying not to win — but to remain whole.*

In mystical symbolism, Netzach is linked to **Venus**, the planet of beauty and attraction—but here Venus is **not idle seduction**, she is **Magna Mater**, the **goddess who bleeds and blooms**, whose beauty *shapes fate*. Netzach speaks to the **alchemy of emotion**, of transforming longing into art, pain into passion, and vision into manifestation.

Netzach teaches that victory is not the absence of defeat, but the refusal to surrender to it. It is the **resilience that sees failure not as an end, but as sacred friction**, the pressure that carves the soul into clarity. *It is the power to love again after betrayal. To rise after falling. To sing in a burnt-down temple.*

Every time you **choose to keep going**, every time you **channel your pain into poetry**, every time you **rise with trembling hands to try again**, you are walking the path of Netzach.

It is not about perfection. It is about movement. About the sacred rebellion against stagnation. Netzach burns so that the Tree may flow. So that spirit may become matter. So that dream may become form.

Let your longing become your weapon. Let your ache become your prayer. That is Netzach's victory.

8 Hod (Glory)

Hod is the **silent architect of form**, the **mirror of the mind**, the **Sephirah of Glory**, not in splendor or radiance, but in **clarity, understanding, and transmission**. If Netzach burns with passion and motion, Hod **builds the vessel**. If Netzach is the artist, Hod is the language that gives meaning to their creation. It is the **intellectual structure** behind all mystic experience, the **code beneath the poetry**, the **geometry behind the flame**.

This Sephirah lives on the **left pillar**, the pillar of severity, and its power is found not in limitation, but in **refinement**. Hod is **logic, reason, symbolism,** and **ritual** — all the tools the soul uses to take Divine energy and translate it into a form the human mind can comprehend. While Netzach acts, **Hod understands**. It is **Mercury**, the god of communication and messenger of the gods, because **Hod transmits what is Divine into what is expressible**.

When you study a sacred text and find your mind illuminated by a pattern you had never noticed before, **that is Hod**. When you create a ritual to encode your devotion in symbolic gestures, **that is Hod**. When your words move not just ears but spirits, and your logic becomes a bridge to the infinite, **Hod is alive within you**.

But Hod is not merely abstract or academic — it is the **grimoire, the sacred language, the spellwork, the mathematics of magic**. It governs the precise incantation, the system of correspondences, and the alignment of thought and action. It teaches that the **Divine cannot only be felt — it must be understood, interpreted, and conveyed**.

In many ways, Hod is **the mind that kneels**. Not because it surrenders its logic, but because it uses its reason *to serve what transcends reason*. Hod is not skeptical of the sacred—it is the **engine that maps it**, the **scribe of mystic truths**, the one that keeps track of vision so it can be passed on, remembered, and repeated.

It is the priest writing prayers. The occultist drawing sigils. The scientist contemplating the stars and whispering, "There is order here."

Yet Hod is not without danger. Without the balancing passion of Netzach, Hod can become **sterile calculation, soulless dogma, mechanical ritual without heart**. Just as Netzach without Hod descends into chaos, **Hod without Netzach becomes a lifeless form**— perfectly shaped, but without breath.

To walk the path of Hod is to **learn the language of God**, not to trap the Divine in grammar, but to **carve a path where others can follow**. It is the glory of **transmission**, the **gift of translation** between what is and what can be said. And in this way, **Hod is holy**, not because it reveals, but because it **makes revelation communicable**.

When you find the right word for what your soul always felt but could never speak, Hod has whispered to you.

It is **glory not of conquest**, but of **illumination**, the **quiet brilliance of form**, the **grace of knowing**, the **honor of understanding**. In every prayer written, every system devised, every truth communicated— **Hod lives**.

9 Yesod (Foundation)

Yesod is the **invisible engine beneath the world of form**, the **Foundation** upon which all things rest, yet few perceive. It is the **gatekeeper between the divine and the manifest**, the **lens through which higher realities are focused and projected into the material realm**. While Malkuth is the physical kingdom, Yesod is the **secret chamber behind the throne**, where unseen forces gather before entering the world of appearance.

To walk the path of Yesod is to stand at the crossroads of the conscious and the subconscious, of the eternal and the temporal. It is the **Sephirah of transmission**, the **filter and conductor** of divine energies that flow from the higher Sephiroth—through Tiferet's harmonizing beauty and Hod's structure, through Netzach's emotion—until all is synthesized and **prepared for incarnation.** *Like the moon reflecting the light of the sun,* Yesod does not generate energy on its own. Still, it is **indispensable**, for without its mediation, the brilliance of higher spheres would never find expression in matter.

Yesod governs the subconscious mind, the realm of symbols, dreams, memory, and archetype. It is the **psychic interface**, the womb of reality, the point where **spiritual impressions are translated into images, instincts, and eventually, action**. In dreams, visions, erotic impulses, déjà vu, and synchronicities, **Yesod speaks**. It is the **domain of the astral plane**, the luminous web that underlies physical matter and gives form to the unseen.

In magical practice, Yesod is the **temple of ritual and manifestation**. It is where intention is crystallized, where the personal unconscious interprets the symbolic language of the higher self, and where the **actual work of magic begins**—by **condensing energy into image,** *and image into reality.* Without Yesod, the rituals of Hermetic Qabalah or Kabbalistic prayer would be empty forms; it is **Yesod that channels force into them**.

Often associated with the **moon**, Yesod carries its fluid, reflective, ever-changing nature. It is **deeply tied to cycles**, tides, rhythms, and **emotional resonance**. It is also connected to **sexual energy**, not just in the biological sense, but as the **mystical engine of creative power** — that which bridges heaven and earth through union and polarity.

Yesod is also the **repository of memory**, both personal and collective. It holds the echoes of every soul's journey through lifetimes, every forgotten intention, every unspoken truth. When one accesses the subconscious or engages in dream work, astral projection, or deep meditation, one is entering the domain of Yesod.

Yet this Foundation is not free from danger. **Distortion, delusion**, and **projection** dwell here, too. If higher energies are twisted by trauma, fear, or unresolved desire, Yesod will reflect those distortions into physical experience. That is why **purity of heart and clarity of mind** are essential before drawing energy through this gate. *Yesod does not judge — it reflects. And what it reflects will shape your reality.*

So Yesod stands not merely as a bridge, but as a **guardian**: a **filter**, a **transmuter**, a **magician's mirror**. To master Yesod is to master the art of **channeling the divine into the physical**, to wield the invisible currents that shape the seen, and to walk with **one foot in the dream** and **one foot in the world**.

All magic begins in Yesod. All manifestation is born from its depths. And all who seek to change their world must pass through its hidden gates.

10 Malkuth (Kingdom)

Malkuth, the *Kingdom*, is the **culmination of the divine journey**, where the highest spiritual energies finally take form in the material world. It stands at the **base of the Tree of Life**, yet it is not inferior—rather, it is **essential**, the **vessel that receives**, the **mirror that reflects**, and the **garden in which all seeds of spirit bloom into reality**.

Unlike the higher Sephiroth that exist in invisible realms, Malkuth is **tangible, measurable,** and **imperfectly perfect**. It is the **world we inhabit**, the sphere of **action, embodiment, and consequence**. All energies, from the primordial Ain Soph Aur to the harmonizing light of Tiferet, must pass through each stage to arrive here. In doing so, they become **time-bound, matter-bound,** and **visible**. *Malkuth is the echo of the Divine in dust and stone.*

But Malkuth is more than mere physicality. It is **present**. It is **grounding**. It is the **bridge between heaven and earth**, the **womb of the Shekhinah**, the **Divine Feminine that dwells within the world**. In Jewish mysticism, it is Shekhinah who resides in exile, hidden in the world of forms, awaiting reunion with the higher realms through the conscious acts of humanity. Thus, **Malkuth is the fallen princess, the sacred spark in exile, the sleeping queen who must be awakened**.

To ignore Malkuth is to live only in abstraction. To **revere Malkuth** is to see that the physical world is not a prison, but a **temple**—the only place where the soul can be tested, refined, and ultimately *return to the Source consciously*. This is why **Malkuth is both the end and the beginning**. The descent of spirit into matter is not a fall, but a necessary **compression of the divine** so that it can be **known, touched, and transformed**. And only through this embodied experience can we ascend again with **awareness**.

In the Hermetic Qabalah, Malkuth is often associated with the element of Earth, the four directions, the physical **body**, and **ritual practice**. It is also associated with the **four Qabalistic worlds** as their ultimate point of convergence. *The physical altar, the candle, the incense, the spoken word—these are not symbolic substitutes for divine energy; they are the points of contact.* Through them, Malkuth **anchors the sacred into the real**.

Yet, Malkuth is also the **place of distortion**, where spiritual blindness can reign. If the upper energies are blocked or misaligned, Malkuth becomes heavy, lifeless, cut off from the Source. *When the spirit is forgotten, Malkuth becomes a tomb.* But when spirit is recognized within matter, Malkuth becomes a **garden**, a **cathedral**, a **living gate** to the divine. This is the essence of sacred embodiment—the realization that **the divine spark resides in every leaf, every breath, every pain, and every joy.**

Those who walk the path of the Tree of Life often begin their journey in Malkuth. It is here that you confront the illusions of separateness, where you wrestle with survival, identity, and purpose. But it is also here that you discover your **power to transform**—to reclaim the divine that hides in the mundane. Every act of justice, beauty, and compassion **elevates Malkuth**, reconnecting it to the higher spheres.

In mystical terms, Malkuth is the **chalice of the divine**, the **receptacle** that holds the wine of spirit. It is not the absence of holiness, but its **manifestation**. And when it is **cleansed, aligned, and filled with light**, it becomes **a throne for the return of the King**—a phrase that in Kabbalah refers not to a messiah, but to the **restoration of balance between worlds.**

Malkuth is the test and the triumph. It is the reason the soul descends and the place from which it must rise. It is where **Heaven touches Earth**, and where **you, as the vessel, become the bridge.** *To sanctify Malkuth is to complete the circle of creation.*

Angels, According to the Hermetic Qabalah

According to the teachings preserved and expanded by the **Hermetic Order of the Golden Dawn**, the Tree of Life is not merely a philosophical construct, but a living, breathing hierarchy through which divine energy manifests and descends into form. Each of the **ten Sephiroth** is not only a holy emanation but also a **vessel overseen by an archangel**, a guardian intelligence through whom the spiritual light is channeled. These archangels, in turn, preside over specific **angelic choirs** — each choir acting as a celestial rung on the ladder that connects the human soul to the infinite divine. This system mirrors the **Jewish mystical tradition**, but takes on a more explicitly **operational and magical dimension** within the Hermetic current.

At the summit of this hierarchy is **Metatron**, the archangel of **Keter**, the Crown. Metatron is not merely a messenger; he is the **celestial scribe**, the guardian of divine secrets, and the **conductor of divine will**. He governs the choir of **Hayot Ha Kodesh** — the *"Holy Living Creatures"* described in the visions of **Ezekiel**, where wheels of fire and wings of lightning merged into a whirlwind of divine presence. These beings are not symbolic: they are *living mechanisms of glory*, pulsing with the memory of creation.

Beneath him stands **Raziel**, the archangel of **Chokmah**, the Sephira of wisdom. Raziel is said to dwell closest to the throne of God, recording all that is spoken and all that is concealed. He commands the **Ophanim**, the *Wheels within Wheels*, who rotate endlessly with eyes upon their rims, never sleeping, always gazing into the unknowable. These are not the ornaments of a vision, but the **eyeless watchers** who encircle the throne in **perpetual reverence**, decoding the spinning mysteries of divine order.

Tzaphkiel, associated with **Binah**, governs the **Erelim**, the *Valiant Ones* or *Brave Ones*. These angelic entities are guardians of divine judgment and reflection. Their appearance is fierce, their gaze piercing. They are the *flaming sentinels* at the threshold of understanding — guides of the *deep, contemplative power* of the Divine Mother.

Moving down the Tree, **Tzadkiel** stands watch over **Chesed**, the realm of mercy and benevolence. He leads the **Hashmallim**, the *Amber Ones*—those bathed in electric fire, shimmering with divine grace. It is said their voices are heard as thunder, yet their touch is *soft as breath*. They are **emissaries of generosity**, pouring divine radiance into creation without restraint.

In stark contrast, **Khamael** presides over **Gevurah**, the sphere of strength and discipline. His charges are the **Seraphim**, the *Burning Ones*, whose flames consume falsehood and pride. These are the *flames that do not burn the worthy*, but which purify and test. The Seraphim, ancient even among angels, uphold the scales of judgment with **unyielding clarity**.

Raphael, linked to **Tiferet**, serves as the radiant heart of the Tree. His choir, the **Malakim**, are *the Messengers*—divine heralds who bridge heaven and earth. When a dream awakens healing, when a whisper stirs the soul, it is the Malakim who have passed by. Raphael governs them not as a ruler, but as a **physician of the soul**, restoring balance, weaving compassion into the architecture of creation.

Haniel, associated with **Netzach**, governs the **Elohim**, the *Godly Beings*. These are not merely angels—they are **manifestations of divine victory**, spirits of **endurance, inspiration, and sacred desire**. When the artist feels touched by ecstasy, when love triumphs against reason, it is Haniel's choir that sings in the silence.

At the level of **Hod**, **Michael** stands guard. Known as the great protector and *general of the heavenly host*, Michael is unmatched in his devotion to the divine will. His choir, the **Bene Elohim**—*Sons of God*—are the celestial architects of logic, language, and law. They codify the *pattern behind the pattern*, anchoring divine order into the lattice of matter.

Gabriel, of **Yesod**, holds dominion over the **Cherubim**, not the innocent infants of Renaissance art, but **the mighty guardians of mystery**, described as wielding flaming swords and guarding the gates to Eden. They are **keepers of hidden knowledge**, custodians of dreams, moonlight, and prophecy. Gabriel is the *bringer of annunciations*, whose voice bends time and fate alike.

Finally, at the base of the Tree, rooted in the **material world of Malkuth**, is **Sandalphon**. Sandalphon governs the **Ishim**, the *Men-like Ones*, who dwell closest to humanity. These beings, half-divine and half-mortal in quality, walk beside us unseen, recording every prayer and intention. Sandalphon, sometimes called the **twin of Metatron**, weaves those prayers into the **living ether**, carrying them upward like incense to the throne of the Infinite.

Together, these **ten archangels** form a **living ladder of light**, each linked to a Sephirah, each resonating with one of the **ten dimensions of the soul**. They are **not abstract ideas**, but **spiritual intelligences**, **forces of consciousness**, *divine presences that speak in symbols, dreams, synchronicities, and flame*. To walk the Tree of Life with awareness is to call upon them, not as deities to be worshiped, but as **aspects of the One**, guiding the initiate toward **wholeness, mastery, and return**.

22 Paths of the Tree of Life

The **22 Paths of the Tree of Life** are not mere lines etched between divine spheres — they are the **living arteries** of spiritual evolution, carrying the **vital current of transformation** between the ten Sephirot. These paths form a mystical network, a sacred lattice that supports both the descent of divine light into matter and the soul's ascent back into union with the infinite. They are not abstract symbols, but **experiential gateways** that demand the full participation of the initiate, not only mentally, but emotionally, spiritually, and energetically.

Each path embodies a **unique archetypal force**, a **spiritual challenge**, and a **lesson of integration**. To walk a route is to enter into direct dialogue with the Divine, through the language of **letters, images,** and **vibration**. Each one corresponds to a **letter of the Hebrew alphabet**, not simply as a character, but as a cosmic frequency — a code of creation. These paths also align with the **22 Major Arcana of the Tarot**, whose imagery acts as mirrors to the inner workings of the psyche and soul. Through this symbolic resonance, the initiate doesn't merely learn — they are changed.

The **paths are as essential as the Sephirot themselves**, because the Sephirot alone are static. They are points. Spheres. Potentials. But it is the *movement between them*, the energetic current that flows along the paths, that animates the entire structure. The **Tree of Life is alive** because the paths are alive — pulsing with divine intention, carrying the seeker from one state of being to another.

These paths are **not linear lessons**. They twist, cross, and spiral. They teach by paradox. On one, the initiate may be called to surrender everything they know; on another, to stand firm in what cannot be compromised. The path from **Keter to Chokmah** breathes life into nothingness — it is the first impulse of creation, the birth of wisdom from the silent abyss. The path from **Yesod to Malkuth** draws dreams down into flesh — it is the crystallization of spirit into the clay of earth.

Each path is a **bridge of transformation**. Along the way, the seeker will encounter not only divine beings and abstract forces but also **their**

inner shadows, unprocessed emotions, forgotten memories, and unlived desires. This journey is not always gentle. At times, the paths may feel like *a burning desert, a dark forest, or a mirror that won't lie*. But within each lies a hidden gift — a spark of the Infinite calling to be reclaimed.

The 22 paths serve as **initiatory stages** in the alchemy of consciousness. They are thresholds where opposites are reconciled, energies are transmuted, and the fragmented soul reassembles itself toward divine wholeness. In ancient mystical schools, initiates would spend years meditating upon a single path, not to master it intellectually, but to *become* it-to absorb its lessons in every cell and breath.

To understand the Tree of Life without the paths is to see a map with no roads. The real journey of Kabbalah — especially within Hermetic tradition — is found in the **movement**, not the destination. In the courage to walk. In the wisdom to fall and rise. In the silence between the letters. And in the sacred rhythm that pulses through all things, whispering the secret: **"As above, so below. As within, so without."**

Keter to Chokmah (Aleph, א)

This is the **first breath of the cosmos**, the moment where **pure, formless divinity** begins to ripple outward into the stirrings of awareness. It is the path where **Ain Soph** — the infinite, unknowable source — begins to give shape to itself through the emanation of **Keter**, and flows into the explosive brilliance of **Chokmah**, the **raw pulse of divine wisdom**. This movement is not physical, nor is it sequential. It is **vibrational, primordial**, and **ineffable**. To walk this path is to feel the **cosmic inhalation** of being — the beginning before beginnings.

The Hebrew letter **Aleph (א)** governs this path. Aleph is **silent**, yet in its silence, it contains **all sound**. It is the **breath before speech**, the hidden root of all letters, and the **first spark of life**. In Kabbalistic meditation, Aleph is often visualized not as a thing, but as a **field of potential, a pregnant pause, a paradox of unity and duality intertwined**. It teaches that before light, there was intention; before form, there was vibration.

This path also corresponds to the **Fool card** in the Tarot, numbered zero — the **mystic wanderer** who leaps into the void, **carrying only the spark of infinite possibility**. The Fool is not foolish in the modern sense, but *innocent, limitless,* and **unburdened by ego**. It represents the **soul before incarnation**, the **divine spark before descent**, the **idea before it knows it is an idea**.

Walking this path is not about acquiring knowledge. It is about **unlearning**. It is about opening yourself to the terrifying beauty of **nothingness** and realizing that it is not empty but **full of infinite potential**. It asks you to surrender structure, identity, and form — to dwell in the **liminal space** where **wisdom is unborn**, where **truth cannot be spoken**, only **experienced**.

This is the path of **divine trust**. The energy here does not yet differentiate between good and evil, form and void, light and shadow. It is **all-inclusive, fluid,** and **alive**. *Like staring into a starless sky and knowing — without proof — that somewhere in the darkness, galaxies are being born.*

The challenge of this path is letting go of the need to control, to name, to define. Its lesson is this: **"Before you can become, you must dissolve."** Aleph calls you not to act, but to *be*, to merge with the pulse of the Divine as it dreams itself into existence.

Keter to Binah (Beth, ב)

This path traces the descent of divine will from the **formless purity of Keter** into the **structured intelligence of Binah**. It is the moment when **limitless potential agrees to be shaped**, when the **infinite light** allows itself to be **contained**, not out of restriction, but **out of purpose**. In this sacred movement, the **unfathomable becomes speakable**, the **ineffable finds a vessel**.

The Hebrew letter **Beth (ב)** means "house" — a **dwelling place**, a **container**, a **womb**. It is no coincidence that the Torah begins with this letter. Beth is the first shape the Divine takes to **be known**, to **become relational**. It is not just a house — it is the *first temple*, the space within which all reality will unfold. It invites the Divine to reside *within*, to become **immanent**, no longer abstract.

This path is also aligned with the **Magician** in the Tarot — the archetype who stands between heaven and earth, channeling the unseen into form. *With one hand pointing to the sky and the other to the ground, the Magician becomes a living bridge.* On the table before him lie the tools of creation — the cup, the sword, the wand, the coin — all emerging from the **One Source**, now given *form* and *function*.

The spiritual current of this path teaches that **limitation is not the enemy of the Divine — it is its expression**. Without form, nothing can be known. Without boundaries, nothing can be created. Just as a womb protects and shapes the unborn, so too does Binah **wrap structure around the luminous formlessness of Keter**, shaping it into *intelligible reality*.

To walk this path is to **honor structure**, not as confinement but as **sacred architecture**. It is to understand that even the most mystical experiences must eventually be integrated into the body, the mind, and the heart. *A flash of revelation means nothing if it cannot be embodied.*

Beth reminds us that **the Divine seeks a home**, and that home is within us. Yet to become that home, we must allow the vastness to *compress*, the infinite to *concentrate*, the idea to *become a word*. This is not a fall, but a *graceful descent* — a decision to *be known*.

The lesson here is one of **acceptance and reverence for form**. Without it, the light would remain unreachable. This path asks you to **honor your limits as sacred**, to see your body, your mind, and your very life as the **Beth** — the **house of the holy**. Through this act of containment, the **Divine becomes real**. Not distant, not abstract — but **living within the boundaries of your becoming**.

Chokmah to Binah (Gimel, ג)

This path is the **bridge between force and form**, between the **dynamic wisdom of Chokmah and the structured understanding of Binah**. In the mystical current of the Tree of Life, it is here that the **primal masculine** energy encounters its **feminine counterpart**, and in that union, **consciousness begins to shape reality**. The movement from Chokmah to Binah is **not a battle between opposites**, but a **sacred courtship** — the dance of **fire and vessel, thunder and echo, seed and womb**.

The Hebrew letter **Gimel (ג)**, meaning "camel," evokes powerful imagery. A **camel survives the desert** not through brute force, but through **endurance, adaptation**, and the **quiet knowledge of rhythm**. It is a symbol of the *inner traveler* — the mystic who **moves between worlds**, carrying divine wisdom across the **barren landscape of unknowing**. Gimel teaches that **crossing the void between inspiration and comprehension** is not a leap — it is a **journey**, and it requires **strength sustained through stillness**.

The Tarot card corresponding to this path is **The High Priestess** — the archetype of hidden knowledge, intuition, and sacred memory. *She sits between two pillars, black and white, Jachin and Boaz — symbols of duality and balance.* She holds the Torah, and at her feet rests the crescent moon, whispering of mysteries not yet revealed. Through her, the chaotic brilliance of Chokmah is drawn down into the **womb of understanding** — not to tame it, but to **conceive** something new from it.

This path is not merely intellectual. It is **alchemical**. It takes **the lightning bolt of insight** and lets it **settle into the chalice**. It transforms **raw knowing into refined meaning**, and through that transformation, the universe begins to take **shape and intention**. Without this path, wisdom would remain *wild and formless*, and understanding would remain *hollow and barren*.

Spiritually, to walk this path is to learn **patience and integration**. It asks the seeker to **hold paradox without collapsing it**, to *listen for meaning in both silence and thunder*. The soul must become the **camel** —

willing to cross inner wastelands, carrying within it the **waters of divine truth**, even when the journey feels **dry and endless**.

This path is also the beginning of **language and structure**, the first step in translating divine will into a **coherent vision**. It is where the blueprint of creation is drafted, not in haste, but with **reverence for precision**. Here, form does not limit — it **honors**. Structure is not oppression — it is **the temple being built**.

In essence, **Gimel** reminds us that there can be no proper understanding without effort, and no true union without tension. The sacred requires both **expansion and containment**, both **lightning and clay**. And so, this path invites the initiate to move with **grace and endurance**, to embrace the journey from brilliance to wisdom, and to **trust the power of sacred duality** — for it is in that **creative tension** that the cosmos sings.

Keter to Tiferet (Daleth, ד)

The fourth path of the Tree of Life is the **direct descent of divine will** into the **core of the soul's beauty and balance**. It is a transmission from **Keter**, the ineffable crown of pure divine intention, to **Tiferet**, the heart-center of **spiritual harmony, truth, and compassion**. This path is not a fall — it is a *gift*. It is the **pouring of infinite light into the chalice of the human soul**, allowing what is divine to **express itself in form** without distortion.

The Hebrew letter **Daleth (ד)** means "door", and this is no ordinary portal. It is the **threshold between the unknowable and the knowable**, the **invitation to step into alignment** with one's **true divine nature**. Daleth reminds us that *to approach the Divine is to accept the invitation to pass through a sacred gate — not with pride, but with humility*. The door stands open for those who are ready to become a vessel for something far greater than themselves.

The Tarot card associated with this path is **The Empress** — the great Mother of creation, embodiment of fertility, abundance, and sensory richness. *She wears the crown of stars and rests amidst wheat and flowing rivers, signaling the manifestation of spirit into nature.* Yet behind her beauty is a **cosmic truth**: she is the one who **makes the invisible visible**, who **midwifes divine potential into the world of form**.

This path bridges the **highest will** of the Creator with the **human capacity for reflection, compassion, and truth**. It is the path by which *the light of the Ain Soph is refracted into the prism of human experience.* In walking it, the seeker learns to *discern between egoic desire and divine will* — to become an agent of **holy balance**, not by denial of the self, but by **realigning the self with the greater pattern**.

Daleth is also associated with the concept of **poverty** in its mystical sense. This is not a lack, but the **poverty of ego**, the **emptiness that makes room for the divine**. As a door is defined by what it allows in and out, the seeker must **learn to become an open vessel**, not cluttered with personal agendas, but clear and spacious enough for the **higher will to flow through**. *Like an open doorway that lets the morning light fill the house, the soul must be stripped of illusion and pride to receive what it was always meant to carry.*

Spiritually, this path teaches **surrender**. Not passivity, but **conscious surrender** to that which is greater. The journey from Keter to Tiferet is **not a descent into limitation** — it is a **descent into beauty**, into the place where *the divine reflects itself like sunlight on still water*. The seeker begins to understand that **to live in truth is not to imitate the sacred, but to become a clear mirror for it**.

This path, when awakened within, grants the power to *bring divine purpose into every act*. The words you speak, the love you give, the work you create — all become imbued with **a sacred resonance**, because you no longer act from separation, but from **connection to the source**. You become the **door through which the light walks into the world**.

And so, Daleth is more than a path — it is a **calling**. A silent, persistent whisper: *"Let me through."* And when the soul answers, it does not become divine — it **remembers it always was**.

Chokmah to Chesed (Heh, ה)

The fifth path of the Tree of Life traces the **streaming of divine wisdom** into the sphere of **unconditional love and benevolence**. It begins in **Chokmah**, the raw, undifferentiated **force of creation**, and flows into **Chesed**, the boundless **mercy of the divine heart**. It is a path of **vision translated into action**, of power softened into **compassion**, and of insight made fertile through **grace**.

The Hebrew letter **Heh (ה)** means **"window"**, and this symbolism is deeply instructive. A window allows **light to pass through**, yet maintains **structure**; it offers **sight beyond the self**, without leaving the house. Likewise, this path invites the seeker to **receive the brilliant light of Chokmah**, not as an overwhelming blaze, but as a **vision tempered by mercy**, seen through the **sacred frame of the heart**. *It is not enough to understand — one must learn to see to give.*

In the Tarot, this path is represented by **The Emperor**, a figure of **divine authority and order**, but one whose power is rooted in the **responsibility to protect and uphold life**. The Emperor sits on a stone throne, holding the scepter of rulership, but his role is not to dominate — *his role is to ensure that wisdom governs justly*. This path teaches that **true power is not control, but stewardship**, and that **divine wisdom without compassion becomes cruelty**.

To walk the path from Chokmah to Chesed is to **learn how to wield spiritual insight in the service of love**. It is not enough to see the pattern of the cosmos; one must **weave it with mercy**, to **bless, heal, and uplift**. *A mystic who hoards revelation becomes a tyrant of the soul, but one who gives from insight becomes a fountain of life.*

Heh also holds mystical significance in the creation story. In Kabbalistic thought, it is the **letter used to form the world**, as in the divine name **Yod-Heh-Vav-Heh**. In this sense, **Heh is the breath of God**, the **exhalation that creates space for existence**. The seeker who embodies this path becomes, in turn, **a window through which divine generosity pours forth**. Their acts of kindness are not charity — they are **emanations of the divine mind in motion**.

There is also discipline in this path. The expansive love of Chesed must be **rooted in wisdom**, not in emotional impulse. It is easy to give unquestioningly, but this path teaches the **maturity of generosity** — *to know when love heals, and when it enables; when mercy uplifts, and when it drowns.* In this way, the wisdom of Chokmah is not lost in the waters of Chesed, but becomes **its guide**, its **inner compass**.

This is the path of **the visionary king**, the benevolent queen, the elder who sees far yet acts close. The lesson is this: **you were given insight not for yourself, but for others**. And when you pour what you've seen into the world — with mercy, with patience, with sacred fire-the window becomes a mirror, and you begin to **see the divine not only above, but reflected in the faces of those you serve**.

Let Heh be the sacred window of your soul. Open it wide. Let wisdom become love, and love become the world.

Binah to Gevurah (Vav, ו)

This path moves from **Binah**, the deep **understanding and structure** of the Divine Feminine, to **Gevurah**, the sphere of **judgment, discipline, and sacred severity**. It is the channel through which **wisdom becomes power**, not power that conquers, but power that defines, protects, and upholds divine order. The Hebrew letter **Vav (ו)**, meaning "hook" or "nail", symbolizes **connection and continuity**. Just as a hook binds two separate parts, this path binds **intellectual structure to practical force**.

Where **Binah** is the great womb of form, where all divine ideas are contemplated, sorted, and given shape, **Gevurah** is the **guardian of these forms**, ensuring they are not diluted, corrupted, or misused. This is not a gentle path. It is a descent from the contemplative silence of Binah into the **tempered fire of Gevurah**, where what is known must be **proven, tested**, and sometimes **cut away**.

In Tarot, this path is traditionally associated with **The Hierophant**, or **The Pope** — a figure who bridges spiritual law and human society. But seen through the lens of this path, it is also the **Judge**, the **Lawgiver**, the mystic who stands not to feel, but to discern. This is the path of the **spiritual warrior**, one who must not only *understand what is right* but also **enforce it**, even when it is difficult, even when it demands sacrifice.

Vav represents the vertical line of descent — from Heaven into form, from idea into discipline. It teaches that **knowledge without discipline becomes indulgence**, and that **compassion without boundaries becomes chaos**. On this path, the seeker learns to **set limits**, not from cruelty, but from **wisdom hard-earned** in the womb of Binah.

There is a sacred solitude on this path. *To judge rightly, you must sometimes stand alone.* You must be willing to **act when others delay**, to **say no when the crowd says yes**, and to **bear the weight of truth** in a world that prefers illusion. But this is not a license for pride or tyranny — for the one who walks this path remembers that **judgment is sacred only when born from understanding**.

In the creation of the world, the Kabbalists say that God withdrew, creating a space — *tzimtzum* — in which existence could take form. This act of restraint, of **divine self-limitation**, mirrors the essence of this path. *To create, we must first contain. To contain, we must first understand.*

This path teaches you to become the **guardian of boundaries** — within yourself, within others, and the world. You learn to **say no to excess**, to **refine your inner fire**, to **sharpen your insight into precise action**. This is the **edge of the sword**, and only those who understand its balance may wield it.

Vav holds the heavens to the earth. It joins **ideal to enforcement, vision to law, insight to responsibility**. It asks you not only what is true, but **what must be done with that truth**.

If you would walk this path, then sharpen your discernment, temper your strength with understanding, and do not flinch from the flame. For only the one who knows when to cut — and why — may hold the sacred blade without being burned.

Chesed to Gevurah (Zayin, ז)

This path stretches between two great opposites on the Tree of Life: **Chesed**, the boundless expanse of divine mercy, and **Gevurah**, the precise restraint of divine justice. Here lies a dynamic **tension** that every seeker must learn to navigate — the challenge of reconciling **love and judgment, giving and withholding, compassion and control**. The Hebrew letter **Zayin (ז)**, which means "sword", captures this tension perfectly: a blade that divides not to destroy, but to reveal what is real.

Zayin cuts through illusion. It exposes **imbalances** — the excessive mercy that enables chaos, the excessive judgment that breeds cruelty. In the journey from **Chesed to Gevurah**, the seeker must learn to hold both forces without letting either dominate. *Too much giving, and you dissolve into indulgence; too much restriction, and the heart withers into coldness.* Zayin demands the **discernment to know when to say yes, and the courage to say no**.

This is not a path of comfort. It is a **refiner's fire**, where your highest intentions are tested by your capacity to act wisely. The one who walks this path learns to **pierce through sentimentality** and to stand firmly in truth, even when it hurts. It is here that the **false dichotomy between love and power begins to dissolve**. True love, the path reveals, is not the absence of limits — it is the presence of boundaries that protect and uplift. And true power is not domination — it is the ability to act with justice, anchored in a **deep inner knowing**.

In Tarot, Zayin is often linked with **The Lovers**, a card frequently misunderstood as mere romance. In esoteric symbolism, however, it represents **the conscious choice between paths**, the union of opposites, and the sacred discernment of what aligns with the soul's true calling. On this path, the seeker is invited to **choose wisely**, not from fear or desire, but from the **clarity of vision that comes only after illusion has been burned away**.

Zayin also teaches that discernment is not a skill — it is a virtue. One must cultivate it with humility, patience, and a willingness to be wrong. *To wield the sword of Zayin is to live with eyes open, heart steady, and conscience transparent.* It is to navigate the razor's edge where

compassion meets consequence, where **the loving embrace must sometimes become the firm hand.**

This path demands **alignment** — not just between Chesed and Gevurah, but within the seeker. You must become both the giver and the judge, both the open hand and the unsheathed sword. *You must learn when to forgive and when to let go. When to nurture, and when to confront. When to hold on — and when to cut away.*

Zayin is sharp for a reason. It is meant to awaken. The one who masters this path becomes **a vessel for divine justice that never forgets mercy**, and **a vessel for divine mercy that never forgets justice**.

To walk between Chesed and Gevurah is to know that love without truth is illusion — and truth without love is brutality. Zayin teaches you to hold both, without flinching.

Chesed to Tiferet (Chet, ח)

This path traces the flow from **Chesed**, the vast outpouring of divine mercy, to **Tiferet**, the radiant heart of the Tree of Life — the sphere of balance, compassion, and spiritual beauty. The Hebrew letter **Chet (ח)**, which means *"fence"*, may seem an odd symbol at first for such a loving and luminous current. But within the sacred geometry of mysticism, **a fence is not a prison — it is a sanctuary**. It delineates what is holy. It guards what is tender. It protects what is becoming.

Chet teaches that **unbounded mercy**, no matter how divine its origin, must be shaped to become **sustainable grace**. The endless generosity of Chesed, while beautiful, can easily overflow and lose its purpose unless it is **channeled through form, intention, and discernment**. That is the essence of this path — to learn the sacred art of *limiting without withholding*, of *guiding without controlling*.

Tiferet is the mirror of divine harmony in the human heart. But harmony is not born from chaos. It is born from love **disciplined** by wisdom. On this path, the seeker must learn how to **create boundaries that do not exclude** but rather **protect the sacred flame** that burns within. It is the path of *the mentor who sets limits out of love, the healer who knows when not to give, the mystic who withdraws to cultivate inner stillness so that their light may one day shine more fully.*

Chet is the shape of the temple door. It marks the threshold you must cross if you are to dwell in the sacred. Not everyone may enter. Not everything may pass through. *To walk the path from Chesed to Tiferet is to become the gatekeeper of your own heart.* You must learn what to allow in and what to keep out. You must **refine your giving** so that it aligns with truth, not ego, not guilt, not the need to be needed.

In Tarot, this path is often associated with **Strength**, not in the crude sense of dominance, but in the quiet, contained force of inner mastery. It is the courage to hold steady. To act with gentleness that is **rooted in power**, not weakness. To be *both tender and unshakable*. Like a fence that sways but does not break in the wind.

Chet also reflects the mystery of **inner discipline**. The capacity to guard your sacred work from distraction. The ability to say *no*, not out of rejection, but as a form of devotion. *To say yes to your higher purpose often means saying no to everything else.* This path carves out the **inner sanctuary** where divine light can dwell, not momentarily, but **permanently**.

And so, Chet teaches that **true love is not measured by how much you give, but by how well you protect what is most sacred** — in yourself and others. To walk this path is to become **a sanctuary for beauty**, not by accumulating more light, but by creating the **conditions where light may flourish undisturbed.**

Chet is the fence around the garden. The boundary around the altar. The silence before the sacred word. It is the architecture of holiness. And the architecture of your transformation.

Gevurah to Tiferet (Tet, ט)

The ninth path on the Tree of Life travels from **Gevurah**, the sphere of divine judgment, power, and limitation, to **Tiferet**, the radiant center of harmony, compassion, and spiritual integration. The Hebrew letter **Tet (ט)** is shaped like a coiled serpent — a symbol that carries many layers of esoteric meaning: *wisdom, regeneration, inner alchemy, and hidden power*.

To walk the path of Tet is to **enter the crucible of spiritual refinement**. Gevurah, with all its intensity, is not meant to punish or destroy. It is the sacred fire that burns away what is false. **Tiferet cannot shine** — cannot reflect divine beauty in its full splendor — **unless the soul has faced the trials of discipline and emerged purified**. This path is the *narrow bridge between severity and balance*, and it demands that the seeker face their **inner resistance** with clarity and courage.

Tet teaches that **true wisdom is born not in comfort, but in challenge**. Like the serpent that must shed its skin to grow, the seeker on this path must *release outdated beliefs, stale identities, and emotional habits that no longer serve their evolution*. Gevurah supplies the force of necessary restriction, but it is through **Tet** that this force is *transmuted* — not into shame or guilt, but into a higher alignment with the divine pattern.

The serpent also represents **Kundalini**, the primal spiritual energy coiled at the base of the spine in many mystical systems. Along this path, that energy begins to stir. Not wildly, not without structure — but **guided through the channel of divine order**. Tet is not the chaos of the snake, but the *order of its sacred dance*.

In the Tarot, this path is frequently associated with **The Hermit** — a solitary figure who carries the lantern of inner light. This is no accident. The Hermit walks alone, not because he is isolated, but because he is **carving an inward path**. He knows that the **actual journey is within**. Tet echoes this lesson: *transformation is not showy, not loud, not external*. It happens **in the quiet chambers of the soul**, where the seeker learns to hold their fire with **restraint**, to speak less and **see more**, to act with **precision**, not impulse.

This path is the test of **character**. Will you crumble under pressure? Or will you allow pressure to **forge you into something finer?** Tet whispers: *What feels like restriction is often initiation. What seems like a loss is sometimes a gift in disguise. And what breaks you might be what ultimately sets you free.*

Gevurah limits. Tiferet unifies. And in between, **Tet transforms**. It coils, not to constrict, but to **concentrate power**. It spirals, not to confuse, but to **lead inward**. Every moment of hardship along this path becomes a mirror, showing you *not what you are, but what you could become*, if only you choose to evolve.

Tet is the serpent in the garden — not the tempter, but the awakener. It is the guardian of the inner gates. And when you walk this path with devotion, you don't slay the serpent... You become it. Wise, focused, and forever changed.

Chesed to Netzach (Yod, י)
The tenth path of the Tree of Life stretches between **Chesed**, the sphere of expansive love and divine benevolence, and **Netzach**, the realm of victory, persistence, and creative force. It is governed by the Hebrew letter **Yod (י)** — the smallest, yet perhaps the most profound character in the Hebrew alphabet. Though minuscule in appearance, **Yod contains the seed of all other letters**, and in the mystical tradition, it is said to embody the **essence of the divine spark** that lies at the foundation of all existence.

To walk this path is to **carry the infinite within the finite**. Chesed pours forth divine grace like an unending river — generous, luminous, and unconditional. However, Netzach demands direction, encompassing endurance, passion, and the capacity to overcome trials through creative expression. The path of Yod is thus the **distillation of grace into focused power** — the sacred act of *making the invisible spark visible* through effort, perseverance, and art.

Yod is not only a spark — it is the **finger of God**, the point from which creation begins. In Kabbalistic thought, this tiny stroke is the **first brush of divine intention**, the flash of potential that precedes the emergence of form. In this path, that same spark is **planted like a seed** into the field of human action. But **will it blossom?** Only if tended with intention. *Only if the heart remains aligned with grace while the hands do the work.*

This is where **spiritual generosity meets divine ambition**. Netzach is often misunderstood as mere victory, but its true nature lies in the **ability to endure** — to hold vision despite delay, to act from love despite challenge, and to manifest *without corrupting the source*. That's what the Yod preserves: **the purity of origin** even as it descends into effort and form.

The Tarot correspondence of this path is commonly associated with **Strength** or **The Wheel of Fortune**, both cards illustrating different facets of this energy. In *Strength*, we see the taming of inner impulses, not through suppression but through *compassionate control* — echoing Chesed's love tempered by Netzach's discipline. In *The Wheel*, we see the cycle of effort and reward, rise and fall — yet the Yod reminds us: **every movement, no matter how chaotic, begins from a point of divine stillness.**

The journey along this path is not always easy. The seeker may feel overwhelmed by the tension between **ideal and reality**, between the **purity of Chesed** and the **earthly trials of Netzach**. But Yod insists that **nothing is too small to carry the sacred**. A single word, a single action, a single intention — *if aligned with the divine* — can transform everything.

This is the path of the **artist who creates not for fame, but from reverence**. The healer who shows up again and again, not because it's easy, but because something sacred compels them. The visionary who refuses to quit — not for glory, but because they feel the weight of purpose in their bones.

Yod is the spark, but also the test: Will you protect the flame through the wind of adversity? Will you remember why you began, even when the road seems long?

To embody this path is to honor the divine in **smallness**. Not in shrinking, but in precision. In devotion. In the **quiet mastery** of one who turns grace into action and vision into victory.

And when that happens — when Yod completes its journey from the heart of Chesed to the victory of Netzach — **what once was potential becomes power. What once was unseen becomes unstoppable.**

Gevurah to Hod (Kaph, כ)

The eleventh path on the Tree of Life extends from **Gevurah**, the Sephirah of judgment, power, and sacred discipline, to **Hod**, the realm of intellect, language, and analytical insight. This bridge is governed by the Hebrew letter **Kaph (כ)**, which means "**palm**." Yet in its esoteric significance, Kaph speaks not merely of the physical hand, but of what it represents — the **interface between power and intention**, between what is held and what is released, between force and form.

To walk this path is to **learn the sacred art of containment**. Gevurah is the burning intensity of divine judgment, the blade that cuts, the fire that purifies. Hod, by contrast, is the meticulous scribe, the architect of thought, the vessel of *logos*. The path of Kaph teaches the seeker to **transmute raw strength into disciplined expression** — to wield power not with violence, but with intelligence.

Kaph is the **palm open to receive**, but also the **palm raised to restrain**. It is the gesture of **offering** and **blessing**, but also a **command**. In this lies its paradox: to possess true strength, one must learn how to **hold back**. In mystical terms, Kaph is the vessel in which divine force is shaped, structured, and *spoken*, turning thunder into word, judgment into wisdom.

In *practical terms*, this is the path of the warrior who becomes a philosopher, the enforcer who becomes a teacher. Imagine a soldier who once knew only the discipline of obedience now discovering the **eloquence of truth**, or a judge who tempers their sentences with understanding born of study and insight.

The Tarot correspondence often linked with this path is **Justice** or **The Chariot**, depending on the system. *Justice* captures the essence of measured judgment — a blade held in balance with the scales of discernment. *The Chariot*, meanwhile, reveals the necessity of **willpower aligned with understanding**, the driver who must rein in wild forces not by brute strength alone, but through focused mastery.

The spiritual lesson of this path is profound and often uncomfortable: **power without clarity leads to destruction**, and clarity without the courage to act is sterile. The seeker on the eleventh path must therefore **learn to unite discipline and intellect**, to forge a will that is both informed and unshakable. *It is not enough to know; one must also do — but do with discernment.*

Kaph also holds a secret in its shape — **a curved hand**, almost as if protecting something fragile. It reminds us that not all power roars. Some of the most **transformative acts of strength** are those that protect, hold, support, or uplift. A whispered truth. A firm boundary. A written word that awakens the soul. *All these are acts of Kaph.*

When one truly integrates this path, **the hand becomes the bridge between divine law and human action**. The palm that once struck now blesses. The force that once destroyed now reveals the truth. The judgment that once divided now illuminates.

To master this path is to **hold the flame without letting it burn** — to carry power not as a weapon, but as a responsibility. For when strength and wisdom finally embrace, *the seeker becomes not just a vessel of divine force, but a conscious co-creator of divine order.*

Tiferet to Netzach (Lamed, ל)

The twelfth path on the Tree of Life stretches from **Tiferet**, the radiant heart of balance and compassion, to **Netzach**, the dynamic force of endurance, desire, and victory. This is the path governed by the Hebrew letter **Lamed (ל)**, which means *"ox-goad"* — a pointed tool used to steer a powerful but stubborn animal along a chosen path. The symbolism is neither random nor mundane. Lamed is the only letter that rises above the line in traditional Hebrew script, as if reaching upward, *always teaching, always aspiring.*

To walk this path is to undergo a **journey of inspired direction**. The seeker is not merely pulled by spiritual beauty (Tiferet) nor propelled by blind desire (Netzach); instead, they are taught to **steer their passion toward purpose**, to align personal will with **the rhythm of the divine**. *It is not enough to feel love or dream of greatness — one must act upon it with direction, focus, and sacred intention.*

This path often feels like the tension between inspiration and execution. The beauty of Tiferet inspires, yes, but Netzach demands **endurance**. Many seekers falter here, not because they lack insight, but because they resist the disciplined motion required to **carry divine vision into the arena of time and space**. Lamed, the ox-goad, urges them onward, not with cruelty but with relentless purpose. It is the symbol of the spiritual teacher — *the inner voice that does not allow you to rest in stagnation.*

In the Tarot, this path resonates with **Strength** or **Justice**, depending on the system, but in the Hermetic tradition, it often aligns with **Strength**. This arcana depicts not brute force, but **compassionate control** — a woman taming a lion, not with chains, but with calm presence and clarity. *It is the lesson that true power is not domination but direction.*

Lamed also connects to the archetype of the **teacher**, and not just any teacher, but the one who appears when the student is ready to be tested, challenged, and evolved. Just as the ox-goad keeps the beast moving toward the goal, so too does Lamed **prod the soul toward its destiny**, even when it resists. It teaches that struggle is not a sign of failure, but rather a sign of momentum.

This path reminds the seeker that **spiritual beauty without endurance becomes sterile**, and **victory without moral direction becomes chaos**. Lamed unites these forces by offering guidance from the heart of Tiferet into the striving force of Netzach. Imagine a poet who, after years of spiritual insight, finally finds the resolve to publish their truth. Or a visionary who transforms compassion into a movement that shakes the world. *This is the current that flows through Path 12.*

At its highest, this path initiates **the alchemy of divine will and human desire**. It teaches that the way forward is rarely easy, but always sacred. And just as the ox is steered not by force, but by persistent nudges, so too must the seeker be ready to **receive guidance from within, from others, and the invisible hand of destiny**.

To embody the lesson of Lamed is to **become the student and the teacher at once**. You learn to act without hesitation, love without attachment, and serve without expectation. For when your will is yoked to the divine, *even the most challenging path becomes the road home.*

Tiferet to Hod — Mem (מ)

This path is carved between **Tiferet**, the center of radiant spiritual beauty, and **Hod**, the sphere of logic, analysis, and linguistic expression. Its letter is **Mem (מ)**, a character deeply associated with *water* — the primordial element of **depth, emotion, reflection, and concealed knowledge**.

Mem evokes the mysterious yet essential nature of water: **fluid, adaptive, yet capable of shaping mountains** over time. As a symbol, it suggests that **actual knowledge is not rigid**, but something that flows, nourishes, and carves its path. Just as water moves between rocks and carries sediment from one region to another, **this path teaches the seeker to take wisdom from the heart to the intellect**, from the luminous center of self (Tiferet) into the finely tuned network of understanding that Hod represents.

Yet this is no simple transmission of facts. Tiferet reflects *spiritual truth*, not data. **To travel from Tiferet to Hod through Mem is to translate mystical insight into human language**, to bring the ineffable into form — *as a poet captures emotion in verse, or a mystic renders visions into sacred geometry*. This path is walked every time you try to **express love as philosophy** or turn inner revelation into a **coherent doctrine**.

As water, memory also represents the unconscious mind, where symbolic dreams and archetypes reside. Hod, with its analytical sharpness, might resist this liquidity at first. However, the path teaches that reason without a soul becomes sterile, just as emotion without structure becomes chaotic. The secret of this path lies in **harmony**: intuition must be *disciplined* by logic, but logic must be *informed* by intuition.

The Tarot card often associated with this path is **The Hanged Man**, a figure suspended upside down, *surrendering to a more profound truth*. He symbolizes the paradoxes of spiritual learning — the need to pause, to invert perspective, to listen not just with the mind, but with the inner tides of the soul. **It's through stillness and surrender that deeper understanding flows**, like water through a narrow stream.

To walk this path consciously is to **learn the alchemical art of translation** — how to speak divine truths in the language of the world, without betraying their essence. Many spiritual leaders, artists, and philosophers find themselves repeatedly passing through Mem, each time refining their message and seeking a purer way to convey what cannot be fully expressed.

In ritual work, this path teaches you to move gracefully between **meditative insight and symbolic analysis**, between **vision and articulation**. *It is the hermit who becomes the scribe*, the visionary who returns from the mountain to write the sacred book.

Ultimately, the thirteenth path reveals that truth must be both experienced and expressed. Mem reminds the seeker that **knowledge flows like water**, and that **the intellect, if it remains open and humble**, can become the vessel for **mystical experience**. The goal is not to reduce mystery to reason, but to let **reason become a mirror** through which **the light of truth may be seen**.

Netzach to Yesod (Nun, נ)
The fourteenth path stretches between **Netzach**, the Sephirah of passion, desire, and victory, and **Yesod**, the subtle yet potent foundation of all material manifestation. At its core lies the Hebrew letter **Nun (נ)**, whose literal meaning is *fish* — a creature long regarded across mystical traditions as a **symbol of life, flow, fecundity, and hidden wisdom**.

Nun swims through the deep waters of potential, **silent and concealed, yet teeming with vitality**. This path is one of *conception*, not only biological, but spiritual and creative. Netzach, burning with inspiration and longing, seeks expression; Yesod, the gateway to the physical realm, provides the **matrix through which desire becomes form**. **Path 14 is the canal of gestation**, where fire cools, and dreams prepare to take shape.

To walk this path is to experience the **translation of chaotic emotion into energetic blueprint**. Netzach's flames — love, ecstasy, ambition, vision — must be distilled into something stable enough to imprint itself onto the matrix of reality. *The artist, impassioned by an idea, begins sketching; the mystic, stirred by a vision, begins crafting ritual.* In each case, **the formless begins to seek a container**.

Nun also speaks to **cycles of death and rebirth**. In many esoteric systems, the fish is seen as a being of the deep, hidden, gestating, and evolving. It **swims through the unseen currents of the unconscious**, a symbol of processes that operate beneath awareness. The path from Netzach to Yesod teaches the seeker that **manifestation requires incubation** — a surrender to unseen rhythms, a willingness to trust the process rather than force results.

The Tarot card traditionally associated with Nun is **Death**, not as an ending, but as **transformation, renewal, and passage**. This may seem surprising, given the themes of fertility and creation, but it is deeply appropriate. **Something must always die for something new to be born.** The fiery surge of Netzach must pass through a kind of surrender before it can become stable and anchored in Yesod. *Old identities, outdated patterns, or scattered desires must dissolve so that genuine creation can occur.*

Energetically, this path is subtle but immensely powerful. Netzach provides the impulse; Yesod, the etheric womb. But without the bridge of Nun, there is no cohesion. Nun **gathers the waters of inspiration** and **infuses them with life-force**, quietly knitting divine passion into the fabric of the astral world, where it awaits final birth in Malkuth.

For the magician, this path is a call to **master emotional alchemy** — to refine raw, overwhelming urges into **disciplined imagination**. For the mystic, it is a reminder that **desire must be purified** before it can serve the spirit. And for the visionary, Nun whispers of the power of the unseen: *"All true creations begin in silence."* Ultimately, Path 14 teaches that **no vision becomes real until it has passed through the waters of transformation**. It urges us to honor our emotions not as ends in themselves, but as **living currents of divine will**, seeking a vessel. And it promises that if we allow those currents to guide us through darkness, surrender, and rebirth, we will arrive at **a foundation strong enough to hold the light of heaven within the world.**

Hod to Yesod (Samekh, ס)

The fifteenth path of the Tree of Life weaves between **Hod**, the Sephirah of intellect, language, and analytical structure, and **Yesod**, the subtle foundation that stores, organizes, and channels energy into the world of matter. This path is governed by the Hebrew letter **Samekh (ס)**, which means *support*, a word that immediately evokes ideas of **safety, structure, and inner strength**.

Samekh is not a passive support, like a beam or a crutch. It is **active containment, protective guidance**, and **inner discipline**. It speaks to the kind of strength that surrounds rather than dominates — like a womb, a sanctuary, or a temple. In the movement from **Hod to Yesod**, the energies of language, logic, and form are taken down into the realm of the subconscious, where they become part of the **blueprint of manifestation**.

This path teaches that **knowledge must be stabilized before it can yield its full potential**. Hod provides clarity and intellectual analysis, but without the grounding function of Yesod, these insights remain **floating concepts**, disconnected from real power. Samekh acts as a **channel**, a **pillar of equilibrium**, ensuring that the refined ideas of Hod don't dissipate in abstraction but are **infused with life and emotional resonance** in Yesod.

In the Tarot, Samekh is aligned with **Temperance**, the card of **alchemy, moderation, and inner harmony**. The angel depicted on the card pours liquid from one chalice to another, symbolizing the **harmonization of polarities** — fire and water, thought and emotion, spirit and matter. This is the essential labor of this path: to **blend the precise structure of Hod with the dynamic emotional reservoir of Yesod**, so that consciousness becomes not only accurate but also **fruitful, impactful, and aligned with the sacred**. Symbolically, the path of Samekh is like a **bridge of crystal suspended in mist** — the mist being the dreamlike, intuitive realm of Yesod, and the crystal representing the sharp light of Hod. Walking this bridge requires both **mental clarity and emotional stability**. It demands that the seeker learn to **trust inner order** even when the outer world is unclear. It's the path of those who are willing to descend into the depths of the self while **maintaining their spiritual compass**.

There's a reason the ancients saw Samekh as the **coiled serpent**, curled within the spine — the **inner axis of spiritual ascent and descent**. This is not a passive resting place, but a **vital support structure**, a spinal column of the soul. When this path is unbalanced, the seeker may become **obsessed with control**, clinging to rigid logic, or descending into compulsive behavior. However, when integrated correctly, Samekh offers a serene and quiet resilience that can withstand immense forces without being broken.

Imagine a mystic writing a sacred chant. The precise words (Hod) must be given form through repetition and rhythm, anchored in the body and the breath (Yesod), so that the chant opens a real doorway to the Divine. That is the work of Samekh — to **hold the form** until it vibrates with life.

Ultimately, this path challenges the aspirant to **weave knowledge into being**, not through brute force or emotional chaos, but through **discipline, sacred routine, and spiritual composure**. It reminds us that **support is not weakness** — it is **the hidden strength that allows all else to rise**. In the silence of Samekh, you learn to walk steadily between mind and mystery, clarity and chaos, without ever losing your balance.

Netzach to Malkuth (Ayin, ע)

The sixteenth path stretches from **Netzach**, the Sephirah of passion, emotion, endurance, and desire, down to **Malkuth**, the realm of physical manifestation — the **Kingdom**, where spirit crystallizes into form. It is governed by the Hebrew letter **Ayin (ע)**, which means *eye*, and thus evokes the power of **vision, insight, and conscious perception**.

Ayin is not merely the physical act of seeing — it is the **awakening of inner sight**, the ability to perceive the hidden patterns behind the world of appearances. When the **fiery drive of Netzach** descends toward **the earth-bound solidity of Malkuth**, it must pass through the gate of perception. It is here that **vision becomes action**, and **creative imagination becomes physical reality**.

This path reminds us that without accurate perception, desire is blind. Netzach is full of longing, beauty, and inspiration — *the impulse to create, to love, to conquer* — but unless that energy is properly **grounded**, it dissipates or burns out. Ayin teaches the mystic to **see through illusion**, to recognize that what we bring into the world reflects **what we hold within**. The creative process must begin with clear sight — not only of what is possible, but of **what is real**.

In the Tarot, Ayin corresponds to **The Devil**, a card often misunderstood. While it may at first seem dark, this arcana reveals a crucial truth: **what we are chained to is usually what we fail to see clearly**. The illusions of control, ego, addiction, and misdirected desire are not inherently evil — they are distortions of divine energy. *The Devil binds us only when we give our power away unquestioningly.* Thus, this path forces the seeker to confront the shadows that emerge when creative energy is not fully integrated.

The eye sees, but it also deceives. On this path, the aspirant must learn to distinguish between **true manifestation and vanity**, between **purposeful creation and compulsive reproduction**. For example, *an artist may be filled with vision (Netzach), but if she cannot ground that vision in craft and action (Malkuth), it remains fantasy.* Ayin challenges her to become not only a dreamer, but a **builder of dreams**.

The descent of divine inspiration into form requires more than just momentum — it demands **clarity of intention, mature vision**, and **courageous honesty**. Ayin reveals that what we see in the world is **a mirror of what we carry inside**. If Netzach is the longing for beauty, Malkuth is the test: *can that beauty survive incarnation? Can it remain true when clothed in flesh and time?*

This is also the path where many spiritual seekers falter. Caught between the emotional force of Netzach and the gritty limitations of Malkuth, they either retreat into dreams or become disillusioned by the imperfect nature of the world. But Ayin urges a different response: **to look deeply**, to confront the real, and to **create anyway**, not despite the flaws of the material, but **through them**.

In its highest sense, Ayin is the *seer's eye* — the eye that pierces through glamour and false light. It teaches that **to manifest is not to escape limitation, but to honor it**. Malkuth is not exile — it is **the throne of spirit**. What good is divine victory (Netzach) if it cannot **touch the soil, feed the body, heal the world**?

Thus, the path of Ayin is **alchemical**: it transmutes emotional fire into embodied expression. It demands **vision with discipline, desire with purpose**, and **awareness without illusion**. In this sacred descent, the seeker becomes an artist of reality, learning not only how to see the world but how to **shape it**.

Hod to Malkuth (Peh, פ)

The seventeenth path descends from **Hod**, the Sephirah of intellect, logic, and structured thought, into **Malkuth**, the physical world — the final emanation and the *Kingdom* of matter. It is governed by the Hebrew letter **Peh (פ)**, which means **"mouth."** This is the path of **articulation, manifestation through language, and the sacred power of the spoken word**.

In the Hermetic Qabalah, Hod represents the realm of **analysis, symbols, and form**, the *architect's mind* that defines structure and detail. Malkuth, by contrast, is the realm of **concrete expression**, the **tangible and manifest**. The path of Peh serves as a **channel that brings thought into form through expression**, whether verbal or symbolic.

Peh is the mouth, and this mouth does more than speak — it **creates, names**, and **commands**. In many traditions, *to name something is to have power over it*. The act of speech becomes an act of creation. Think of the Genesis narrative: *"And God said, Let there be light."* Creation begins not with action, but with **utterance**. On this path, the seeker learns that the **word is a bridge between mind and matter**, between abstraction and action.

This is not just metaphorical. Peh teaches that your **thoughts are made real through your voice**, whether that voice is literal, such as *writing, chanting, praying,* or symbolic, such as *designing, coding, directing others, or storytelling*. When you speak, you **shape reality**. When you remain silent, your inner vision dies on the altar of potential.

The Tarot card associated with this path is **The Tower**, often seen as one of the most disruptive and feared cards in the deck. Yet within that destruction lies revelation. The Tower is a **violent clearing**, a tearing down of illusions built upon weak foundations. It is **truth unleashed**, a *divine utterance* that strikes the false structures of ego, ideology, and dogma. Just as Peh is the mouth, **the Tower is the shout that cannot be ignored**, the thunderous *"enough"* that shakes what must fall.

Thus, this path warns the seeker: *your words have power*. A lie repeated becomes a structure. A truth withheld becomes a prison. The spiritual challenge here is not only **to speak**, but to **speak rightly** — *with precision, responsibility, and awareness of impact*. In an esoteric sense, Peh also connects to **magical utterance**: *incantation, invocation, the casting of a spell* — all of which require clarity, will, and exactness. *Sloppy speech weakens magic; precise articulation conjures worlds.*

Walking the path from Hod to Malkuth means learning to **translate insight into impact**. For example, *a mystic may understand profound cosmic truths (Hod), but if she cannot teach, inspire, or embody those truths in action (Malkuth), they remain sterile*. Conversely, *a builder may create vast monuments (Malkuth), but without divine intention or vision (Hod), those works become hollow shells.*

Peh teaches the necessity of *language as the carrier of divinity*. In daily life, this can mean writing a book that conveys sacred truth, speaking a brutal yet healing truth to a loved one, or choosing silence when words would distort the message. Each is an **act of conscious expression**. Each is a **magical gesture**.

To walk this path is to become a *mouthpiece of divinity*, to let the **logos- the divine Word — pass** through you and shape the world. It is to **marry mind and matter through the breath of speech**, to **exhale truth into clay** and shape it into form.

But it also demands that you *demolish false structures* — beliefs, behaviors, habits — that no longer serve your path. Like The Tower, **the actual word may burn**. But what it leaves behind is **clarity, purity, and a ground solid enough to build anew**.

Peh is not gentle. It is surgical. It is the divine voice cutting through the noise. It asks: *What will you speak into being? What lie will you tear down? What truth are you brave enough to say out loud?* This is the mouth of the magician, the oracle, the prophet — the one who speaks *not to be heard, but to transform.*

Yesod to Malkuth (Tzaddi, צ)

The eighteenth path connects **Yesod**, the Sephirah of the subconscious, dreams, and energetic blueprint, to **Malkuth**, the material world — the domain of sensory experience, physicality, and action. It is governed by the Hebrew letter **Tzaddi (צ)**, traditionally translated as *"fishhook"*. This small but potent symbol holds profound implications: it is **the act of drawing something hidden out from the depths and bringing it to the surface,** much like pulling a fish from deep water into the light.

Yesod is the place of reflection, of **unmanifest potential**, where energies from the higher Sephiroth are filtered, shaped, and stabilized before they can become real. It is the **foundation**, but not the actual structure. It's where symbols, desires, images, and intentions incubate — like dreams waiting to be born. **Malkuth**, in contrast, is the world we live in — the **consequence** of all that has come before. The body, the senses, the soil beneath your feet, the computer screen you're reading from — all belong to **Malkuth**. It is **completion**, but also a **beginning**.

The fishhook — **Tzaddi** — represents this precise moment: when **something from the invisible realm is pulled into manifestation**. It is the archetype of *birth*, of *expression*, of *revelation*. Just as a fisherman casts his line into the unknown, hoping to retrieve something of value, the seeker learns on this path to *cast intention into the realm of the unseen and draw it into physical reality*.

In mystical terms, this is **the path of manifestation magic**. Not theoretical understanding. Not planning, but **bringing spiritual ideas into the tangible** — turning visions into structures, words into books, prayers into action. *For example,* a ritual conceived in Yesod only becomes real when performed with the body in Malkuth. A vision of healing only changes the world when turned into a medicine, a message, or a mission.

This path also demands **integrity** — not moral perfection, but **alignment with one's values**. When your inner world (Yesod) and your outer actions (Malkuth) are in **disharmony**, nothing truly manifests. You fish in murky waters and pull up **only shadows**. But when your intentions are clear, when your energy is undivided, you begin to pull **light** into form.

The Tarot card traditionally associated with **Tzaddi** is **The Star**, although in some esoteric systems, its position was debated. **The Star** is the emblem of **hope, clarity, inspiration, and divine connection flowing into the world**. It speaks to an open channel between heaven and earth, between imagination and embodiment. The Star pours living water — not into the heavens, not into Yesod — but into the world. *Into Malkuth.* This is not a dream. It is **the dream made flesh**.

On a personal level, this path teaches you to **ground your power**. It is not enough to *meditate, visualize,* or *wish*. You must **act**. You must **walk, touch, speak**, and **build**. The sacred is not only in the stars — it is in the sweat of your labor, in the mundane rituals of daily life. *The way you clean your space, the way you cook your food, the way you keep your word — these become acts of magic.*

In the descent from Yesod to Malkuth, you are asked to become a **conduit** — one who translates spirit into form. This is where many seekers falter. It is easy to remain in dreams, in the soft mists of potential. It is harder to **commit to the heaviness of earth**, to **dig your hands into clay and shape it**.

And yet this is what Tzaddi requires: that you take the **hook of intention** and draw out something **real**. It could be small — a candle lit with reverence, a poem whispered to the wind, a boundary set with love. Or it could be vast — a healing sanctuary, a sacred garden, a book that changes lives.

But one thing is sure: if you do not complete the descent, **you remain unfinished**. Your magic remains theory: your potential, just a cloud.

Tzaddi is the final alchemy. **You do not just dream the divine. You become it. In this world. In your body. In your actions.** That is the only way heaven descends to earth, through you.

Tiferet to Keter (Qoph, ק)

The nineteenth path stretches from **Tiferet**, the heart of the Tree and the seat of beauty, harmony, and inner truth, all the way up to **Keter**, the Crown — the ineffable source of divine will and unmanifest potential. This is not a path for the unprepared. It is the vertical axis that links the **center of the soul** with the **origin of all existence**, and it is governed by the Hebrew letter **Qoph (ק)**, which means *"back of the head."* This simple image is layered with meaning, for it is in the back of the head, the hidden side of consciousness, that the **subconscious mind resides**.

Tiferet is the mirror of the divine within us — it is where personality begins to dissolve into purpose, where selfishness is refined into service, and where fragmented desires are gathered under the banner of truth. But Tiferet still *knows* itself. There is still an "I" that strives to be good, balanced, and spiritual. The journey from Tiferet to **Keter** demands the sacrifice of even that identity. This path is the call to **surrender all self-awareness**, to **step beyond thought**, beyond even the idea of being a seeker, and to **enter into the silent ocean of divine will**.

Qoph is the doorway through which one must pass when the ego has been refined, but not yet annihilated. It is the narrow passage between self-realization and **self-erasure**. The Zohar describes this transition as "entering behind the veil," because this is where the veil between the manifest and the unmanifest, between the created and the Creator, becomes **permeable**.

Imagine standing in the stillness of dawn, before a vast, endless horizon. There are no more questions, because the one who asked them has begun to fade. There are no more prayers, because the one who prayed is dissolving. There is only the quiet pull of light — the upward gravity of the Crown.

The Tarot card associated with Qoph is **The Moon**, a card traditionally seen as mysterious, deceptive, even dangerous. But on this path, its meaning deepens. The Moon represents the **twilight of consciousness**, when reason fails and intuition must guide the way. The seeker does not ascend to Keter through logic or effort, but through **receptivity, surrender, and purification**. It is in the **night of the soul**, when the ego no longer provides direction, that one begins to feel the gravitational pull of the Divine.

The back of the head — Qoph — also points to that which is **behind us**, unknown to our conscious sight. It represents the realm of **dreams, archetypes, forgotten truths**, and pre-linguistic awareness. To walk this path is to navigate this **liminal zone**, where the subconscious becomes the bridge to the supraconscious.

There is danger here. Not every seeker is ready to lose their center. The ascent to Keter is a form of **death**, not of the body, but of identity, attachments, even one's spiritual pride. It is not rare to reach this threshold and turn back, overwhelmed by the *terrible silence* of the Crown. For in Keter, **there is no more "you"**. There is only **Will — unspoken, unformed, and infinite**.

Yet for those who persist — for those who dissolve and allow themselves to be reformed — **the reward is not ecstasy, but union**. The heart (Tiferet) merges into the Will (Keter), and **life becomes an extension of the Divine's unfolding**. *You do not act; the Divine acts through you. You do not speak; you become the voice of the ineffable.*

This is why mystics of every tradition describe this state not as a peak, but as a **disappearance** — *the candle extinguished by dawn, the river swallowed by the sea, the final breath before stillness.* And from this stillness, everything is born.

So Qoph, though a small letter, governs one of the most significant transitions of all: **from beauty to emptiness, from knowledge to silence, from self to source**. It is not a path one walks once, but one that reappears **at every threshold of spiritual growth**, demanding ever-deeper levels of surrender.

To walk the path of Qoph is to say, not "I will find the Divine," but **"I will become empty so that the Divine may find me."**

Chokmah to Tiferet (Resh, ר)

This path connects **Chokmah**, the primordial spark of divine wisdom, to **Tiferet**, the heart of the Tree, the seat of beauty, harmony, and compassion. The Hebrew letter **Resh (ר)**, meaning *"head"*, governs this channel, not merely as the seat of intellect, but as a symbol of **vision, clarity, and spiritual leadership**.

To walk this path is to **bring the unformed flash of insight down into the realm of integration**, where divine brilliance becomes **wisdom-in-action**. Chokmah is pure, undifferentiated force — a lightning bolt of inspiration, masculine and generative. But it lacks form. It does not explain; it simply *is*. Tiferet, on the other hand, is the **mediator**, the place where divine forces are balanced, refined, and expressed in beauty. This path is the bridge between *brilliance* and *embodiment*.

Resh, the head, does not symbolize dominance or ego. In the Kabbalistic sense, **authentic leadership means service** — the capacity to hold a vision high enough to inspire others, yet humble enough to reflect their needs. *The head leads the body not through control, but through guidance and responsibility.* Similarly, this path challenges the seeker to take the **raw flame of divine will** and transform it into an inner compass that others can both feel and follow.

The Tarot card corresponding to Resh is **The Sun**, a symbol of illumination, joy, and revealed truth. On this path, the Sun is not merely light — it is the **gift of clarity** after spiritual blindness. Chokmah is like staring directly into a blinding light; Tiferet, by contrast, is the **radiant glow that warms rather than burns**. This transition mirrors the mystical movement from incomprehensible knowing to **living insight**.

To walk the twentieth path is to **become a conduit** for divine wisdom without distorting it through pride or confusion. Many falter here, *believing the vision is theirs*, or rushing to act without temperance. But the initiate who learns to listen as much as to speak, to reflect as much as to shine, discovers the secret of this passage: **leadership is a function of inner alignment**.

Imagine a mystic who receives a sudden, overwhelming flash of insight during prayer — the nature of the universe unfolding before them. If they rush to speak, they lose it. If they try to possess it, it disappears. But if they let it settle into the heart, like sunlight diffusing through still water, that insight becomes a new way of living. This is the teaching of Resh.

This path also initiates the **journey of the prophet,** the healer, the spiritual guide. It is not enough to *know*. One must be able to **embody wisdom without ego**, to walk with **radiance and humility**, to speak with **power and stillness**.

Resh also hints at **rebirth**. The shape of the letter suggests a turning — a *return to origin*. This is fitting: every ascent of this path brings the seeker **closer to their true essence**, not through the accumulation of knowledge, but through shedding illusion. The wisdom of Chokmah, when filtered through Tiferet, becomes **not something you teach, but something you** *are*.

Thus, Path 20 is not merely a corridor of intellect. It is a **refining fire**, demanding purity of motive, integrity of heart, and constancy of inner vision. It asks you to **stand at the center of the Tree, not to be seen, but to reflect the Divine Light clearly**, like a mirror polished by suffering, devotion, and truth.

To walk this path is to become **a radiant presence**, guiding others not with force, but with **the silent gravity of inner certainty**.

Binah to Tiferet (Shin, ש)

This path, which stretches between **Binah**, the sacred chamber of divine understanding, and **Tiferet**, the radiant heart of the Tree, is governed by the Hebrew letter **Shin (ש)** — a letter of fire, transformation, and purification. It is the path of alchemy: where **raw understanding is refined into luminous beauty**, where the seeker does not merely comprehend, but is *transformed* by what they learn.

Binah is structure, discipline, the womb of all form. It is the **Divine Mother**, the force that gives shape to the wild flash of Chokmah. It contemplates, analyzes, and defines. But Binah is also distant, high upon the Tree, removed from the emotional warmth of the lower Sephirot. **Tiferet**, by contrast, is empathy, balance, and divine compassion — the place where the abstract becomes **alive and relational**.

To move from Binah to Tiferet is to carry the weight of divine understanding *through the fire* — to descend not with arrogance or cold intellect, but with a heart illuminated by clarity. The letter **Shin**, with its three flames, has long been associated with the **sacred fire that purifies**, not destroys. This is not the fire of wrath, but of **revelation** — the kind that *burns away what is false* so that truth may shine.

The Tarot card linked to this path is **Judgement** — a card not of condemnation, but of **awakening**. It is the moment of *inner resurrection*, when the soul hears the call to rise above the grave of unconsciousness, just as Judgement speaks of rebirth through fire. Hence, this path demands **the death of illusions and** a **refinement of identity**.

Imagine a mystic who has studied deeply, who understands the laws of the universe with exquisite precision. And yet they remain untouched in their soul — dry, rigid, distant. But one day, through suffering or awe, something in them breaks open. The knowledge once held in the mind flows into the heart. It changes how they speak, how they love, how they suffer. This is the work of Shin.

This path does not ask for passive devotion. It **challenges** the seeker to **take what they know and burn it in the furnace of the heart**. It teaches that **understanding is sterile without love**, and that **beauty without wisdom is blind**. The journey from Binah to Tiferet is not linear — it is a **crucible**. The ego is confronted, the intellect humbled, the heart opened. And through that fire, the seeker emerges **more fully themselves**.

Shin is also the letter inscribed on the **forehead of the High Priest** in Kabbalistic vision — it marks one who has undergone inner purification and can now act as a vessel of divine will. The flames of Shin are not random: they point upward, signifying **aspiration**, a desire to **return to Source**, even while rooted in embodied compassion.

This path refines not only thought, but **character**. It burns away selfish ambition, prideful certainty, and spiritual coldness. What remains is **Tiferet** — a center of gravity so luminous that others are drawn to it, not by force, but by resonance.

To walk this path is to *let fire pass through you*. It is to allow divine insight to move beyond theory into **humility, service, and inner radiance**. It is the path of the **spiritual artisan**, who crafts not temples of stone but sanctuaries of presence, *where others may glimpse the divine simply by being near you.*

Thus, Path 21 is the sacred firewalk of the Tree — where **intellect bows to beauty**, and the seeker becomes not a master of knowledge, but a **living flame of insight**, shaped by suffering, softened by grace, and illumined by divine love.

Keter to Malkuth (Tav, ת)

This path, which stretches between **Binah**, the sacred chamber of divine understanding, and **Tiferet**, the radiant heart of the Tree, is governed by the Hebrew letter **Shin (ש)** — a letter of fire, transformation, and purification. It is the path of alchemy: where **raw understanding is refined into luminous beauty**, where the seeker does not merely comprehend, but is *transformed* by what they learn.

Binah is structure, discipline, the womb of all form. It is the **Divine Mother**, the force that gives shape to the wild flash of Chokmah. It contemplates, analyzes, and defines. But Binah is also distant, high upon the Tree, removed from the emotional warmth of the lower Sephirot. **Tiferet**, by contrast, is empathy, balance, and divine compassion — the place where the abstract becomes **alive and relational**.

To move from Binah to Tiferet is to carry the weight of divine understanding *through the fire* — to descend not with arrogance or cold intellect, but with a heart illuminated by clarity. The letter **Shin**, with its three flames, has long been associated with the **sacred fire that purifies**, not destroys. This is not the fire of wrath, but of **revelation** — the kind that *burns away what is false* so that truth may shine.

The Tarot card linked to this path is **Judgement** — a card not of condemnation, but of **awakening**. It is the moment of *inner resurrection*, when the soul hears the call to rise above the grave of unconsciousness, just as Judgement speaks of rebirth through fire. Hence, this path demands **a death of illusions**, a **refinement of identity**.

Imagine a mystic who has studied deeply, who understands the laws of the universe with exquisite precision. And yet they remain untouched in their soul — dry, rigid, distant. But one day, through suffering or awe, something in them breaks open. The knowledge once held in the mind flows into the heart. It changes how they speak, how they love, how they suffer. This is the work of Shin.

This path does not ask for passive devotion. It **challenges** the seeker to **take what they know and burn it in the furnace of the heart**. It teaches that **understanding is sterile without love**, and that **beauty without wisdom is blind**. The journey from Binah to Tiferet is not linear — it is a **crucible**. The ego is confronted, the intellect humbled, the heart opened. And through that fire, the seeker emerges **more fully themselves**.

Shin is also the letter inscribed on the **forehead of the High Priest** in Kabbalistic vision — it marks one who has undergone inner purification and can now act as a vessel of divine will. The flames of Shin are not random: they point upward, signifying **aspiration**, a desire to **return to Source**, even while rooted in embodied compassion.

This path refines not only thought, but **character**. It burns away selfish ambition, prideful certainty, and spiritual coldness. What remains is **Tiferet** — a center of gravity so luminous that others are drawn to it, not by force, but by resonance.

To walk this path is to *let fire pass through you*. It is to allow divine insight to move beyond theory into **humility, service, and inner radiance**. It is the path of the **spiritual artisan**, who crafts not temples of stone but sanctuaries of presence — *where others may glimpse the divine simply by being near you*.

Thus, Path 21 is the sacred firewalk of the Tree — where **intellect bows to beauty**, and the seeker becomes not a master of knowledge, but a **living flame of insight**, shaped by suffering, softened by grace, and illumined by divine love.

Kabbalistic Correspondence Table: Hebrew Letters and Numbers

This chart reveals the deep correspondences between the **22 letters of the Hebrew alphabet**, their **numerical values** (as understood through Gematria), and their **symbolic meanings** within the Kabbalistic tradition.

Each letter is more than a sound or a mark—it's a key to understanding the **hidden architecture of reality**. In Kabbalah, **numerical values** are not arbitrary; they uncover **subtle layers of meaning** embedded in sacred texts and mystical teachings. Through Gematria, letters transform into numbers, and numbers become pathways of spiritual insight.

The **symbolism of each letter** reflects universal archetypes mapped onto the **Tree of Life**, guiding the seeker through stages of transformation, initiation, and return. For example, *Aleph* (1) speaks of **origin and unity**, *Beth* (2) of **duality and containment**, and *Tav* (400) of **completion and truth**.

Together, these correspondences form a **mystical language**—a bridge between word and number, matter and spirit, thought and manifestation. The table serves as a **core tool** for decoding esoteric texts, meditating on divine structure, and attuning to the **vibrational essence** of Hebrew itself. It unifies **the linguistic, numerical, and archetypal realms into a single,** living system of sacred knowledge.

Letter	Name	Numerical Value	Symbolic Meaning	Archetype/Connection
(Aleph) א	Aleph	1	Ox, unity, beginning	Divine breath, the oneness of creation
(Beth) ב	Beth	2	House	Creation of space, containment
(Gimel) ג	Gimel	3	Camel	Journey, self-nourishment, balance
(Daleth) ד	Daleth	4	Door	Entry into new realms, thresholds
(Heh) ה	Heh	5	Window	Vision, revelation, spiritual insight
(Vav) ו	Vav	6	Hook	Connection, binding of energies
(Zayin) ז	Zayin	7	Sword	Discernment, struggle, cutting away
(Chet) ח	Chet	8	Fence	Protection, boundaries, sacred space
(Tet) ט	Tet	9	Serpent	Wisdom, transformation, renewal
(Yod) י	Yod	10	Hand	Divine spark, the seed of creation
(Kaph) כ	Kaph	20	Palm of hand	Receiving and giving, action
(Lamed) ל	Lamed	30	Ox-goad	Guidance, learning, spiritual discipline
(Mem) מ	Mem	40	Water	Flow, cleansing, the unconscious
(Nun) נ	Nun	50	Fish	Life, fertility, evolution
(Samekh) ס	Samekh	60	Support	Stability, foundation, cyclical protection
(Ayin) ע	Ayin	70	Eye	Perception, insight, awareness
(Peh) פ	Peh	80	Mouth	Speech, expression, manifestation
(Tzaddi) צ	Tzaddi	90	Fishhook	Drawing forth, seeking, introspection
(Qoph) ק	Qoph	100	Back of head	Subconscious, the unknown, dreams
(Resh) ר	Resh	200	Head	Leadership, vision, beginnings
(Shin) ש	Shin	300	Tooth	Fire, transformation, divine energy
(Tav) ת	Tav	400	Cross, mark	Completion, truth, universal connection

Chapter 5

INNER FRAMEWORK OF KABBALISTIC MYSTICISM

The mystics of Kabbalah have long drawn a profound and deliberate distinction between two fundamental dimensions of the Divine: the **hidden, unknowable essence** and the **revealed, knowable manifestation**. At the core of this dichotomy stands the concept of **Ein Sof**—a Hebrew phrase that means **"Without End."** This name designates **the Infinite aspect of God**, an aspect so utterly transcendent and unbounded that it lies beyond any conceivable form, description, or attribute. **Ein Sof is not a "He," nor even a "She."** Kabbalists often insist that **referring to this Infinite Source as "It" is more appropriate**, despite the limitations of the Hebrew language, which does not possess a neuter gender. This emphasis reveals a fundamental truth: **Ein Sof cannot be personalized, contained, or made relatable through the language of human experience.**

To speak of **Ein Sof** is not to describe a character or a personality—it is, instead, to acknowledge the presence of an ultimate reality that defies all limitation. *It is not that we say God is this or that; it is that we confess we do not, and cannot, know what God is.* This is **the Divine as pure potential, formless and boundless**, untouched by creation yet sustaining it from beyond.

Because of this unbridgeable gap between the **Infinite Creator** and the **finite creature, Kabbalists caution against making Ein Sof the object of prayer or direct meditation. There is no relationship**—not in the human sense—between that which is utterly beyond comprehension and that which is contingent, shaped, and temporal. One does not commune with the abyss of infinity; instead, one must find pathways through which the infinite *chooses* to become immanent.

These pathways are the **Sephirot—ten luminous vessels**, or archetypal **emanations**, through which divine energy flows into creation. While **Ein Sof** remains **veiled and untouched**, the Sephirot represent **the facets of the Divine that are accessible, interactive, and intelligible** to the human soul. *Imagine a blinding sun — too brilliant to gaze upon directly — but whose rays, when refracted through a prism, reveal the hidden spectrum of colors. The Sephirot are these refracted rays — divine attributes revealed in forms we can contemplate and reflect upon.*

In this way, **God expresses two fundamental "natures"**: the **unknowable essence** (Ein Sof), and the **knowable manifestations** (the Sephirot). The former is eternal, formless, and without predicate; the latter are **structured, relational, and dynamic**—a bridge between the world of spirit and the world of form.

The word **Sephirot** itself holds several layers of meaning, each of which deepens our understanding. In its earliest usage, it was linked to **"numerals,"** emerging from the mystical text known as the **Sefer Yetzirah**, or **"The Book of Formation."** This association with numbers emphasizes the idea that **the Divine structure of the universe is mathematical, ordered, and precise.** Each Sephirah corresponds to one of the **ten cardinal numbers**, echoing the Pythagorean intuition that **number is the essence of reality**.

Yet the Hebrew root **"safar"** also means **"to tell" or "to recount."** According to many Kabbalists, this suggests that **each Sephirah "tells" us something about God**, revealing a dimension of the Divine psyche or personality. Through the Sephirot, God narrates the story of existence—not in words, but in emanations of light, will, mercy, judgment, beauty, and so on. *They are the ten divine utterances through which the world is continuously spoken into being.*

Another evocative interpretation connects **Sephirot** with **sappir**, the Hebrew word for **sapphire**. This poetic link conjures the image of the

Sephirot as **gemlike illuminations**—radiant facets of divine light that shimmer through the veil of the cosmos. As such, the Kabbalistic path becomes a journey through **a celestial gematria**, in which each **radiance** reveals something precious, eternal, and luminous about the Source.

Many translators and commentators have struggled to render the term "Sephirot" into English with accuracy and grace. Some have proposed **"spheres," "emanations," "radiances,"** or even **"attributes."** Yet none of these fully capture the **simultaneous abstraction and intimacy** embedded in the term. One might suggest the word **"calculi"**—from the Latin, implying both *counting* and *structured reasoning*—to reflect the symbolic and numerical dimensions of the Sephirot. Still, **all translations fall short**, because **the Sephirot are not merely ideas to be analyzed, but realities to be lived, experienced, and internalized.**

Ultimately, the Sephirot are not objects; they are **processes, forces, archetypes—the very architecture of divine manifestation**. They are the **inner dynamics of God made legible**, the luminous lattice upon which the soul may ascend. In contemplating them, we do not reduce God to understandable terms, but rather **allow God to reveal aspects of the Divine self** that invite human participation. Through them, **we do not define God—God defines us**.

connections of the sephirot

The **Sephirot** are not simply abstract metaphysical principles — they are the **living connective tissue between the Infinite and the finite**, the unseen and the seen, the Creator and the created. Through them, the **unfathomable unity of God remains intact**, even as God engages in an **intimate relationship with the world**. This paradox is essential in Kabbalistic thought: **how can the One who transcends all things dwell within all things?** The answer lies in the ten emanations — **the Sephirot**.

A true practitioner of Kabbalah does not direct prayers to **Ein Sof**, the **Infinite, Hidden God**, because **Ein Sof is beyond attributes, beyond comprehension, beyond even relationship**. The Kabbalist instead prays *through* the Sephirot, those **manifest gateways of divine energy** that express **God's will, wisdom, mercy, and justice** in ways that the human heart can know and the soul can reflect.

This distinction is not trivial. It's **the very foundation of mystical understanding**. When you speak of God's kindness, wrath, beauty, or justice — **you are not describing Ein Sof**. You are describing **the qualities and attributes that are manifest within the Sephirot**. To say that God loves, punishes, acts, or even *thinks* is to tell the Divine *as it is expressed through the Sephirot*, not the boundless, formless essence that lies behind them. **The God of the Bible — the one who walks, speaks, grieves, and rejoices — is not Ein Sof**. It is the **personal and relational aspect of God as reflected in the Sephirot**.

Thus, **nowhere in the scriptures is Ein Sof mentioned by name**. The biblical texts are saturated with interactions with the knowable God, not the unknowable Source. The **Bible speaks of God in human-like terms**, not because God is human-like, but because **the Sephirot serve as vessels of divine expression** that we, in our human condition, can grasp.

The **Sephirot make possible the meeting of two opposites: the eternal with the temporal, the unmanifest with the manifest, the limitless with the limited**. They are the **divine interface**, the bridge across the cosmic divide. To understand this, imagine the relationship between **your soul and your body**. *You do not see your soul; you cannot measure it or weigh it. Yet its presence is undeniable.* You are aware of your soul through the life it animates in your body—**your breath, your gestures, your voice, your thoughts**. Your body is not your soul, yet **without the body, your soul cannot act in the world**. This is how the **Sephirot function for Ein Sof**.

The Sephirot are the divine limbs, channels, and garments through which Ein Sof breathes, moves, and creates. You cannot see Ein Sof, just as you cannot see your soul—but you can witness its **movements, echoes, and shadows** in the world, just as you see your soul's impact through the motion of your body. *Each Sephirah is like a sacred organ, each with a unique function, yet all serving one soul. So too, the ten Sephirot express the One Divine.*

And just as the body cannot fully grasp the mystery of the soul, **no single Sephirah can contain the fullness of the Infinite**—yet through their interplay, we begin to perceive the rhythm of eternity flowing into time.

Kabbalah is not a doctrine. It is a revelation cloaked in mystery. It has evolved over centuries, passed down through whispers and symbols, embroidered with layers of wisdom drawn from **ancient myths, sacred geometry, esoteric rituals, and arcane cosmologies**. It is a path that draws from the wells of many traditions yet flows in a direction all its own—**toward union with the Divine, toward knowing the unknowable**.

And yet, **Kabbalah is also a science of the soul.** Hidden within its arcane diagrams and cryptic texts lies **an astonishing wealth of information about the nature of life, the universe, and even matter itself**. *Long before modern physics postulated the atom or quantum fields, Kabbalistic manuscripts hinted at the structure of particles, parallel realities, the curvature of space, and the spectral nature of light.* These are not vague poetic gestures—they are **precise glimpses** into truths science would only later confirm.

Many scientists and philosophers have found themselves **accidentally echoing Kabbalistic principles** in their explorations. **Terms and concepts rooted in Kabbalah—such as vibration, light, unity, and polarity—appear time and again** in serious metaphysical and scientific discourse. And this is no coincidence. **The language of Kabbalah speaks not only to the mystic but to the mathematician, the physicist, the seeker of structure within chaos.** It is **a cosmic blueprint.**

This is part of the **eternal seduction of Kabbalah**: it does not offer answers, it provides more profound questions. It does not hand you a final truth—it **invites you into an unfolding spiral of insight**. *It dares you to unlearn what you believe you know and to step into a mystery that has no floor, no ceiling, only layers upon layers of revelation.*

Mystery is not the absence of meaning—it is the presence of too much sense. Kabbalah draws you into this excess of meaning, where every symbol bleeds into another, where every truth hides a more profound reality. For centuries, those seeking ultimate understanding have turned to these teachings. Some have joined secret orders, hoping for illumination. Others have walked the lonely path of the mystic, guided only by dreams and visions. But all were **magnetized by the possibility of *experiencing* the Divine, not merely believing in it.**

At the heart of Kabbalah lies one supreme mystery, from which all others flow: **the secret of the Godhead**, also called in Aramaic *raza de-mehemanuta*—"the mystery of faith." This is **the center from which the Sephirot spiral outward, the hidden fire behind the veil**, the **silent presence at the center of all being**. To approach it is to stand at the **edge of what can be known**, and to leap—not with certainty, but with awe. From this leap, from this center, **all actual knowledge flows.**

The four dimensions

The Four Worlds of Kabbalah, known collectively as **Olamot** (singular: *Olam*), represent the descending stages of **Divine manifestation** from the Infinite into the realm of physical existence. These worlds are not spatial locations, but rather **states of consciousness**, degrees of **Divine revelation and concealment**, and levels of **spiritual reality**. They reflect how the **light of Ein Sof** — the Infinite Divine Presence — is progressively **filtered, veiled, and structured** to allow for creation, free will, and ultimately, the experience of individuality.

Each world corresponds to a specific **mode of spiritual operation** and is linked to aspects of the **soul's psychology**, the **human senses**, and the **Tree of Life**. In their descending order, these four worlds form a **cosmic ladder** from the Divine to the mundane, and also represent the framework by which the soul descends into the body, and by which it may ascend again toward unity with the Source.

The four worlds are:

- **Atziluth** (אֲצִילוּת) – *The World of Emanation*
- **Beriah** (בְּרִיאָה) – *The World of Creation*
- **Yetzirah** (יְצִירָה) – *The World of Formation*
- **Asiyah** (עֲשִׂיָּה) – *The World of Action*

Together, these form the acronym **ABiYA** (אבי"ע), a key term in Kabbalistic texts. These are not merely metaphysical categories — they are **filters through which Divine consciousness is refracted**, each more distant from the Infinite, and yet each essential in the architecture of creation.

Each world represents a distinct **stage in the process of Divine self-limitation**, or **Tzimtzum** (צמצום), a Kabbalistic concept introduced by **Isaac Luria**. *Tzimtzum* refers to the **contraction** or **withdrawing** of Divine light to make "space" for creation. This does not mean God is absent — instead, the **Infinite Presence veils itself**, permitting finite reality to emerge, much like **the sun behind a curtain still provides warmth, but no longer blinds the eye**.

From the first great *Tzimtzum*, a **vacated space** (ḥalal ha-panuy) emerges. Into this conceptual space, Divine light shines through the **Kav** (a narrow ray or line), gradually **structuring the emanation** of the spiritual worlds. These emanations do not depart from Ein Sof, but **unfold as garments or expressions** of the Infinite, **revealing and concealing the Divine in precise measure**.

In **Atziluth**, the Divine light remains **pure, undivided, and almost unfiltered**. It is the world closest to the Infinite, a state of near-total unity. Here, there is **no absolute separation between God and creation**, only an **emanation of archetypal forces** — it is the realm of pure being. *Imagine a painter conceiving a masterpiece – not yet drawing, just knowing the vision in their mind. That is Atziluth.*

In **Beriah**, the world of **Creation**, we find the **first sense of separateness**. This is where **the Divine idea becomes a distinct entity**. It is the world of the **Throne**, the **supernal palace**, where the **primordial soul begins to take form**. This is the realm of the **archangels** — spiritual beings born from the clarity of Divine thought. *It is as if the painter chooses a canvas and gathers materials, preparing to bring the vision to life.*

Yetzirah marks the world of **Formation**, where **shape, emotion, and structure begin to form**. This is the world of **angels**, of **emotive forces**, and **symbolic constructs**. The Sephirot in Yetzirah begin to take on **individual character**, and the **divine forces interact and build the inner scaffolding of creation**. *Here, the painter begins to sketch and block in the outlines, choosing shapes and gestures.*

Finally, in **Asiyah**, the **world of action**, the Divine light is **most concealed**, and the structures formed above now take on **material substance**. This includes both the **spiritual dimension of Asiyah** and its **lowest aspect**, known as **Asiyah Gashmi** — the **physical world**, our reality. Here, the Divine is present, but **almost entirely hidden**, clothed in **matter, time, and space**. *This is where the painter finishes the work,* *rendering the image in vivid color on canvas — it is no longer a dream but a reality in the world.*

Kabbalistically, **each world correlates to a part of the human psyche**:

- Atziluth: **Will and essence**
- Beriah: **Intellect and conception**
- Yetzirah: **Emotion and relational experience**
- Asiyah: **Action and embodiment**

And to the **four senses**:

- Atziluth: **Speech** (Divine communication)
- Beriah: **Sight** (vision of creation)
- Yetzirah: **Smell** (the subtle discernment of emotion)
- Asiyah: **Hearing** (the concrete reception of outer sound)

There is, however, a **fifth world**, often considered **beyond even Atziluth: Adam Kadmon, the Primordial Man** — the **first configuration of Divine light after the Tzimtzum**, and a **pre-Sephirotic, transcendent state of awareness**. It is so elevated that it cannot be fully described — it serves as a **bridge between Ein Sof and Atziluth**. It is said to correspond to the **Divine Will before differentiation**.

In **Isaiah 43:7**, all Four Worlds are alluded to:
"Everyone that is called by My name and for My glory (Atziluth) I have created (Beriah), I have formed (Yetzirah), even I have made (Asiyah)."

This descending structure **illustrates how Divine reality becomes increasingly veiled, allowing free will and multiplicity to emerge while remaining** connected to the Source. As Hasidism teaches, **God is not in the world —** *the world is in God.* Hence, **God is both concealed and present**, both *HaMakom* (the Place) and *the One who transcends all place.*

Ultimately, these Four Worlds are not just **cosmic zones**, but **spiritual maps for inner transformation**. They invite you to journey upward — from **action to formation, from emotion to intellect, from intellect to essence**. And in doing so, you move not only through the architecture of reality but also **through the architecture of your soul**, returning to the Infinite from which you came.

About Enumeration and the Divine Architecture of the Worlds

The mystical structure of existence, as explained in **Kabbalah**, is not a random layering of spiritual concepts, but a **precise and intentional framework** shaped by the flow of **Divine light**, known as *Ohr*. One particular expression of this light — **Ohr Mimalei Kol Olmin** — is the creative **immanent light** that **fills all the worlds**, each according to its **spiritual capacity**. This light does not flow uniformly; instead, it adapts to the nature of each world, **filling it only as much as it can contain without being overwhelmed**.

All **Ten Sephirot**, along with their **Twelve Partzufim** (personae or Divine "faces"), unfold across these worlds — **except Adam Kadmon**, which remains too lofty for full manifestation. The Sephirot are *modalities of Divine expression*, and the Partzufim are their complex configurations — **Divine archetypes** that channel and personalize the Infinite energy.

Each world, while permeated by Divine light, is **dominated by particular Partzufim and Sephirot**, giving that realm its **unique psychological and spiritual signature**. These worlds form a **chain of descent**, from the most abstract to the most tangible, known as the **Seder Hishtalshelut** — the orderly progression from the Infinite into the finite. The process unfolds not through abrupt separation, but by *constriction*, known in Kabbalah as **Tzimtzum** — a term that means "contraction" or "condensation." It refers to the deliberate **concealment of Divine light** so that Creation may appear as *something other than God*, while remaining within the Divine will.

Adam Kadmon — *The Primordial Man* — stands beyond even the Four Worlds. It is not a "world" per se, but a **pre-cosmic blueprint, the first emergence after the initial Tzimtzum**. The name is symbolic: "Adam" alludes to the **upright configuration** (*Yosher*) of the Sephirot in the form of a human being. This metaphor highlights the order and purpose inherent in the structure of existence. "Kadmon" means *primordial* or *first of all firsts* — this is **the most pristine projection of Divine Will**, rooted still in **Ein Sof**, the Infinite.

The light of Adam Kadmon is called **Tzachtzachot**—*luminous, pure, crystalline*. It is a light **without vessels**, a radiant, **unshaped essence**, carrying the seeds of all future realities. It is **the source code of existence**, still unmanifested, yet already containing the entire **Divine plan of creation**. In Lurianic terms, **Adam Kadmon corresponds to Keter Elyon**, the Supernal Crown—the realm of **Will beyond comprehension**, inaccessible to the lower worlds. For this reason, when Kabbalistic texts speak of "the Four Worlds," **Adam Kadmon is omitted**, for it transcends even emanation.

Then begins the chain of **the Four Worlds**, the **cosmic descent** from the Infinite to the finite:

Atziluth (*World of Emanation*)
Also meaning *closeness*, Atziluth is the realm **closest to Ein Sof**. The Divine light here is **so overwhelming and pure** that individual consciousness is **dissolved** in the **Bitul HaEtzem**—the nullification of essence. *Imagine a drop of water dissolving into the ocean – so fully unified with the Source that it cannot recognize its separateness.*
The **Sephirot fully manifest** here, yet their existence is **entirely transparent to Divine will**. This is the world of **Divine unity**, where **Wisdom (Chokhmah)** dominates. The ego does not exist in Atziluth. All that is here *knows itself only as God's emanation*, not as a created being. **Malchut**, the lowest sephira, is the **Divine speech** through which creation begins— *"Let there be light"* —but even that speech is still soaked in infinity.

Beriah (*World of Creation*)
Beriah introduces **separateness**—it is the world of **Creation ex nihilo**, *something from nothing*. Yet even here, beings experience **Bitul HaMetzius**—a nullification of existence rather than essence. Souls and angels in Beriah *recognize their reality*, yet they live in **constant awe of the Divine presence**.
Here, **Understanding (Binah)** is the dominant Sephira—the beginning

of **intellectual consciousness**. This is the world of the **Divine Throne**—a metaphor for how Atziluth's light sits upon Beriah, *as a King upon a throne*, still sovereign but now **refracted through structure**. Beriah is also known as the Higher Garden of Eden and is considered a realm of **Divine intellect**.

Yetzirah (*World of Formation*)
Yetzirah brings **structure and emotion** into the unfolding creation. What was conceived in Beriah begins to take **form, shape, and relational energy**. This is the world where **angels abound**, where **souls develop the capacity for feeling**—love, awe, reverence.
Here, **Chesed (Loving-kindness)** and **Yesod (Foundation)** are dominant. Souls in Yetzirah are engaged in **worship** as a **striving toward God**, marked by **emotional devotion** rather than pure intellectual clarity.
Imagine the stirring in the heart when one prays or sings or yearns for truth — that's Yetzirah at work. This world is **closer to ours**, yet still spiritual, and is vital to the **circulation of Divine vitality** between realms.

Asiyah (*World of Action*)
Asiyah is the **completion of creation**. Here, form becomes **function**, intention becomes **execution**. The Divine vitality is now **so hidden**, so **clothed in concealment**, that existence appears to stand alone. And yet, even here, the **Sephirot operate**, and the **Divine animates every moment**.
In its **spiritual dimension**, Asiyah remains infused with Malchut, the kingship that governs and structures all. Angels here are **active**, fulfilling tasks and carrying out Divine decrees.
Below this is **Asiyah Gashmi**, the **physical world**, our universe—the world of **time, space, matter, and limitation**. Here, Divine light is **veiled behind veils**, and yet still **present in every atom**, animating, sustaining, willing the world into being at every instant.

The **Four Worlds** are not merely theoretical—they form the **inner scaffolding of reality**, and the **ladder of spiritual ascent**. Each world is a **layered stage** through which consciousness can **descend into embodiment**, or **return to its Divine source**. The words *higher* and *lower* do not mean spatial distance—they reflect how **close or distant** each realm is from **Divine revelation**.

In mystical language, **the worlds are garments**, and **Ein Sof is clothed within them**, each layer **hiding and revealing**, like light through stained glass. Kabbalah teaches that **through meditative ascent**, through alignment with the **Sephirot**, one can traverse these worlds, not as places to go, but **states of being to awaken**.

Each level of the soul correlates to these worlds—**Nefesh** in Asiyah, **Ruach** in Yetzirah, **Neshamah** in Beriah, and **Chayah** in Atziluth. Beyond them all is **Yechidah**, the soul's spark in Adam Kadmon—so lofty it can never fully manifest in this world, only **glimpse itself in rare moments of transcendence**.

Thus, enumeration in Kabbalah is not about **counting for its own sake**, but about **understanding the blueprint** of creation. The Ohr is the Divine light; the Sephirot are its instruments; the Partzufim are its faces; and the Worlds are its **symphony in time**. All serve one purpose: to allow the Infinite to **dwell in the finite**, and for the **finite to remember the Infinite** from which it came.

Chapter 6

ANGELS, ASTROLOGY, AND THE HIDDEN FORCES OF KABBALAH

You've heard of *karma*, the principle in Hindu philosophy that whatever energy one sends into the world, through thoughts, actions, or intentions, must eventually return to them. In Kabbalah, a similar concept exists, but it is cloaked in different language and grounded in the mystical dynamics of divine justice. Here, actions ripple through spiritual realms, echoing back not only into the soul's future lifetimes but also into the very fabric of creation itself. **Every deed, every word, and even every thought** is recorded in the spiritual architecture of the cosmos. Nothing vanishes. Nothing is forgotten. The universe, according to Kabbalah, is a finely tuned system of cause and effect. This system does not operate blindly, nor is it mechanical. Instead, **it is overseen by spiritual intelligences**—forces of consciousness known as *malakhim*, or angels. These are not the soft-faced beings with feathered wings depicted in religious art. In Kabbalistic understanding, **angels are not individuals but emanations—fiery currents of divine will**, each fulfilling a specific task in the celestial design. Some carry judgment, others mercy. Some guide, others test. Their form is not fixed but symbolic, **formed by their function,** *just as a flame takes the shape of the air that contains it.*

These entities dwell not in a separate heaven far removed from our experience, but in **higher levels of reality interwoven with our own**. The worlds of existence, as outlined in Kabbalistic doctrine, are not different locations but different degrees of consciousness. We live in the lowest realm—**Asiyah**, the World of Action—where divine energy becomes solid, dense, and tangible. Above us is **Yetzirah**, the World of Formation, the abode of angels. Their world **is not distant—it is parallel**, vibrating just beyond the reach of ordinary perception. Those who awaken spiritually may, at moments, pierce the veil and sense these presences—not as visions, but as **overwhelming pulses of clarity, trembling insight, or sudden awe**. Angels, in this context, **are not seen but known**. They reveal themselves to those whose souls have been refined, who have cleared the noise of ego and illusion enough to perceive the divine frequency. Astrology, too, finds deep resonance within Kabbalah, though not in the mundane, fortune-telling sense. It is not about **predicting trivial events**, but about **understanding the divine signatures encoded in the heavens**. The stars are not gods. They are **glyphs written in the sky**, sacred scripts reflecting the unfolding of spiritual cycles. Each planet embodies a force within the soul, and **each zodiac sign is a gate**—*a lens through which divine light refracts into specific energies.*

The ancient sages taught that **Abraham himself was a master astrologer**. Still, he transcended it—not by rejecting it, but by understanding that the soul, when united with divine will, could rise above its celestial programming. In other words, the stars may *influence*, but they do not *rule*. To the Kabbalist, astrology is a map, not a prison. **It reveals the path, but not the traveler's destiny.**

Other concepts tied to Kabbalah echo through ancient mystery traditions—the idea of **spiritual correspondence**, where physical events reflect spiritual truths. The belief in **parallel universes**, now echoed by modern physics, is rooted in the principle of names as keys, where each Hebrew letter holds a vibrational frequency and a divine code. To speak a name with awareness is to open a doorway, to **summon an archetype** into consciousness. Kabbalah is not a collection of beliefs. It is a **system of transformation**, one that decodes the hidden architecture of existence. **Nothing is random. Nothing is meaningless.** The angels know this. The stars reflect this. The soul longs for this. And once the seeker begins to walk the path, guided by these ancient truths, they will never again see the world as merely material. Everything breathes. Everything speaks. Everything burns with hidden fire.

The angelic form

In Hebrew, the word **malach** does not simply mean "angel" in the way most people imagine it—it means **messenger**, and this subtle distinction changes everything. Angels are not winged beings of sentimental art. In the language of Kabbalah, **they are spiritual forces, channels of energy, carriers of divine will.** They are not "people with wings"; they are *instructions made manifest*. Each one exists for a **single, specific purpose**, and unlike humans, they have **no free will**. An angel does not debate, hesitate, or doubt. It **executes**.

There are two fundamental categories of angels according to the Kabbalistic tradition. The first are those **created directly by the Divine**, known as *God-made angels*. These are primordial messengers crafted to fulfill **defined cosmic roles**. For instance, *Malach Hamavet*, the Angel of Death, exists solely to fulfill the sacred and terrifying task of **separating the soul from the body** at the moment of physical death. He doesn't question. He doesn't feel pity. He carries out divine justice without deviation, with precision born from a higher order.

But the second category is far more mysterious, and far more relevant to you.

Kabbalah teaches that human beings **continually create angels, not metaphorically, but** literally, in the spiritual realms. These are known as **artificial angels**, or *spiritual charges*. Every time you think a thought, **speak a word**, feel an emotion, perform an act, or even dream something powerful, **you are forming an angelic entity**. *They are not fantasies. They are real structures of consciousness.* They spring from you like breath, like fire from a flint. **They are alive.** And once created, **they are attached to your soul forever.**

This means that you are *never* alone. You walk this world and sleep each night surrounded by a **host of invisible beings**, beings you brought into being. Some are luminous, warm, and expansive. Others are dark, twisted, and cold. *A harsh word shouted in anger creates a malignant form, while a selfless act births a messenger of light.* And here is the paradox: **both are you**. They are the *residue* of your choices, and they gather in your soul's wake like sparks or shadows.

But not all anger creates a dark angel. Not all love creates a pure one. **It's not the emotion—it's the intention.** *Anger channeled righteously to protect the innocent is a sacred force. Love twisted into manipulation births poison.* Every act is weighed not just by its external shape, but by the **fire that fuels it**. That is why Kabbalists insist on **deep inner work**, because the unseen is often more powerful than the seen.

What happens when the soul leaves the body?

The body returns to Earth. But the soul—**eternal, indestructible**—ascends. And in its wake, it carries everything it ever created: **all the angels, all the charges, good or bad**. You don't die alone. You rise accompanied by a choir of your own making. If you spent your life asleep, unaware, consumed by selfish impulses, your soul will be **encrusted with malformed angels**, parasitic energies that now cling to you. But if you've awakened—even late, even broken—you carry with you an army of light.

Here enters the holy concept of **teshuvah**—*return*. This is **not just repentance**. Teshuvah is the spiritual technology that allows you to **reshape your past**, not by time-travel, but by shifting the spiritual pattern behind your actions. *Time is not linear in Kabbalah.* All of existence is **now**, and through sincere transformation, you can **reach back into the past**, illuminate it with present awareness, and redeem what was once corrupted.

This is not a poetic metaphor. It is **spiritual physics**.

Teshuvah means recognizing your mistake, not with shame, but with the **clarity and pain that gives birth to transformation**. If your regret is genuine, if your desire to change stems from the depths of your being, **you don't just become clean—you become powerful**. Because **those malformed angels are transformed**. *Your negative creations do not vanish – they are purified, reconfigured, elevated.* They become **beings of light** built from your darkness. And in doing so, *you become more than one who never sinned – you become the alchemist of your soul.*

That is why the Kabbalists taught: **the one who has sinned and truly repented stands higher than one who has never fallen**. Because that person carries a host of **redeemed energies**, they have seen the abyss and still turned toward the light. They have taken the very matter of their failures and **turned them into divine messengers**.

But beware: this law of teshuvah cannot be **manipulated**. Some thought they could deliberately sin and then feign repentance to *game the system*. But **you cannot deceive the Infinite**. Ein Sof sees through all masks. It knows your every intention before you speak it. *Trying to fake teshuvah is like a child with chocolate all over her face insisting she didn't eat the cake*. The Divine does not punish such attempts — it simply reveals them as hollow.

So remember: you are always creating. You are a **source of emanation**. Each moment of your life is a **ritual of summoning**, and your soul is a **temple crowded with spirits born of you**. Choose well. Speak with care. Feel with awareness. And if you fall — rise with fire. Because in Kabbalah, your past is not a prison. It is **a field of sparks**, waiting for your light.

Kabbalah and astrology

Astrology and Kabbalah are not separate systems. They are twin reflections of a deeper, unified cosmic language that reveals how your soul is woven into the fabric of the universe. While astrology offers a personal *life map* through the birth chart, **Kabbalah presents the blueprint of reality itself**, tracing the spiritual architecture that sustains both the cosmos and human consciousness.

At the heart of Kabbalistic cosmology lies the Hebrew alphabet—a sacred code of 22 letters. These are not mere symbols or phonemes; they are **vibrational frequencies**, each one infused with divine power. These 22 letters **correspond directly with the 22 Major Arcana of the Tarot,** *another esoteric map of transformation and revelation*. But this sacred number does not stop there. In Kabbalistic astrology, the 22 letters are divided into three sacred categories that map directly onto the zodiac, the planets, and the elements:

- **Twelve simple letters** align with the *12 signs of the zodiac* and *12 months of the year*. These govern the rhythm of time, identity, and personality.

- **Seven double letters** correspond to the *seven visible classical planets*—the celestial bodies that exert direct influence on fate, emotion, and experience.

- **Three mother letters** represent the primal **elements** of *Air, Water, and Fire*. The fourth element, **Earth**, is *not listed because it is not absent — it is everything*. It *contains* the other three and **manifests** their energies into the physical world.

These cosmic correspondences don't float in abstraction—they are deeply **embedded in your body and psyche.** The Four Kabbalistic Worlds—**Atzilut, Beriah, Yetzirah, and Asiyah**—mirror the four elements and **the four levels of consciousness**:

- **Atzilut**, the World of Emanation, is *pure fire*. It represents the **divine spark**, the realm closest to **Ein Sof**, where nothing is separate and all is fused in essence.

- **Beriah**, the World of Creation, is *air*. It is the *mental realm*, the plane of **pure archetypes**, governed by the clarity of thought, intellect, and divine reason.

- **Yetzirah**, the World of Formation, is *water*. It is the realm of **emotion, desire, and dream**, the inner architecture of feeling.

- **Asiyah**, the World of Action, is *Earth*. It is the world of **manifestation**, the only realm visible to our senses, where divine intent solidifies into matter.

Now, enter the **Tree of Life**, a diagram that is not merely symbolic but **an anatomical model of your soul**. It is also **a celestial map**, illustrating how the ten Sephirot—or attributes of the Divine—are interconnected not only with spiritual states but also with **planets, elements, the body, and even the Ten Commandments**. You are not separate from the cosmos. You *are* a microcosm, **a temple walking on earth**.

Let us begin at the crown and descend.

- **Keter**, the crown, sits atop the skull. It represents **pure potential**, the unformed spark of divine will. It is above comprehension, the point where **Ein Sof touches reality**, and is often left *unspoken, unreachable*. It is the source.

- **Chokhmah**, the right brain, is the flash of **raw wisdom**—*inspiration like lightning*, sudden and overwhelming. Associated with **Uranus**, it is the wild force of insight before words.

- **Binah**, the left brain, is **understanding**. It is the womb that **receives Chokhmah's lightning** and gives it shape. Linked to **Saturn**, it is the container, the matrix, the form-maker.

- **Da'at**, the hidden Sephirah, is the *bridge* between the supernal and the accessible. It is **knowledge**, and yet it is paradoxical: the more you seek it, the more elusive it becomes. Da'at is the mystery of the One that is *unknowable yet intimate*.

From the head, we move to the arms:

- **Chesed**, the right arm, is **kindness and grace**. It flows outward like a benevolent river. It carries the expansive qualities of **Jupiter** and the mystical compassion of **Neptune**. It gives without measure.

- **Gevurah**, the left arm, is **severity, discipline, and strength**. It is Mars in its righteous form — *cutting through illusion*, defining, defending, and saying **"no"** when no is needed. Where Chesed opens, Gevurah constrains.

These two are balanced in the chest:

- **Tiferet**, the heart, is **beauty, balance, and harmony**. It is the radiance of the **Sun**, the central point that integrates emotion, intellect, and spirit. *It is where your will meets divine design.* It is not passive beauty, but **beauty that unifies and illuminates**.

Descending to the legs:

- **Netzach**, the right leg and kidney, is **endurance and victory**. Venus rules it, but not the Venus of pleasure — instead, *the Venus of love that persists*, that survives heartbreak, and keeps moving toward the light. It is an action born of faith.

- **Hod**, the left leg and kidney, is **glory and splendor**, ruled by **Mercury**. It is the precision of language, the elegance of logic, and the clarity of thought that stabilizes emotion. It is the humility that *knows how to receive and organize*.

Below the waist, you find the foundational forces:

- **Yesod**, the sexual organ, is **the foundation**, the **Moon**, the reflective gateway where *all above must pass before becoming real*. It is desire, magnetism, intuition, and the point where dreams begin to crystallize.

- **Malkuth**, the feet and mouth, is **the Kingdom**. It is **Earth**, not in the mundane sense, but in the **alchemical sense**: the vessel, the temple, the final expression. It is not lowly; it is sacred. It is where the divine breath **walks and speaks**.

Each Sephirah also has **a planetary correspondence, a unique energy, an angelic guardian,** and **a moral lesson**. They are not abstract ideas. They are **living realities**, encoded into your body, psyche, and spiritual path. *Your chart shows your challenges, your strengths, and your tendencies — but the Tree of Life shows the road home.*

The synthesis of **astrology and Kabbalah** allows you not just to read your fate, but to **transform it**. When you align your actions with the higher qualities of each Sephirah — when you become aware of their planetary pulses and archetypal patterns — you stop reacting to life and start **participating in the divine unfolding**. You move from being a leaf blown by astrological winds to becoming **a conscious gardener of your soul**.

Mother letters

The Mother Letters — Aleph, Mem, and Shin — are not merely letters. They are **primordial frequencies**, the **first pulses of Divine articulation** before language, before time, before form. In the structure of the **Tree of Life**, these letters traverse the horizontal branches, bridging **opposites across the spheres**, balancing the vertical descent of energy and the diagonal flow of creation. Each of these three letters is **an elemental force — Air, Water, and Fire** — and together, they breathe the soul of existence into being.

Aleph (א) is the silent breath of the ineffable. It is **the breath before creation**, the echo of potential. Unlike other letters, Aleph has **no inherent sound** — it is the space between vibration, the pause before speaking, the *invisible inhale that feeds all utterance*. It is not emptiness, but **fullness, too subtle to be grasped**. In mystical teachings, Aleph symbolizes **Air**, not as wind or movement, but as the **medium of all life** — *the unseen element that touches everything and is touched by nothing*.

Aleph is said to dwell **in the upper chest**, between the shoulders, hovering over the heart like a poised falcon, watching in stillness. *It does not command. It allows.* Its energy is **balance, purity, and equanimity**. The sages say Aleph contains within it the tension between Fire and Water — it does not resolve them, it **holds their contradiction**, allowing life to exist in dynamic harmony.

You can awaken Aleph in yourself by **bringing awareness to your heart**. *Close your eyes. Let your breath soften. As you inhale, imagine your chest opening like wings. As you exhale, let a faint "ahhhhh" pass through your lips — not a sound, but a release. Do this slowly, three times. Not to achieve, not to summon. To remember.*
Aleph is the spark behind all sparks, the origin that never claims attention, yet without which nothing could be.

Mem (מ) is **the womb of creation**, the mother of waters, the deep. In Hebrew, *mayim* (water) begins and ends with Mem — **a letter that curves inward, guarding sacred mystery**. Mem is the flow of feeling, of inner truth, of intuition that *rises not from logic, but from the depths* *beneath thought.* It is the **element of Water**, and just like the ocean, it **holds memory, emotion, sorrow, tenderness, and infinite power**.

The sacrum resides in the pelvis, specifically in the **sacral basin** of the human body. This is not a passive place. It is the seat of **creative potential**, the matrix of both physical and spiritual birth. When Mem awakens, it **connects you to the ancient currents** of all who have dreamed before you, all who have wept, all who have felt the unseen presence of the Divine flowing through their blood.

Mem is also the beginning of *maggid*, the word for **spiritual guide or angelic messenger**. It is through Mem that you hear what no ear can perceive — the **whispers of spirit, the songs of the soul, the murmur of your own higher self**.

To invoke Mem, let your awareness sink into it. *Sit with a straight spine, yet soft. Focus on the bowl of your hips. Inhale deeply into the belly. As you exhale, let the sound "mmmmmmm" hum from your lips. Let it vibrate through your bones, into your spine, into the earth. Repeat slowly, three times.* **Mem is not a stream — it is an ocean.** You don't swim through it. You **drown in it, willingly**, to emerge renewed.

These two letters, Aleph and Mem, are not just sounds. They are **practices of presence, temples of breath and vibration**. Aleph is the air that awakens awareness. Mem is the water that carries it deep. One opens the sky, the other submerges the soul. Together, they form part of **the sacred triad of the Mother Letters**, weaving heaven and earth through the body, anchoring the infinite into the physical.

To work with them is not to recite — but to **embody**, to **remember**, to **return**.

immanence healing

The Healing of Immanence is not a technique. It is a state. A remembrance. A surrender.
To engage in this process is to abandon the illusion that healing is a reaching, or that there is a place you must arrive at. **You do not fix. You do not force. You become.**

In this sacred mode of Kabbalistic healing, you begin by **envisioning the root of the Tree of Life**—*not as a symbol or concept, but as a living presence within your body and awareness.* This root, grounded in the **element of Earth**, holds no radiance of its own. It does not shine. It does not rise. Instead, it *receives*. It **contains**. It is the **sacred vessel**—*a place of gravity, stillness, and total Presence.*

You, as the healer, **become this root**. You embody its stillness. You hold the field. You are not reaching toward transcendence; you are not trying to elevate the soul above pain, above matter, above time. *You are not even trying to heal.*

You are remembering.

You are remembering that **Ein Sof—the Infinite—is not "out there."**
It is **here**.
It is **now**.
It is **this**.

The pain? Divine.
The longing? Divine.
The breath, the body, the trembling? All Divine.

There is nowhere that Ein Sof is not.

In this healing, you do not ask "what is wrong." You do not diagnose. You do not dissect the wound. Instead, you sit in full awareness, holding space with the **radical certainty that nothing is missing,** nothing is broken, and everything–every **cell, every shadow, every silence**—already has the presence of the Divine. **Healing happens not because something is added, but because the illusion of separation dissolves.**

You become the container. You hold the soul of the other like a mirror, reflecting to them what they have forgotten: **that they are whole. That they are seen. That they are already held by something vaster than words.**

This is **Immanence**. The Divinity that does not sit on a throne above the worlds but pulses within them. The Shekhinah that walks among the broken, the hidden, the mundane. In this healing, you invoke Her not by calling, but by becoming still enough that She *emerges* through you.

If you are a **Kabbalistic astrologer**, this becomes your map. You do not use astrology to name wounds. You do not use the chart to point out what is "wrong." You let it reveal what is already **perfectly designed**. Every planet, every aspect, every house is a **portal into Divine consciousness**.

The chart does not judge. The chart does not condemn. It simply speaks. And you listen—not with the mind, but with the whole of your being. You let the Tree of Life be your frame, your vessel, your lens. **Kabbalah means "to receive,"** and that is your sacred role: *to receive what already is. Not to correct it. Not to change it. To witness it with reverence.*

There is no illness to be solved. There is no sin to be scrubbed clean. **There is only the Divine, in different garments.**
And when you see it clearly—*in yourself, in the other, in the trembling of the world*—healing happens without a single word.

Not because you did something.
But because you became the Place where the Divine could be remembered.

chapter 7

OHR EIN SOF - LIGHT WITHOUT END

Ohr, meaning *"light"* in Hebrew, is not merely illumination in the physical sense. It is the **core metaphor** through which Kabbalah seeks to communicate the **invisible yet pervasive** radiance of the Divine. The plural of Ohr, **Ohrot**, or **Orhos**, reveals how this light flows in multiplicity, while remaining rooted in **a singular, unknowable Source**. In Kabbalistic mysticism, **light is not just a symbol—it is a transmission, a living breath, a whisper from the Infinite**.

When Kabbalists speak of **Shefa**, meaning *"flow,"* or *Hashpa'ah*, *"influence,"* they are not describing something static or decorative. They are speaking of **the Divine current that nourishes existence**, like blood through the veins of Creation. And yet, rather than these terms, the sages often prefer **Ohr**, not just for its elegance, but because its **gematria**—its numerical value—is the same as **Raz**, the Hebrew word for *mystery*. This is not a coincidence. It is a revelation: **Light is mystery, and mystery is Light.**

Kabbalah uses two great metaphors to speak of the unknowable Divine: **Ohr** and **Sephirot**. The **Ohr** is the *emanation*, the radiant overflow. The **Sephirot** are the *vessels*, the facets, the structures through which this light becomes legible. The relationship between these two is like that of soul and body: **the soul flows, the body shapes**. And so it is with Divinity. One must learn to read the **flow** as much as the **form**.

What makes **Ohr** so compelling as a metaphor is its **intangible yet perceptible nature**. We cannot hold light, and yet it fills every space. It **delights the soul, brings clarity to the mind**, and **travels across space at unimaginable speed**, all the while **remaining rooted in its source**.

Light can be refracted, bent, or dimmed, but it is never separated. This teaches the mystic something essential: **You may feel distant from the Divine, but you are never disconnected.**

Consider *tzimtzum* — the great **Kabbalistic concept of Divine contraction**. Just as clouds or curtains can veil light, the **Ohr Ein Sof**, the Infinite Light, **withdraws itself**, allowing a space in which finite things can appear to exist. And yet, even in withdrawal, **the Source remains present**. Just as white light contains within it **all the colors**, so too does **Ohr** contain the full spectrum of the **Sephirot**. *Chesed* (Lovingkindness), *Gevurah* (Severity), *Tiferet* (Beauty) — each one is a beam from the same original radiance. **They are distinctions of perception, not separations of essence.**

The contrast between **Ohr** and **Ma'Ohr** — between **light** and **luminary** — is profound. **Ohr** is what shines. **Ma'Ohr** is that from which it shines. In human terms, one might think of a flame and its glow. But in the Kabbalistic sense, this metaphor collapses, because in the Divine realm, **the Source and its emanation are not separate things**. Unlike earthly light, which can be switched off, **the Divine cannot cease to shine**. It is **not capable of withholding its presence, for to do so would be to deny its very nature**.

And yet, here lies the paradox: **The light of Ein Sof fills all things, and yet it is hidden.** It is hidden not because it is absent, but because we lack the perception to see it. Our senses are tuned to the material, to the fragmented. But the **Kabbalist trains herself to perceive the unity behind the veil**, to gaze past the multiplicity and into the blazing, silent core of Being.

Creation did not happen because God had to act. **It was not the obligation — it was a will.** The **Ohr Ein Sof** emanated not because the Source was lacking, but because **Divine generosity is infinite**. The world is not a necessity. It is a **gift**.

This realization brings us to the concept of **Bittul**, the **nullification of the self before the Infinite**. From the perspective of the Ein Sof, **there is no distance, no hierarchy, no separation**. All things are contained within it like rays in the sun. And so the work of the Kabbalist becomes clear: **to nullify the ego, to erase the illusion of separation**, to become as light itself—**transparent, radiant, inseparable from the source.**

Scripture affirms this eternal truth: *"I, the Eternal, I have not changed."* This verse is more than reassurance. It is an ontological key: **the essence of God does not fluctuate, and therefore all emanations, all lights, all Sephirot are merely modes of relationship, not transformations of Being**. To know this is not to grasp a doctrine. It is to stand trembling at the edge of the Infinite, **bathed in a radiance that precedes all form, all time, all language.**

This is the **Ohr Ein Sof: not a light that you see, but a light that sees you**. Not a metaphor, but **the very breath of Mystery**, whispering through every atom of your being, calling you—not to understand, but to **become**.

Light Without End

Ein Sof, in Hebrew, means **"without end," "limitless,"** or simply **"Infinite."** In the sacred language of Kabbalah, this is not just a poetic title. It is a profound declaration of the Divine Essence—**a Being beyond all conception, beyond all qualities, beyond even the idea of being.** *Ein Sof is not a "thing" that exists within creation – it is that which transcends existence itself.* From this **unfathomable Essence**, all that is emanates. From its infinite depths, **the Sephirot**—the ten archetypal attributes or vessels—**pour forth**, not to define the Divine, but to make what is unknowable *accessible* to the finite mind and to sustain the unceasing **flow of life-force** into all planes of reality.

Yet, **a critical distinction** must be made: the difference between **the light that flows from Ein Sof—Ohr Ein Sof—and the Source of that light, the Luminary Itself.** The light is **the emanation, the overflow,** the radiant self-expression of the Infinite. But **the Luminary is not the light.** It is the **origin beyond all manifestation, the silence behind all music, the presence that remains even when all else vanishes.**

Kabbalah is not pantheistic. It does not claim that God *is* the creator. Instead, it affirms that **everything emanates from the Divine, but the Divine is beyond all that it emanates.** There is no separation—yet there is distinction. This paradox, this tension between the One and the Many, **between the Infinite and its expressions, is the mystery of dualism** at the heart of Kabbalistic cosmology. *Just as sunlight and the sun are not identical, yet inseparable, so too are the emanations from Ein Sof inseparable from their Source, and yet not the Source itself.*

Beyond the **ten Sefirot**, which act as lenses through which **Divine Light** shines into creation, there exists **a more primordial light**—a light that predates even structure, even formulation, even the concept of creation itself. This is **Ohr Ein Sof, the Infinite Light**, unbounded, unformed, undivided. It is not filtered through the Sefirot. It is **pure being, pure awareness, pure love**, radiating from the Infinite **not because it must, but because it wills to do so.**

Here arises a question that has **perplexed mystics for centuries:** *How can God be revealed through Ohr Ein Sof even before creation? How can there be radiance before there is anything to receive it?* For does not light imply the presence of both a source and a vessel? A **ruler**, after all, can only be called such if there are **subjects to be ruled**. This puzzle seems to challenge the very foundation of Divine emanation.

But Kabbalah reveals a more profound truth: **the Infinite Light is not for the sake of others—it is the Divine Self-knowledge.** Ohr Ein Sof is not God's light *to* creation; it is God's light *within* Itself. In this eternal, timeless radiance, **Ein Sof contemplates Itself, knows Itself, loves Itself.** This **pre-creation illumination** is **a mirror of infinite awareness**, a divine unfolding of all potential within the Divine Mind. There are no others yet, but there is the fullness of possibility. **All that will ever be is already present in the silent thought of Ein Sof.**

Creation, then, is not an accident. It is not a necessity born of lack. It is **a deliberate act of Divine Will.** Through self-contemplation, **Ein Sof unfolds the structure of reality**, from **Ohr Ein Sof** to the **Sefirot**, from **Sefirot** to the **worlds**, and from the **worlds** to **souls, angels, planets,** and **flesh**. This movement from the ineffable to the manifest is **not a descent**, but **an expression**—like breath from the lungs, like ink from a quill, like fire from a flint. It is **the Infinite recognizing itself in a thousand masks.**

And so we return to **Ein Sof**—not as a concept to be grasped, but **as a silence to enter, as a light to be swallowed by.** It is the root of all mystery, the womb of all becoming, the **light behind all lights**. You do not pray *to* Ein Sof. You dissolve *into* it. You do not seek to define it. You desire to be **emptied** of all that blocks it. And when you are no more, **only it remains**, shining without end.

Tzimtzum

Ohr Ein Sof, the Infinite Light, is beyond all comprehension, beyond all limitation, and all division. **Its essence is absolute infinitude**, unbounded in quality, quantity, and purpose. Every emanation that arises from it, every act of creation, every world, and every soul — all are permeated by its limitless presence. Yet paradoxically, **if all things remained fully immersed in this Infinite Light, they could not truly be called "creations"**. They would not possess autonomy, individuality, or self-awareness. **They would be utterly nullified (in Hebrew, *Bittul*) within the radiant immensity of the Divine**, like a drop dissolved into the sea, losing even the memory of its separateness.

To resolve this paradox, to allow the emergence of **finite consciousness from infinite Oneness**, a series of profound spiritual operations had to unfold. This process is known in Kabbalistic tradition as **Seder Hishtalshelus**, the *Order of Emanation*, a chain of descent through which the Infinite becomes manifest in the finite.

At the core of this descent lies the concept of **Tzimtzum** — a word that means *contraction, withdrawal,* or *concealment*. The Ohr Ein Sof, to allow creation, had to **withdraw or recede**, leaving a conceptual *vacated space*, called **Chalal**. This does not imply literal absence, as the Infinite can never be *truly* absent. Instead, it signifies a concealment of its overpowering presence from the *perspective of the created*. This is a critical distinction: **Ein Sof did not cease to exist in the Chalal — it simply concealed Its Light in such a way that the illusion of separation could arise**.

This **First Tzimtzum**, as articulated by Rabbi Isaac Luria, the Arizal, and expanded upon in Lurianic Kabbalah, is a foundational doctrine in the mystical unfolding of the universe. It is the primal cosmic act of self-limitation, an **intentional Divine withdrawal** for the sake of love: *the Infinite making room for the Other.*

But this was not enough. Following the First Tzimtzum, **a new light had to emerge**, one that was neither as boundless nor as overwhelming as the original Ohr Ein Sof. This light is known as the **Kav** — a *Ray* or

Line of Divine Light, a diminished but focused beam of consciousness that entered the Chalal to initiate and sustain creation. The **Kav** does not fill the void with the same all-consuming intensity as the original Infinite Light. Instead, it *measures itself,* allowing for **gradual revelation, diversity, form,** and **structure.**

This **Kav Light**, in contrast to the boundless Ohr Ein Sof, is **relatable** to the worlds. It permits the arising of **levels**, of **differences**, of **hierarchies of being**. Through this Ray, the Divine becomes **Immanent**—*not less Infinite, but concealed in such a way that finite minds can engage with It.* The Ray shines by the needs and limitations of each world, each soul, and each situation, ensuring that **Divine Presence is accessible**, even in realms far removed from the Source.

Imagine a sun so blindingly brilliant that no eye could ever gaze upon it. The Kav is like a filtered beam of that sun, passing through stained glass – diffused, colored, refracted – so that each created being may receive only what it can bear, and no more.

Yet even as it descends, the Kav is never disconnected from its Source. **The Ray remains tethered to the Infinite**, even as it weaves the tapestry of time, space, matter, and consciousness. It retains within itself the memory of the Whole, even as it plays the role of the part. And so, in every breath, in every atom, in every moment, **Divine Immanence is secretly glowing**, surrounded still by **Divine Transcendence**, waiting for the mystic to awaken and *see.*

Thus, creation is not a fall from grace, but a **sacred concealment**. The worlds are not separate from God, but **expressions of God's desire to be known, loved, and discovered in multiplicity**. The finite emerges not to deny the Infinite, but to make it knowable. And the Kabbalist, through meditation, ritual, study, and love, seeks to trace the **light of the Kav** back to its **source in the Ohr Ein Sof**, and from there into the unspeakable mystery of **Ein Sof Itself**, the **limitless wellspring of all that was, is, and will be.**

Keilim and Ohrot Vessels of Lights

Vessels and Lights — or in the sacred language of Kabbalah, **Kelim and Ohrot** — represent one of the most fundamental dynamics in the architecture of the universe. Every **Sephirah** on the Tree of Life is composed of two interdependent elements: **a vessel (kli, plural kelim)** and **a light (or, plural ohrot)**. These are not mere poetic symbols, but the very framework through which **Divine consciousness becomes manifest** in the created worlds. The vessel contains, limits, and shapes. The light fills, flows, and radiates.

The **light**, drawn from the **Ohr Ein Sof**, is pure, undifferentiated, and infinite. It is **Divine Will, Divine Wisdom, and Divine Compassion** all at once, yet in potential, formless like the whiteness of a page before the letters appear. **It is the absolute, unified essence of revelation**, the raw presence of the Infinite that seeks expression. But light, without form, cannot be grasped. To reveal the Divine in a way that is perceivable, understandable, and actionable within creation, **there must be a kli — a vessel**.

Each Sephirah possesses its vessel, a unique spiritual structure that gives form and function to the Infinite Light within it. *The difference between Chokhmah and Binah is not in the light itself — it is in the vessel that receives and filters that light.* Like water poured into different-shaped glasses, the **content remains the same, but the presentation and interaction change. Chesed's vessel channels the light into boundless kindness**, while **Gevurah's vessel focuses the same light into restraint and discipline**.

In this way, **Divine Revelation** is not uniform. It becomes differentiated, **custom-tailored to its purpose**, *just as light passing through a prism separates into distinct colors, each beautiful and essential.*

In Kabbalistic thought, the name **Ban** — one of the **Divine Names formed by the permutation of the Tetragrammaton** — is associated with this process. It refers to a specific configuration of Divine energy linked to **manifestation and receptivity**, *particularly as the light descends into vessels.* In this context, Ban symbolizes the **Divine Immanence,** expressed through the ship, representing the way the Infinite is experienced in a finite form.

The concept of vessels also runs deep in Jewish tradition, extending beyond the mystical. In the **Halachic (Jewish legal)** sense, the word **kli** appears frequently in discussions, especially in laws regarding **Shabbat**, where even objects not typically thought of as "containers" are defined as kelim based on their utility or capacity to hold function. But in **Kabbalah**, such language is elevated. **These vessels are no longer merely physical objects — they are metaphysical realities**, containers of cosmic purpose and spiritual intentionality.

The revelation at Mount Sinai serves as the ultimate example of light meeting vessel. It was not just a historical moment, but a metaphysical event in which **the Infinite Light of Divine Wisdom poured into the boat of human perception**. This revelation includes not only the **Written Torah**, but also the **Oral Torah** — and within it, the **mystical tradition of Kabbalah**.

The **Oral Torah**, when approached through the lens of **Kabbalah and Hasidic philosophy**, reveals its deepest layer — the level known as **Sod**, the *secret dimension*. Here, even the simplest verse or law can be seen as **a vessel for sublime metaphysical insight**. Every halachic narrative becomes an **encoded expression of Divine energy**, and every legal detail hints at higher cosmic structures.

This integrative approach, where **Peshat (literal meaning), Remez (allegorical meaning), Derash (homiletical meaning), and Sod (mystical meaning)** are **woven together**, forms a unified tapestry of spiritual truth. The vessel (kli) is no longer a static container, but **a dynamic process of reception, limitation, and transformation**, through which **Divinity becomes knowable**.

In **Hasidic thought**, this synthesis is especially emphasized. The vessel and the light are not just external opposites, but **aspects of a single spiritual movement** — the light desires to give, and the ship desires to receive. Yet the ultimate state is not the separation between the two, but their **fusion** — the vessel **transforms** the light, and the light **fills** and **uplifts** the vessel. This interplay becomes the **foundation of**

spiritual life, *mirroring how the soul seeks to channel the Divine through the limitations of the body, time, and action.*

Thus, **Kelim and Ohrot are not simply cosmological models — they are blueprints for human transformation.** Every thought you refine, every act you perform with intention, every emotion you transmute, is a vessel being shaped to hold more light. And in this way, you are not only a student of Kabbalah, but **a living Sephirah — a vessel of Divine light unfolding within the world.**

Ohr — the Divine Light — is not merely illumination, but the *very expression of spiritual vitality,* the **revelation of Divine reality** as it descends from the highest levels of the Infinite into the layered structure of existence. At every stage of descent, this **light cloaks itself in vessels** (*kelim*) suited for each realm, allowing it to be received, interpreted, and manifested.

Yet, despite this descent, **Ohr remains fundamentally in a state of Bittul** — *nullification*. It is not autonomous. It is not self-referential. It remains always oriented *back* toward its origin, its **source in the Ein Sof**, the **limitless Divine essence**. This longing to return, this **tension of yearning,** is called **Ratzo** — the spiritual impulse to **ascend**, to dissolve again into the infinite ocean of Being. It is the **soul's pull toward unity.** *Like a flame leaping upward from a candle, Ohr moves with a natural urgency toward its root.*

But light cannot dwell forever in ascent. The Will of the Divine is not that existence should vanish into mystical union. **The Will is for the light to descend.** To be clothed. To become real within form. This counterforce, this necessity of **Shuv** — **return,** brings the Ohr **back down** into the vessel. **Shuv is the return to purpose,** the movement into the world of form, the world of **action**, the world of *tikun, repair*. It is through **Shuv** that the **Divine Will is ultimately fulfilled.**

This dynamic — **Ratzo and Shuv** — is not only a cosmic rhythm, but **a mystical choreography,** eternally echoing through **the entire structure of creation.** The angels themselves move by it. As described in **Ezekiel's vision of the Merkavah (Divine Chariot),** the beings of light **"ran and returned."** *They surged toward God in ecstasy, and then returned* *to their station, their duty, their role within the cosmic design.* So too with the soul of man. *In moments of deep prayer, meditation, or awe, we experience Ratzo — we want nothing but to merge, to leave the world and cling to the Light.* But in the very next breath, Shuv calls us back. *Back to the task. Back to the world. Back to where the Divine longs to dwell.*

This is not exile. This is a mission.

The purpose of creation, according to **Kabbalah**, is not for the higher worlds. It is **not** for the realm of angels. **It is for this world — the** realm of **Asiyah**, where **action, matter, choice**, and **imperfection** exist. The Divine desire, as expressed through the **Ohr Ein Sof**, was not to create endless sublime worlds of perfection, but rather to bring the Divine into **the lowest**, most hidden of realms. *To have a dwelling place **here**, in the work of man, in the grit and glory of embodied life.*

And so the light must descend. *Shuv must occur. The light must agree with the vessel.*

In this framework, your **soul is the light**, and your **body is the vessel**. The soul is **exiled**, yes — but with sacred intent. Your desires, your dreams, your struggles are all *the light being trained through the vessel*, not destroyed, but transformed. It is precisely through this interplay that the **Divine is revealed in the world**.

Even the structure of the **Seder Hishtalshelus**, the **chain of descent** from the Infinite to the finite, mirrors this principle. Each world is formed by the unfolding of **the 10 Sephirot**, Divine attributes that shape the realities of each level of existence. At the bottom of each world's Sephirotic ladder lies **Malchut — kingship**, the **manifestation**, the final stage. And that **Malchut becomes the Keter — the crown — of the next world.** *What was completed becomes a new beginning. What was fulfillment becomes origin.*

This pattern continues infinitely. In each world, light births form. Form reveals new light. **Every revelation contains the seed of the next ascent.** Each **Sephirah** becomes a *womb* for the next. This is not just metaphysical theory — it is the inner pattern of all growth, healing, and transformation in your own life. *The descent into the body, the challenges* *of daily existence, the tension of choice — all are stages in the sacred oscillation of Ratzo and Shuv.*

The **Divine drama** is not happening somewhere else — it is happening **in you**. When you breathe in and long for something greater, that is Ratzo. When you open your eyes and act with integrity, with love, with presence, that is Shuv. The purpose of it all is not escape, not transcendence alone — but **integration, embodiment, divine indwelling**. And in that, **the world is made holy**.

Ohr and Ma'Ohr

Ohr, or **Divine Light**, originates from **Ma'Ohr**, the **Luminary**, the **source** itself. This distinction between the *radiance* and the *radiant* is one of the most profound in Kabbalah. The **Ohr** is not separate from the Ma'Ohr. Yet, it is the **manifestation**—the **expression** of the **Divine Being** in a form that can *enter creation*, be *perceived*, and eventually *transform* what it touches. In traditional Kabbalistic teaching, the metaphor—or **mashal**—used to explain this relationship is the **sun and its light**. The **sun** represents the Ma'Ohr, and the **sunlight** represents the Ohr. *They are not two entities, but one reality expressed in different modalities — source and emanation.*

Yet even this analogy falls short. **Sunlight**, as we experience it here on Earth, is **not the full radiance** of the sun. It has passed through a **nartik**—a **sheath**, a kind of **shield**—which **dims, filters**, and **modifies** the intensity of the original light. This filtered light is known in Kabbalah as **Ohr HaNartik**, the **Light of the Sheath**. This concept reveals something crucial: *the light that reaches our world is not the raw, unbounded intensity of the Divine — it is a tailored, moderated form* designed for the survival and integration of the created realms.

Ohr HaNartik is **not nullified** in the same way as the original Ohr is. The light from the sun, after being filtered through the atmosphere, no longer holds the **same intimacy** with its source. It is **distant, modified**, and, crucially, **capable of giving form to finite reality**. In contrast, the **Ohr that remains within the Ma'Ohr**—the sunlight still within the sun—is in a state of **total Bittul**, or **nullification**, to its source. It does not "exist" as an independent entity. It *is* the sun. This distinction underpins the metaphysics of **creation and concealment**, the **dance between revelation and limitation** that defines the **Divine strategy** of existence.

In the **language of Divine Names**, this difference is symbolized by **the Tetragrammaton**—the holiest, unutterable Name of God—and **Elokim**. The **Tetragrammaton** represents the **Divine Essence, unconcealed, limitless, creative in essence**, and **unified with its light**. Elokim, by contrast, represents **Divine Constriction**—it is the **shield**, the **nartik**, the *channel* through which the Divine Light becomes **concealed enough** to *allow creation* to perceive itself as **independent**. If the **Tetragrammaton alone** were revealed in creation, *nothing would exist with self-awareness*, because the *infinite light would dissolve all form into its source. It would be like trying to see your shadow in the heart of the sun — it is overwhelmed, erased by the light itself.*

This leads to one of the central paradoxes of Kabbalah — **the mystery of Divine Unity**, which is understood through two distinct perspectives. The **Upper Divine Unity** (Yichuda Ila'ah) views creation **from a divine standpoint**. In this view, **creation is illusory** — nothing exists but the Ein Sof. *All differentiation is swallowed up in the Infinite Light.* This is the perspective of **Bittul HaMetzius** — the **nullification of essence**. Just as **sunlight within the sun** has no identity apart from the sun, **all of creation, in the Divine gaze, is still inside the source**. This is the root of what philosophers would call **acosmism** — the belief that the universe, in truth, is not ultimately real, but **a veil** over the only actual reality: **the Divine Infinite**.

But there is another perspective, just as valid: the **Lower Divine Unity** (Yichuda Tata'ah). This is the **perspective of creation** itself. From here, the **universe exists**, and yet, it exists only because the **Divine life-force** is being *constantly channeled into it*, moment by moment. Existence is **sustained**, not **autonomous**. The **Ego**, or **Yesh**, seems real, but is **dependent**, like a candle flame glowing brightly in a room flooded with sunlight — it is visible, but only because of contrast. This is **Bittul HaYesh**, the **nullification of the something**, where we recognize our **smallness** and **utter dependency**, but not our total nonexistence.

This distinction is also reflected in the structure of the **Four Worlds**: **Atzilut, Beriah, Yetzirah,** and **Asiyah. Atzilut,** the highest realm, is *not truly a creation*, but an **emanation** of the Divine. It carries the **Upper Unity** — a **nullification of essence**. Below it, **Beriah** (Creation), **Yetzirah** (Formation), and **Asiyah** (Action) are truly created worlds, where **self-awareness increases** and **nullification decreases**. *The lower the world, the greater the concealment, and yet — the greater the potential for transformation.*

This structure is mirrored in the **Creation narrative** of Genesis. In the **first account**, the Divine Name **Elokim** is used exclusively. "And Elokim said..." is repeated for each day of creation. This reflects the **Divine concealment**, the **moderated light**, the **filtered Ohr HaNartik** necessary to allow the finite to emerge. Each **day** of this narrative corresponds to one of the **seven lower Sephirot**, the emotional attributes through which **Divine energy channels into form**.

It is only in the **second narrative** of creation that **the Tetragrammaton** appears—*and it appears in **combination** with Elohim.* "The Lord God" — YHWH Elokim—now signifies the **unification of opposites: transcendence and immanence, infinity and limitation, revelation and concealment, Ma'Ohr and Nartik**. This synthesis is not accidental—it is essential. *Both Names, both modalities, are required for Creation to exist and be real.*

When **God speaks to Moses**, it is through **the Tetragrammaton**. The **Essence reveals itself**, now that Moses has reached the level of **receiving Divine instruction directly**. But the world cannot yet withstand such unshielded radiance. Thus, throughout all creation, **Elokim** remains necessary, a **curtain** that makes **existence possible** without blinding it with too much light.

Only **Ein Sof**, the **Divine Essence**, can create *yesh me'ayin*—something from nothing. This **act of creation ex nihilo** is beyond all levels of Ohr. It belongs to the Ma'Ohr alone. Yet, for that **primordial light** to enter reality, to give *shape*, to give *form*, to allow us to even speak of a "world"—it must **pass through Elokim**, the **filter**, the **vessel**.

This is the mystery of the **Divine Name**—*not as an identity, but as a process, a technology of being*. And it is through this duality—of **Name and Light, of Concealment and Revelation, of Unity above and Unity below**—that the **drama of Creation continues to unfold**, moment by moment, breath by breath, within you, around you, and through every act of awareness.

Mimalei means *"filling"* and **Sovev** means *"surrounding"*, but these are not mere spatial terms. In the language of Kabbalah, they describe **two radically different modes** of Divine presence—**immanence** and transcendence. Though they may sound geometrical or physical, these adjectives are **highly metaphorical,** pointing to the nature of how **Divine Light** permeates—or does not permeate—creation. They are not measured in distance, but in **relationship.**

Sovev Kol Almin—translated as *"Surrounding All Worlds"*—refers to a type of Divine Light that is **transcendent, non-specific,** and **non-differentiated.** It is not limited by the capacity of the world it touches. It doesn't "enter" the vessels or forms of creation, because it is **above form, beyond containment.** It is **Infinite Light** (*Ohr Ein Sof*) in its most sublime function—present *everywhere* but **not graspable,** not limited by the laws of each realm. It is the Divine that **overflows boundaries,** like *a light so vast that it cannot be poured into any particular cup, only hover around it with overwhelming brilliance.*

This surrounding light **precedes** even the **Tzimtzum**—the initial contraction described in **Lurianic Kabbalah** that allowed creation to occur. Sovev Kol Almin continues to be **present throughout all levels** of existence, but always as something **too vast to be contained.** It is **revealed only in moments of miracle, divine intervention, or transcendence,** where the **normal laws** of existence are **suspended.**

Think of it like this: *a soul, in its most valid form, is not bound by the body, nor by time or space.* Similarly, the **Torah,** being of Divine origin, exists **beyond all worlds,** and is studied in every realm according to that realm's capacity—*like one book, read in many languages, each translation accurate to its world.*

On the other side is **Mimalei Kol Almin**—*"Filling All Worlds".* This is the **immanent** aspect of Divine Light, the light that **enters, saturates,** and **gives form** to each world according to its **unique vessels.** This light originates not from the unbounded essence of Ohr Ein Sof, but from the **Kav**—the **Ray** of light that reentered the **vacated space (Chalal)** after the **First Tzimtzum.** It is the **specific, contracted, purpose-driven** Divine force that animates the **details** of creation.

Mimalei Kol Almin is what creates the *distinctions* between realms— physical and spiritual—and gives each its particular **form, structure,** and **vitality.** To reach the lower worlds, this light must pass through countless **veiling, filtering,** and **contractions,** referred to as the **Second Tzimtzumim**. It is **limited** not because it is weak, but because **limitation is necessary** for anything to exist as something other than God.

In **Hasidic philosophy,** this **lower light** is not secondary—it is the **primary focus.** Since the **ultimate purpose** of Creation is fulfilled in the **weakest of realms,** it is precisely this light—the one that **fills**—that must be engaged, transformed, and uplifted. *By taking the physical and revealing the spiritual within it, we make Mimalei the vehicle for redemption.*

The **direct light** descending from above—**Or Yashar**—is known in Kabbalistic language as the **"arousal from Above"** or **"masculine waters"**. This metaphor is drawn from the Torah itself—in *Genesis 1:6-8,* where the **firmament separates the upper and lower waters**. This **masculine flow** expresses the **Sephirah of Chesed**—*Divine Kindness*—which gives **limitlessly,** without judgment, without consideration of the vessel's worthiness. It pours out **Divine grace,** ever-flowing, abundant, unrestrained.

But Chesed must be balanced. The **Sephirah of Gevurah,** *Judgment,* acts as the counterforce. It examines each vessel, each situation, each soul's preparedness—and then **restrains** or **measures** the light accordingly. Without Gevurah, the unfiltered light would **overwhelm creation,** just as sunlight without atmosphere would **burn the earth**.

This **descent of light,** this Divine grace, **only occurs in response to an ascent from below**. This **reflected light** is called **Or Chozer,** the **"feminine waters",** or **"arousal from below"**. It is what we **offer upward**—our **prayers,** our **actions,** our **intentions,** our **rituals,** our **mitzvot**. Every ethical deed, every word of Torah, every act of love or compassion, rises like **vapors** to the firmament, *calling down the rain of blessing*. It is the **Divine mirror**—when the lower reaches upward, the higher responds.

This dance between **masculine** and **feminine waters,** between **Or Yashar** and **Or Chozer,** forms the **spiritual logic** behind **reward and punishment** in Jewish belief. Not in the simplistic sense of transactional morality, but in the **profound alchemy of interaction** between **Divine response** and **human intention**. The **greater the ascent of feminine waters, the greater the delight** and **reciprocity** in the Upper Worlds. It is **joy**, not judgment, that stirs the heavens to respond.

Kabbalah may sound **radical**—indeed, it is among the most **esoteric theosophies** of any mystical system—but it remains **conservative** in its devotion to the **halachic framework**. The **Torah**, the **mitzvot**, the **festivals**, the **structure** of Jewish life—these are not dismissed as externalities. They are **essential vessels** that make the **Divine flow possible**. The **rituals are technologies**, and the **commandments are cosmic levers**.

Lurianic Kabbalah, in particular, teaches that each of us has the power not just to receive light, but to **repair** it. This is **Tikkun Olam**—*repairing the world*. Every soul has a **unique spark**, a **portion of Divine purpose**, and when we play our part—*even if we don't fully understand it*—the **structure of reality shifts**.

Even those unaware of the **deeper metaphysics** behind their observance still affect the heavens. The **ascending waters** don't require intellectual mastery—they require **intention, devotion,** and **sincerity**. And once they rise, the Divine responds. Always.

It is this **mutual yearning**, this **reciprocity**, this **mystical marriage of immanence and transcendence**, of **Mimalei and Sovev**, that fuels the cosmic cycle of **creation, blessing,** and **redemption**. Creation is not a finished act—it is an **ongoing relationship**. *And you are part of it.*

chapter 8

FIVE LEVELS OF SOUL WORLDS IN KABBALAH

Some teachings within Kabbalah speak of the soul as having **three distinct levels**. In comparison, others expand this understanding to include **five primary levels**, and still others hint at even higher, more concealed dimensions. These **levels are not separate entities**, but **interwoven layers** of the same soul, each revealing a deeper, more refined aspect of our **Divine essence**. They represent a spiritual ladder, a structure that reflects how the Infinite Divine Light descends into finite form, and how the human being can ascend from earthbound awareness to cosmic unity. The soul is not just a spark—it is a **multi-dimensional emanation** of the Divine, clothed in the garments of body, mind, and heart.

The first and most accessible level is **Nefesh**, which corresponds to the realm of **action** and the physical body. It is the **animating life-force** present in all living beings, even animals. Nefesh is what **drives the body**, allowing you to breathe, move, digest, sleep, and survive. But beyond biology, it is also the level of **habit**, of instinctual reaction. *When you feel anger before you understand why, when you react without thinking, when your body flinches before your mind catches up – that is Nefesh in motion.* It is the most grounded part of the soul, intimately tied to the **Sephirah of Malchut**, where **Divine kingship** is expressed through manifestation in the world. It is through Nefesh that a person begins their spiritual work, *not by transcending the world, but by sanctifying it.*

Above Nefesh is **Ruach**, the spirit or **emotional self**. Ruach is the seat of **moral discernment, character**, and **emotions**, encompassing love, fear, courage, shame, and compassion. It is the part of the soul that strives, struggles, and grows. Ruach gives you a sense of **inner identity**, and it allows you to **choose between right and wrong**. It is the spiritual engine behind **teshuvah**, the capacity for return and transformation. *When you feel a sudden pang of conscience, when your heart swells with empathy, when you are moved to tears by beauty or sorrow – that is Ruach stirring within you.* This level of soul is associated with the **Sephirot of Tiferet and Gevurah**, which balance emotion and judgment. It is in Ruach that we find the battleground of the soul's refinement.

Beyond Ruach is **Neshamah**, the **breath of God** within us, the level of the soul associated with **intellect, contemplation, and higher wisdom**. This is not the thinking mind that calculates or reasons, but the **supernal intellect** that perceives truth without filter—the **Divine intuition**. Neshamah enables a person to grasp spiritual ideas, meditate on the Infinite, and experience awe before the Divine mysteries. It is through Neshamah that we gain **clarity**, a clear mirror that reflects Divine light into consciousness. *When you sit in stillness and a truth arises within you unprovoked, when you understand a sacred text not with the mind but with the heart, when you feel connected to something larger than the self – that is Neshamah speaking.* This level is associated with the Sephirah of Binah, understanding, and is considered the first of the "upper" soul levels, typically awakened through **Torah study, prayer**, and **inner purification**.

Some stop here, at three levels. However, more profound Kabbalistic teachings reveal two additional ones. These higher levels are so **subtle and transcendent**, they are rarely experienced fully in this lifetime— but they are **always present**, like dormant seeds.

The fourth level is **Chayah**, the **living essence**, a soul-force that transcends conscious thought. Chayah is the dimension of the soul that is **directly aware of the Divine**, not as a belief, not as a philosophy, but as a **living presence**. It is the state of **being in unity** with the Divine will, beyond selfhood. *It is what moves the tzaddik who acts without* *hesitation, because the will of God and his will are the same.* Chayah flows through moments of **prophetic vision, sacred ecstasy**, and **divine inspiration**. It is associated with the **Sephirah of Chokhmah**, Divine Wisdom, the **spark of insight** that flashes like lightning, too vast to hold but too real to deny.

And finally, there is **Yechidah** — the **singular one**, the **essence of the soul**, the **pure spark of Ein Sof** within each person. Yechidah is not a level of consciousness — it is **beyond consciousness**. It is not something one "has," but **something one is**. In the most profound moment of connection, Yechidah **does not know God** — **it is God**, or rather, it is the **point in you that never left God**. Yechidah cannot be accessed through intellect, action, or emotion. It reveals itself in **total surrender**, in **oneness**, in the **annihilation of ego**. *In moments of absolute selflessness, when the boundaries between "I" and "Thou" collapse, when you no longer seek because you have become the seeker and the sought — this is Yechidah made visible.* It is connected with **Keter**, the crown, the unknowable will of the Divine.

Though the levels appear to ascend — Nefesh, Ruach, Neshamah, Chayah, Yechidah — they are also **simultaneously present** in every soul, **nested like concentric circles**, or **vibrations within a chord**. Every person, regardless of knowledge or merit, contains all these layers. The spiritual path is not about gaining a soul, but about **unveiling what was always there**.

To speak of five levels is not to fragment the soul, but to **recognize its unfolding**, from the **earthly to the infinite**, from **body to Source**, from **the breath you take in this moment** to **the breath that created the cosmos**.

Kabbalah reveals that **human consciousness is never static**. It **rises and falls**, flowing like a river between moments of Divine closeness and states of distance, between illumination and concealment, between **soul and self**. The soul journeys not in a straight line, but in **waves of ascent and descent**, like breath moving in and out of the body. One may begin a day tethered to the lowest aspect of their soul — **Nefesh**, the domain of instinct, survival, and the physical — only to experience moments later a sudden elevation into **Ruach**, the world of emotion and morality, or even glimpses of **Neshamah**, the clarity of spiritual insight. *Have you ever felt thoroughly grounded and bodily one moment, then suddenly moved to tears by a prayer, a piece of music, or an act of kindness the next? That's the soul in motion.*

No soul remains on one level forever. Even the most seasoned mystics, the deepest meditators, the most awakened beings—those who live and breathe the sacred truths—experience **shifts**. They ascend through passionate study, disciplined devotion, and inner purification, yet **they too fall**. It is not failure; it is part of the cosmic rhythm. The world pulls us down, not as punishment, but as part of the **dance between concealment and revelation**, between the **body's gravity** and the **spirit's desire to soar**. Kabbalists call this movement the secret of **ratzo v'shov**—running and returning. *Even Moses, in his grandeur, ascended Mount Sinai only to descend again to the people.*

Kabbalah teaches that **intellect must rule over emotion**, not the other way around. Emotions, though powerful and holy, are **lower in the hierarchy** of the soul's structure. They are transient, reactive, and shaped by memory and mood. Intellect, when refined and elevated, serves as the vehicle to **transform emotion into alignment** with Divine Will. *It is not about suppressing the heart, but about guiding it.* In moments when the emotions rage, when anger or desire threaten to overtake, it is the **light of Neshamah**—spiritual understanding—that must lead.

Reaching the level of **Chayah** is **exceedingly rare**. It requires a lifetime of **relentless inner work**, stripping away illusion, enduring trials, and surrendering ego again and again. Chayah is not just insight; it is **awareness of the Divine presence as the only reality**. At this level, one is no longer pulled by the tides of intellect or emotion. They **see clearly**, not through logic or feeling, but through **Divine perception**. Their soul no longer speaks of God as an idea or a yearning, but as a **presence so real it dissolves all other identities**. Few reach it, and those who do become vessels of a light that few can bear to look upon.

But above even Chayah is **Yechidah**—the hidden crown of the soul, the **spark of absolute unity**. This level cannot be "reached" in the usual sense. It cannot be "understood," "felt," or even "experienced" in the way we know experience. **Yechidah is the soul's Divine core**, where

God and soul are not two things. There is no separation, no distinction, no awareness of self at all. This is not a spiritual state but an ontological truth. One does not live in the state of Yechidah and remain a separate individual. To dwell there is to **cease being a 'self' at all**. *This is the domain of the tzaddikim who have fully merged into the Divine, or of the soul after death, when its garments fall away and only essence remains.*

Yet, even if we do not reside constantly in Chayah or Yechidah, their **presence lives within us**. The path is not about climbing once and remaining above—it is about **moving, returning, refining, purifying**. The **goal is not escape**, but **transformation**. The **purpose of your soul's journey** is to **perfect the vessel**—your body, your habits, your actions—until it becomes **transparent to the Infinite Light**. You do not ascend into Divinity by abandoning the world. You bring the Divine **down** into the world, into your speech, into your hands, into how you treat others. You make the Infinite **visible through the finite**.

In truth, your task is not to become someone else, but to **reveal who you already are beneath the veils. You are Divine**, and your soul carries the spark of **Ein Sof**. Your spiritual journey is the unfolding of that truth—**from concealment to revelation**, from scattered fragments to oneness. *Each time you meditate, each time you forgive, each time you choose light over shadow, you rise a little closer to that oneness.*

Kabbalah demands this of you: **To know the potential of your soul**, and to never stop climbing, falling, and climbing again, for every descent brings a new ascent. And every ascent reveals **another hidden spark** waiting to be redeemed.

According to Kabbalah, the **masculine and feminine polarities** of the cosmos represent **two fundamentally distinct orientations of consciousness**. The masculine archetype perceives **from above to below**—a vantage point rooted in **transcendence**, where the world below is negligible, even illusory, in the overwhelming presence of the One. In this state of awareness, the **Infinite Light—Ohr Ein Sof—** shines with such intensity that *nothing else is real by comparison.* The world does not exist as separate; it is **nullified**, absorbed in the blinding unity of Divine Oneness.

In contrast, the feminine gaze moves **from below to above**, a consciousness that **acknowledges the world** in its multiplicity but sees within it the glimmer of the Divine. From this perspective, **everything is a reflection** of the Source. The mountains, the rivers, the pain, the longing—all of it **points back to God**. This is not a lower or weaker vision—it is a **devotional consciousness**, filled with yearning, perception, and nuance. *Think of the mystic who sees the sacred in the soil, the lover of God who weeps at the sound of birdsong. That is the feminine gaze.*

These two orientations—**Above to Below**, and **Below to Above**—are not separate doctrines, but **two modes of the same Divine intelligence**. At their meeting point is the **Essence of Ohr Ein Sof**, the place **beyond polarity**, beyond gender, beyond even being. And yet, this essence radiates into form, descending as masculine and feminine consciousness.

The masculine mind **descends into man**, into the drive to **conquer, to shape, to impose order** on the chaos below. But in doing so, it may lose the capacity to feel the pulse of life. The feminine descends into woman, into the mystery of **nurturing, receiving, constraining light** within form. Her light is held tight, hidden in judgment, **gevurah**, restrained but powerful. She is not weak—**she contains the world**. But without balance, **her judgments can harden** into unyielding barriers. *A woman who has locked her heart becomes iron, and yet within her is a molten sea of compassion, waiting for the sweetness of union.*

When the masculine and feminine unite, a **rectification occurs**. The man brings **chesed**, the sweetness that softens her gevurah. The woman brings **binah**, the deep understanding of how to hold, nurture, and channel Divine light into form. This union is not just romantic—it is **cosmic perfection**, the reflection of **Ein Sof** in dual embodiment.

In the act of **conception**, this union mirrors the highest mysteries. There are always **three partners in the formation of a soul**: the mother, the father, and **the Infinite**. The Divine breathes a soul into the world—but this breath must descend **through a garment**, a sheath, a protective vessel. This garment—**the soul's suit**—is not random. It is **shaped by the thoughts, the intentions, the purity or distortion** of the parents at the moment of conception. *If the parents are unified, selfless,* *and noble in their desire, then the suit is smooth and luminous, and the soul finds easy passage into the world. If they are distracted, self-indulgent, fragmented, the suit is tangled – and the child will struggle with limitations not their own.*

This soul, whether new or returning, must pass through the veil. If the soul has lived before—as most have—it carries **echoes of previous incarnations**: wounds, knowledge, regrets, strengths. It's "suit" contains these karmic impressions, and they shape the life to come. *Imagine a bright light trying to shine through a stained garment. The light is pure, but the garment affects what can be seen.*

Even when no child is born from the union of man and woman, **something is conceived—souls, energies, sparks** in higher realms. Every sacred act, every moment of union, **ripples through creation**. And those ripples will **return**. There is no waste in the spiritual economy of the universe.

Modern interpretations of Kabbalah, particularly those from the **Jewish Renewal movement**, have offered more **egalitarian readings** of these archetypes. Scholars like **Shlomo Carlebach** and **Zalman Schachter-Shalomi** emphasize the **Shekinah**, the feminine presence of God, as not merely a vessel, but central and even primary in the spiritual unfolding. These modern mystics use **feminine names for the Divine**, speaking of God not as a remote king, but as an indwelling mother, a **womb of mercy**.

This approach has drawn **controversy**. Critics argue that it distorts traditional Kabbalistic texts, which often portray the feminine as incomplete, in need of redemption, or as a means of absorption into the masculine. The **Zohar** and classical sources usually speak of the Shekinah as a **limb** of the greater body of Divinity—something **needing repair**, to be **reunited** with the masculine face of God, **Ze'ir Anpin**.

And yet, buried in these same texts are hints of **radical unity**. In **Lurianic Kabbalah**, the feminine is destined to become **whole**, autonomous, and **able to stand face to face** with the masculine. In the beginning, she was **within him**, hidden. Later, she stands **outside him**, receiving his light. But in the end, she becomes **equal**, "a full stature" — **qomah shleimah** — and they unite in **body opposite body**, not as master and servant, but as **authentic counterparts**.

This is the secret of **cosmic redemption**. It is not only the soul of man that ascends. **It is the soul of woman, the feminine in all of us**, that must be lifted, **completed, dignified**, not absorbed into the masculine, but **embraced as essential**. Every act of compassion, justice, beauty, intuition — **every act that honors the Divine feminine — hastens this union**. The trembling of Ze'ir Anpin before the Shekinah is **the trembling of the Divine before wholeness**. God yearns for His Bride to rise and meet Him.

Still, the classic Kabbalistic texts do not frame **gender liberation** as their central concern. The system remains rooted in **hierarchies**, roles, and cosmic orders. But even within those forms, the mystic **can find freedom**. The masculine is not man, and the feminine is not woman. **They are energies, forces, and lenses through which the Infinite makes itself known.**

And in the union of those forces, in the trembling and merging of opposites, in the silent place where **Above meets Below**, the true face of **Ein Sof** appears — not male, not female, not one or two, but **a singularity beyond all names**.

Nefesh

Nefesh is the **foundational layer of the soul**, the most **earthbound**, the most intimately connected to the **physical body,** and the **realm of action**. In many contexts, especially in the Torah or general speech, the term "soul" is often used interchangeably with *nefesh*, because it is the aspect of the human being most directly **involved with life itself** — the breath, the blood, the **movement**, the *drive to survive*. Yet in the **Kabbalistic map of consciousness**, nefesh is only the **lowest rung** on a grand ladder of the soul's ascent toward Divine union.

Nefesh is not intellectual. It is not spiritual in the contemplative sense. It does not grasp great truths or receive visions. **It acts. It responds. It desires. It lives.** The nefesh is what gives the body its **animation**, its **warmth**, its **instinctive reactions**. It is the level of soul that **we share with animals**, with plants, even with the elements. *A deer fleeing from danger moves because of nefesh. A vine turning toward the sun follows the pull of nefesh.* It is the **life-force** that dwells **within all creation**.

In humans, the nefesh is **located in the blood**, as the Torah states: *"For the soul (nefesh) of the flesh is in the blood."* This deep association with the **vital fluids** of the body underscores the intimate connection between nefesh and the processes of digestion, fertility, locomotion, sex, and survival. It is **visceral, impulsive,** and **reactive**. Nefesh does not reflect — it *hungers, fears, craves, strives*. It does not understand God, but it may still feel **awe in thunder** or **joy in food**, both raw, unfiltered spiritual experiences without form or articulation.

The **world of Asiyah**, the world of action, corresponds to nefesh. This is the lowest of the Four Worlds in Kabbalistic cosmology. It is the **realm of doing,** of **mechanics,** of **physical laws,** and **daily repetition**. A person whose soul primarily operates on the nefesh level is one **rooted in instinct**. They may live **entirely by routine**, defined by **material needs, social roles,** and **bodily desires**. This does not make them evil or less than others, but it does mean that their **spiritual light is concealed**, wrapped in layers of habit, fear, appetite, and survival reflexes.

Yet even within nefesh lies the **Divine spark**. It is not to be despised. It is the **gateway**, the **raw clay**, the **earth** from which the rest of the soul may rise. A person must begin with nefesh. It is **through nefesh that we learn to choose**, even if at first those choices are crude — *to work instead of steal, to care instead of harm, to remain faithful instead of giving in to lust*. Each time nefesh is **elevated**, purified, trained toward restraint or devotion, it becomes **refined**, and the next level of soul begins to emerge through it.

Many religious practices — **such as kosher laws, Shabbat observance, ritual purity, and ethical discipline — are designed to elevate nefesh, channeling** its **animal energies** into sacred service. The same drive that makes one **hunt for food** can be transformed into a **yearning for meaning**. The same force that wants **sex for pleasure** can be made to seek **union for love and creation**. This is the **alchemical transformation** that begins at the level of nefesh. *The work of the mystic starts in the kitchen, not in the clouds.*

Those who neglect nefesh, who seek only the higher worlds while ignoring their **bodily obligations**, fall into delusion. They **float without roots**, and their spiritual insights become **ungrounded**. The nefesh must be **honored** — not worshipped, not indulged, but **disciplined, respected**, and ultimately **offered**. When the nefesh learns to bow, to serve, to align with something greater, it becomes the **foundation stone** for the Temple within. Only when nefesh is **stable** can the higher aspects of the soul — **ruach, neshamah, chayah, and yechidah** — descend and inhabit the body.

In the end, **no part of the soul is separate from God**. Even nefesh, the lowest, carries **Divine life-force** within it. It is the **breath of the world**, the pulse of the earth, the beat of instinct that keeps us alive until the soul remembers why it came. And when nefesh is awakened, purified, and aligned with its higher nature, it becomes **the servant of the throne**, the **earth that reflects the heavens**.

Ruach

Ruach is the **second layer of the soul**, situated above **nefesh**, and is often translated as **"spirit."** Yet this translation hardly does justice to the profound, turbulent, and sacred nature of **Ruach** in the Kabbalistic worldview. While **nefesh** animates the body and governs movement and survival, **Ruach is the breath of identity, the storm of the heart, the wind of emotion and morality.** It is the level at which the human being becomes fully **human**, not just biologically alive, but capable of **feeling, choosing,** and **relating**.

Ruach resides in the **world of Yetzirah**, the World of Formation. This is the realm where raw spiritual energy begins to take on **shape**, where **structure, relationship,** and **meaning** emerge. If Asiyah, the world of nefesh, is the body of a letter, **Yetzirah is its vowel**, its sound, its breath. Ruach is the **air between words**, the **atmosphere of the self**, the medium through which the higher levels of soul begin to reach into the human experience. Ruach is the **seat of emotions**, but not only the emotions we commonly understand. These are not fleeting mood swings or momentary urges. In Kabbalah, **emotions are sacred vessels**, the means through which the Divine interacts with the world. Every feeling—**awe, compassion, courage, sadness, hope, love, humility, anger, mercy**—is a **mirror** of one of the **Sephirot**. When you feel, you are not merely reacting; you are **touching archetypes, tasting God's inner world.** *Think of a moment where you felt overwhelming compassion for a stranger.* That warmth, that pull toward kindness—this is **chesed**, the Sephirah of loving-kindness, flowing through your **Ruach**. Or recall a time when you stood before something immense—a mountain, the ocean, a funeral—and felt utterly small. That trembling is **yirah**, awe, a sliver of **Gevurah**, the Sephirah of discipline and judgment. These experiences are not incidental. They are **invitations**, whispers from the Infinite filtered through your inner world. While nefesh is impulsive and reactive, **Ruach carries memory, reflection, and choice.** It is the part of you that **wrestles with morality**, that **questions**, that seeks to understand *why* something matters. Ruach doesn't just want to *live*—it wants to **live rightly**. It asks *What is good? What is just? What does God want of me?*

But Ruach can also be **unstable**, like wind. It **rises and falls, howls and stills, builds and destroys**. A person dominated by **Ruach** may feel deeply, but also swing wildly between extremes. *One day, they may burn with sacred passion, and the subsequent collapse in despair.* To dwell in **Ruach** is to enter the **soul's battlefield**, where every feeling can either bring you closer to God or drag you deeper into ego.

This level of soul is where **ethics** are born. When the nefesh wants something—food, sex, power—it is the **Ruach** that must discern whether that desire is holy or harmful. This is where the **Torah meets the heart**. It's not enough to follow rules robotically; **Ruach must feel their truth**, internalize their wisdom, and willingly choose them. When **Ruach aligns with the Divine**, it becomes a **loyal servant of higher will**. When misaligned, it becomes the **storm that ruins the Temple within**. The beings who dwell in **Ruach** are not just alive—they are **self-aware, emotionally rich**, and capable of **empathy, loyalty, awe, repentance**, and **love**. These traits are the fingerprints of Ruach. To dwell in Ruach is to know that **your choices matter**, that **your inner world shapes the outer world**, and that **your relationship with others is a sacred dance reflecting the One**.

Ruach is also where **prayer** becomes transformative. *When you pray from your nefesh, you may go through motions. But when Ruach prays, the soul trembles.* Tears flow, hands shake, breath shortens—not because you want to be seen by others, but because something inside is rising toward the Divine, and it hurts to remain small.

Still, Ruach is **not yet the summit**. It is **the bridge**, the **windy middle path** between body and spirit, between nefesh and neshamah. **If you stop at Ruach**, you may become a spiritual narcissist—complete of feeling, but still ruled by the self. But if you **refine your Ruach**—if you **temper your emotions with wisdom**, and **offer your feelings as sacrifices to a will beyond your own**—then **you begin to open the gates of Neshamah**, the soul's next unfolding.

And so, Ruach is the **moral soul**, the **emotional soul**, the **relational soul**. It is not always peaceful. But it is where **Divine sparks are stirred, conflicts are redeemed**, and **love becomes a ladder toward Heaven**.

Neshama

Neshama is the **third level of the soul**, a realm **loftier, more refined, and more illuminated** than the nefesh and ruach. If nefesh is the soul that animates the body, and ruach is the soul that breathes and feels, **neshama is the soul that thinks, understands, and intuits the Divine.** It is the soul's access point to **intellect, contemplation,** and **spiritual awareness**. In Kabbalah, it is associated with the **World of Beri'ah**—the **World of Creation**, where pure Divine **ideas and blueprints** first come into form. Unlike the lower levels of the soul, which are tangled with the body and emotions, the **neshama stands somewhat apart from physicality**. It is the **breath of God breathed into man**, as the Torah says in *Genesis 2:7*: "And He breathed into his nostrils the breath of life." That *breath* is **neshama**—a more **sublime, heavenly** spark that **knows the truth** without needing to learn it. **It does not wrestle with good and evil the way Ruach does.** It sees. It knows. It perceives the Oneness beneath appearances. In a moment of profound insight, when the veil is thin and your thoughts feel infused with something *not of this world*, you are **touching neshama**. *Imagine walking under the stars and being struck not just by their beauty, but by the feeling that you are part of something infinite — that there is meaning, design, intention. That sensation comes from neshama.* **Neshama is the home of Da'at, Binah, and Chokhmah**—the higher powers of the mind known as the **intellectual Sephirot**. It is where **intuition, understanding,** and **integration** meet. While ruach might feel awe, **neshama comprehends it**. It is what allows us to understand **Torah**, not merely on a moral or emotional level, but as a **revelation of the structure of reality itself**. Through **neshama**, a person begins to glimpse the patterns of the Infinite, the architecture of the Sephirot, the language of the Divine Mind. Whereas ruach lives in tension, torn between emotion and ego, **neshama is serene** because it **knows its origin**. It comes from **a purer realm**, and **it remembers the Garden**. Those who access this level often carry a quiet **certainty**, a kind of **inner clarity** that doesn't need external validation. They are **drawn to truth** not for argument, but for alignment. **Their faith is not blind; it is informed by insight and understanding.** However, few people live from neshama consistently. Most experience it only in moments—when praying with deep kavannah, when studying sacred texts and suddenly *understanding something they've never been taught*, when immersed in nature or silence and *feeling the presence of something beyond name*. These are moments when the **neshama rises**, speaking softly through the noise of body and heart.

Neshama is also the soul's compass. It always points upward, always toward **Ein Sof**, even when the rest of the person is lost or distracted. While nefesh might crave comfort and ruach might be swept up in passion or despair, **neshama quietly longs for return**—for teshuvah, for alignment, for **cleaving to the Divine**, known in Kabbalah as **devekut**. This level of soul is also associated with **Shabbat**, the day of rest, where a person receives what the sages call a **neshama yeterah**, an "additional soul." This refers not to the addition of more nefesh or ruach. Still, there is **an intensification of neshama**, a heightened state of consciousness in which the spiritual becomes more palpable and the material fades in urgency. *On Shabbat, you may feel thoughts come more easily, feel more aware of God, or find that the world feels lighter.* That is **neshama drawing closer**. Yet for neshama to function fully, it must be **nurtured**. While it comes from above, it lives *within* the human being. If ignored, it may remain **dormant**. **Through study, silence, prayer, and holy acts**, you awaken the neshama. It is like a **lamp hidden within stone**: the fire is there, but you must **strike it**. That strike is your discipline, your yearning, your surrender. To live from **neshama** is to begin to **think like the soul** rather than the self. It is to look at others and see not their actions, but their essence. It is to encounter life and ask *not what does this mean to me*, but *what is being revealed here from above*?

Neshama is not your personality. It is not your memories. It is not your will. It is the part of you that was never born and will never die. It is your share in **eternity**, your window into **divine thought**, your bridge to all that lies beyond perception. And yet, even **neshama** is not the summit of the soul. It is only the **gateway to Chayah and Yechidah**, the higher reaches where the soul doesn't just know God—it *becomes* part of the Divine itself. But without **neshama**, the lower soul is blind. It is **the eye of the soul**, the light by which we see the path, even in darkness.

Chaya

Chayah is the **fourth level of the soul**, and it stands far above the more familiar aspects of human consciousness. While **nefesh** animates the body, **ruach** feels, and **neshamah** thinks and perceives divine ideas, **chayah is the soul's direct connection to the living presence of the Divine**—a level so elevated, so radiant, that it does not descend fully into the body. It surrounds the person like a **halo of light**, remaining partially hidden and inaccessible in ordinary awareness. It corresponds to the **World of Atzilut**, the **World of Emanation**, where there is **no separation** between the Creator and the emanated reality.

Those who access **chayah** do not merely believe in the Divine—they experience it. Not as a concept. Not as a feeling. But as an **immediate, undeniable truth**. They are not guessing, nor are they hoping. They are **living from the direct experience of the Infinite**, even if only in fleeting moments. While **neshamah sees Divine patterns, chayah sees only Divine presence**—the raw, unmediated vitality of Ein Sof, the Infinite.

This level of the soul does not speak in words or concepts. It does not argue. It **knows**. *Imagine standing on the edge of a cliff at dawn, the sky catching fire with color, and suddenly losing all sense of being separate from the wind, the earth, the light. There is no "you" observing. There is only what is.* That is a glimpse of chayah.

Chayah means "life-force," but not the same life-force that animates movement. It is the **life that flows from source to vessel without interruption**, pure, unfiltered, and too powerful for the human psyche to contain in its fullness. Only the **purest of vessels**, refined by spiritual effort, humility, and radical inner transformation, can safely bear even the edges of this level.

The tzaddikim, the truly righteous, are said to **live close to chayah**. Their presence radiates something inexplicable, a light that stirs others without them even having to speak. They **transcend the ego**, not by suppressing it, but by becoming so transparent to the Divine that the ego is no longer needed. In their presence, others feel elevated — not by their words, but by **who they are**.

Accessing **chayah** does not require more knowledge, but **less obstruction**. It is not about knowing more Torah — it is about **becoming Torah** — the **Torah of silence**, of **breath**, of **presence**. Chayah cannot be captured in doctrine, only reflected in being.

This level of soul is beyond the dualities of emotion or thought. It does not care for questions of worthiness, success, failure, or fear. It does not measure. It flows. It radiates. It **emanates** like light from a flame, **boundless, intimate, undeniable**. Yet this does not make Chayah aloof or untouchable. On the contrary, when you access it, even slightly, it evokes a deep compassion that is not sentimental but rooted in the understanding of **the unity of all things**. You no longer feel sorry for others. You feel *with* them. You **become them**, and they become you because the separations collapse.

To access this level is to feel **the breath of Ein Sof moving through you**, not as inspiration, but as **identity**. You don't worship the Divine — you become **a conduit**. You don't pray for connection — you are **already connected**.

But Chayah cannot be summoned. It appears only when **the vessel is ready**. And the ship is readied by **bitul**, self-nullification — not in weakness, but in surrender. You must become empty of self, of story, of pride, and of grasping, to be filled with what **cannot be possessed**.

And so, the Kabbalists teach, even if you live your entire life without fully tasting **chayah**, every mitzvah, every breath of prayer, every conscious act of love — **they prepare you**. They polish the mirror. They quiet the noise. And when the moment is right — perhaps in prayer, or death, or ecstasy, or in a silence so vast that even thought dares not speak — **chayah touches you**. And in that moment, **you remember who you are**. Not the you that is separate and striving, but the you that is always and already one with the Source. **You are not in the world. The world is in you, not** as ego, but as soul. That is **chayah**: the life of all life, the light behind the light, the whisper of the Infinite echoing through your form.

Yechida

Yechidah is the **fifth** and **most transcendent level** of the soul, the **crown of human consciousness**, and the **spark of absolute unity** that lies **beyond even individuality**. Unlike the other four levels — **nefesh, ruach, neshamah,** and **chayah** — which correspond to the Four Worlds of Action, Formation, Creation, and Emanation, **yechidah does not correspond to any realm**. It transcends them all. It is not *in* the world. It is *before* the world. **It is not a part of you — it *is* you, beyond you.**

The word **"yechidah"** comes from the Hebrew root *yachad*, meaning **oneness, singularity, absolute unity**. At this level, there is no longer a "self" experiencing God, no longer a soul perceiving the Divine, an "I" about a "Thou." There is only **oneness**. The distinction between Creator and created dissolves, not in blasphemy, but in sacred realization. **God is not near you. God is not with you. God is *you*.**

This is not a metaphor. This is not philosophy. This is **reality**, *raw, unfiltered, and unbearable to the ego*. It is the truth behind all truths, a whisper older than time: that **your soul is not a spark cast far from the flame — it is the flame itself**, clothed in the illusion of separation for the sake of revelation.

Yechidah is not something you "reach." It cannot be achieved through study, willpower, or effort. No spiritual practice, however sincere, can *create* the yechidah. It has always been there, **silently watching behind the masks**, waiting. The ego cannot approach it. The intellect cannot understand it. The emotions cannot contain it. Even the loftiest mystical states — visions, ecstasies, revelations — *still occur within the lower four levels*. **Yechidah is when all states fall away**, and only **being** remains. *No fire. No voice. No vision. Just pure, absolute, undivided Presence.*

Those rare souls who are said to have **touched the yechidah** — *the prophets, the greatest tzaddikim, those who burned with divine madness and clarity* — did not become "holy" by adding spiritual credentials. They became nothing. **They were not elevated. They were erased.** And in their erasure, they **shone with the light of the One that remains when all else disappears.**

This is why **yechidah is called the "point of contact" with the Divine.** Not contact like two fingers touching, but like **a drop of water returning to the sea**. There is no boundary anymore. You cannot say where the drop ends and the ocean begins. You **can no longer say "I."** Only **"Ehyeh asher Ehyeh"**—*I Am That I Am*—remains.

At this level, even the most sublime experiences of the soul-the love of ruach, the wisdom of neshamah, the ecstasy of chayah—are seen as **veils, refractions, echoes** of the original light. *Imagine a mirror shattering into ten thousand pieces, each catching a sliver of the sun, and then slowly, impossibly, becoming whole again. That is the return of the soul to its yechidah.* Not in death, necessarily, but in **radical unity**.

This unity is not peaceful—it is overwhelming. *It is not gentle—it is total.* It is the light Moses encountered on Sinai that burned too bright for flesh to bear. It is the fire the mystics feared yet longed for. It is the place where **free will dissolves into Divine Will**, where **every action becomes holy**, not because it follows a rule, but because **it arises from the Source itself**.

In the soul's descent into this world, **yechidah remains untouched, unchanged, unsullied**. It is not damaged by sin. It does not age. It is not born and does not die. It does not speak, but every whisper of conscience and every tremor of awe that stirs within you *comes from its silence*. You can live your whole life never knowing it, yet **it knows you**, always. And though we live in a time of concealment, of distraction, of ego, **every moment holds the potential to awaken yechidah**. Not through mastery, but through **surrender**. Not by climbing the ladder, but by **falling into God**. In a single instant of **pure surrender, true teshuvah, radical love**, or **utter brokenness**, the veil can tear. The light rushes in. And for one breathless moment, you *remember*. Not as a memory, but as **the thing that remembers all things**. That is **yechidah**. The soul's secret. The Divine's reflection. The still point where **you never were**—because **only God is**.

chapter 9

THE SEFER HA-ZOHAR

The **Zohar**, also known as the *Book of Radiance*, is the most iconic and enigmatic text in the Kabbalistic tradition. The word *Zohar* itself appears in the Bible, first in the **vision of Ezekiel** (*Ezekiel 8:2*), where it signifies a form of **shining brightness**, and again in the *Book of Daniel* (*12:3*), in the verse: *"Those who are wise shall shine like the brightness of the firmament."* The term thus evokes the image of **radiance**, of a **supernal illumination**, not only physical but also spiritual — an **inner light** that pierces the veils of ordinary understanding.

Composed in a rich and arcane Aramaic, the **Zohar is not a single book** but rather a **vast anthology** of mystical commentary, allegorical narratives, homiletic discourses, and poetic exegesis, spanning multiple volumes and comprising **well over a thousand pages**. It offers an intense, symbolic reflection on the **Torah**, layer by layer, **revealing hidden structures, divine dynamics, and esoteric truths** beneath the plain words of Scripture.

While not the earliest known Kabbalistic work — that title belongs more appropriately to texts like the *Sefer ha-Bahir* — the Zohar has become the **quintessential expression of Kabbalah**, the book through which the soul of Jewish mysticism found both depth and fame. It owes much of its modern renown to the scholarship of **Gershom Scholem**, the groundbreaking academic who elevated Jewish mysticism to serious intellectual study, and to the **translators** who labored to bring its luminous obscurity into English, though even then **much remains veiled**.

The Zohar claims to have been revealed to **Moses on Mount Sinai** and then transmitted orally across generations until Rabbi Shimon recorded it **by Bar Yochai** in the 2nd century. He, according to legend, received the mysteries while hiding in a cave for thirteen years with his son, immersed in asceticism and divine study. Yet **modern scholarship** suggests the Zohar was composed in **13th-century Spain**, most likely by **Rabbi Moshe de León**. The use of ancient Aramaic in that time and region was highly unusual, leading many to believe it was a **deliberate stylistic device** to grant the text an aura of antiquity. In a controversial story, De León's widow is said to have confessed that her husband authored the book himself, attributing it to Shimon bar Yochai to increase its spiritual and commercial value. But such accounts remain **shrouded in hearsay**, and **for the mystic**, the **authenticity lies in the message**, not in the manuscript's origin.

What does the Zohar teach? At its heart, the Zohar is an unveiling — a **revelation of the architecture of the cosmos**, the **hidden dimensions of the Divine**, and the **sacred mechanics of creation**. It speaks of **Ein Sof**, the Infinite, and of the **Sephirot**, the divine emanations that bridge the gap between **infinite light** and **finite world**. It speaks of **Creation not as a historical event**, but as a **constant unfolding**, a divine speech reverberating through all dimensions. It reminds us that **words and numbers are sacred**, forming the very **fabric of reality** — *as above, so below*, the vibrations of speech and thought ripple through the **upper and lower realms alike**.

Much of the text unfolds through **allegorical sermons**, often tied to the weekly Torah portion. **Characters from the Bible become spiritual archetypes**, with each action a symbol and each verse a gateway to another world. *Abraham becomes Chesed*, the force of **kindness**; *Jacob becomes Tiferet*, the **harmonious balance**; *Pharaoh becomes egoic resistance to divine flow*. The Zohar treats every human story as a **cosmic reflection** and every mundane event as a portal to a **holy encounter**.

One of the Zohar's central doctrines is **devekut** — *cleaving to God*. For the mystic, this is not achieved through asceticism alone, but through **study, prayer, ritual, and love**. The soul becomes a **lover**, and the Divine a **bride**. The act of mystical union is expressed through **erotic**

metaphor, where the **Shekinah**, the **Divine Feminine Presence**, longs to reunite with the **Holy One**, and the Kabbalist acts as a **bridge**, facilitating this reunion through **contemplation and commandment**. Just as the union of man and woman can create a child, so too can the **union of human soul and Divine Presence birth new light** in the world.

The **Zohar's view of language is revolutionary**. Speech is not a tool, but a **force of creation**. *When you speak with intention, you reshape the world.* When you pray, you're not asking — you're **participating** in the unfolding of reality. And when you study Torah in its mystical layers, you're not reading — you're **weaving light into vessels**.

For the **Kabbalist**, the Zohar is not just a book — it is **a spiritual technology**, a **living text**, one that **transforms the reader** as much as it explains the cosmos. Its language is dense, often cryptic, and **utterly non-linear**. *You don't read the Zohar the way you read a novel.* You circle it, return to it, allow its light to **seep in slowly**, sometimes through confusion, sometimes through sudden flashes of insight that pierce the heart.

Tradition held that one should be **over forty years old**, married, and deeply learned in Torah and Talmud before even approaching the Zohar. It was deemed too **powerful**, too **destabilizing** for the unprepared soul. Yet today, many are drawn to it earlier, not out of hubris, but from **a calling**, a **magnetic pull toward the mystery of being**.

The influence of the Zohar cannot be overstated. It laid the groundwork for the **Lurianic Kabbalah**, with its intricate cosmologies of *Tzimtzum* (divine contraction), *Shevirat ha-Kelim* (shattering of the vessels), and *Tikkun Olam* (restoration of the world). It shaped **Hasidism**, which took its cosmic visions and brought them into the **human heart**, translating mysticism into **joy, prayer, and psychological elevation**. Even **Christian mystics** found echoes of their Trinity and Incarnation in its pages.

The **Zohar continues to live** because it is **not a relic**. It is a **mirror**. And in its mirror, **the soul sees itself in its most valid form** — *as a spark of the Divine*, descending, forgetting, remembering, and rising again.

To study the Zohar is to enter a **labyrinth of fire**, but if one goes with sincerity, humility, and love, one finds not confusion but **light**.
The kind of light that doesn't merely illuminate a page... but illuminates the soul.

The Acceptance of the Zohar in Judaism has long been a subject of both reverence and dispute. Traditionally, many believed — and still believe — that God revealed the Kabbalistic teachings **to the patriarchs of the Hebrew Bible**, such as **Moses, Abraham**, and other foundational figures. These divine mysteries, too profound for casual interpretation, were not immediately inscribed but instead passed down **orally through the generations**, held close by the sages and whispered only to the worthy. According to this view, the teachings eventually coalesced into written form in the hands of **Rabbi Shimon bar Yochai**, one of the most celebrated mystics of the second century, who, *according to legend*, transcribed them after years of divine isolation in a cave.

However, in modern academic circles, particularly following the work of **Gershom Scholem**, the father of scholarly Jewish mysticism, the **authorship of the Zohar has been a subject of intense debate**. Scholem and others proposed that **Moses de León**, a 13th-century Spanish Jewish mystic, was the actual author or redactor of the Zohar. His writing in **antiquated Aramaic** — a language largely defunct at that time — was likely **a literary artifice**, intended to lend the book an aura of ancient authenticity.

Yet even among scholars, there are competing theories. Some assert that **an older, foundational text may have existed**, and that Moses de León and others built upon it, **gradually expanding and layering interpretations** until it became the vast compilation we know today. This raises the possibility that **the Zohar is not a singular voice**, but a **chorus of mystics** working within the same visionary tradition, each contributing fragments of light to the collective flame.

Still, the **Zohar's acceptance within Judaism has never been universal**. While **Hasidic and many Sephardic traditions embrace it wholeheartedly**, other **Orthodox, non-Hasidic**, and particularly **non-Orthodox denominations** have taken a more skeptical stance. Among them, some **dismiss the Zohar as pseudepigraphical** — that is, **falsely attributed** to an ancient sage to grant it authority. These critics argue that **de León may have projected his mystical worldview onto the persona of Rabbi Shimon bar Yochai**, not maliciously, but to enhance the spiritual impact of the text.

Certain Jewish groups, such as the **Dor Deah movement, explicitly reject the Zohar** and its teachings, considering them **later accretions** that distort the purity of Torah and Talmud. After the explosive failure of the **messianic pretender Sabbatai Zevi**, who Kabbalah had deeply influenced Kabbalah and later converted to Islam, many **Portuguese and Spanish Jewish communities purged the Zohar and its influence from their liturgies**. This was a profound moment of disillusionment, where **mysticism was seen as dangerous**, even **heretical**. In the centuries that followed, some of these liturgical elements were slowly reintroduced. Still, the scars of that historical trauma remain in the cautious stance of specific communities toward Kabbalistic texts.

Despite this, even some **non-Orthodox siddurim and prayer books today include passages from the Zohar, demonstrating that while the historical origin may be disputed, the spiritual insights offered by the text are** still **deeply valued**. Some Jewish educators argue that **truth in mysticism isn't always about historicity** — *it's about resonance.* If a mystical vision resonates with the soul and aligns with core teachings, it may be spiritually valid, **even if its author remains debatable**.

Outside Judaism, the **Zohar has found a surprising and often passionate audience**. **Spiritual seekers**, whether religious or secular, are drawn to its **rich metaphors, cosmological architecture, and existential questions**. They come not necessarily for Jewish law, but for insight into the **purpose of life**, the **nature of consciousness**, and the **interplay between spirit and matter**. *Why are we here? What does suffering mean? What lies beyond this world?* These are the eternal questions that **the Zohar dares to confront**, and it is precisely this universality that has allowed the text to reach beyond its original context.

However, from a **traditional rabbinic perspective**, the Zohar was not written for the world at large. It was meant to **guide the Jewish people** through **Exile**, to **illuminate the Torah** with hidden light, and to **deepen the meaning of mitzvot**, the sacred commandments. The Zohar repeatedly emphasizes the centrality of Israel's spiritual journey, and its perspective is one of Jewish cosmic responsibility, rather than universal metaphysics. This **creates tension** between its status as an esoteric Jewish text and its broader appeal to mysticism.

The **criticism** of the Zohar intensified in the modern era. In **1851, Adolf Jellinek** launched one of the first sustained academic critiques, followed by **Heinrich Graetz**, whose monumental *History of the Jews* cast further doubt on the traditional narrative of authorship. But it was **Scholem** who brought the full weight of historical methodology to bear. By 1941, he concluded decisively that **Moses de León had authored the Zohar**, citing clear **linguistic errors in Aramaic, the use of Spanish sentence structures**, and **geographic misunderstandings** about the land of Israel.

Scholem's critics, however, argue that **his conclusions may have been too rigid**. While he convincingly identified **non-ancient influences** in the Zohar, it remains possible that **de León was compiling and interpreting far older oral traditions**, or that he acted as a **channel** through which a **mystical collective voice emerged**.

Many scholars now believe that **the Zohar was a group effort**, created by **a mystical school led by de León**, or that it may represent a **fusion of authentic spiritual insight with fictional literary devices** — a **sacred mythopoesis**, rather than a fraud. In ancient times, it was **common to attribute teachings to revered sages** — not out of deceit, but as a **sign of humility**, or a **gesture of continuity** with the past.

Scholem, in his *Encyclopaedia Judaica* article, analyzed the **Zohar's sources** and showed that while **much of it is original**, it draws heavily from earlier Jewish texts. The Zohar incorporates **Babylonian Talmudic teachings, Midrash Rabbah, Midrash Tanhuma, Pesikta**

de-Rav Kahana, Pirkei de-Rabbi Eliezer, and **Targum Onkelos,** among others. The author — whoever he was — **did not always quote precisely,** but **translated and reframed these sources in his mystical idiom.**

Notably, he **neglected some key rabbinic sources,** such as the Jerusalem Talmud and halakhic midrashim. He showed little awareness of other mystical texts, including the Alfabet de-Rav Akiva and the **Yalkut Shimoni.** Yet he **did refer** to more obscure esoteric works, such as the **Hekhalot Rabbati, Sefer Zerubbabel,** and the **Baraita de-Ma'aseh Bereshit.** He also created entirely **fictitious works within the text,** such as *Sifra de-Hanokh* and Sifra de-Rav Hamnuna Sava, among many others — yet these invented books **function not as fraud,** but as **mystical frameworks,** symbolic doorways into higher realms.

In the end, whether **revealed on Sinai** or **penned in 13th-century Spain,** the **Zohar endures** because it **burns with a peculiar, undeniable light.** It is not history. It is **cosmic midrash.** It is the **language of the soul,** cloaked in symbols, **calling the reader to ascend** beyond the mundane and glimpse the hidden architecture of existence.

chapter 10

THE SEFER YETZIRAH

Sefer Yetzirah, often translated as the **Book of Formation** or **Book of Creation**, stands as one of the most enigmatic and foundational texts in the landscape of Jewish mysticism. It is considered the **oldest known Kabbalistic treatise** that has come down to us, a document veiled in mystery and speculation, both in terms of its **authorship** and its **true purpose**. While modern readers frequently associate it with **Kabbalah**, many early scholars and sages viewed it instead as a **work of sacred linguistics and cosmological mathematics**, a manual for understanding how the **divine blueprint** was encoded into the very letters of the Hebrew alphabet.

The name "**Yetzirah**" itself is deeply symbolic. Unlike "Briah," which connotes **creation ex nihilo** (creation from nothing), "Yetzirah" implies **formation** — shaping what already exists into structured order. This distinction is not trivial: it suggests that the **divine creative process**, as revealed in this book, did not begin from a void, but from an ineffable source already imbued with potential. **Forming**, rather than creating, is an act of intelligent design, of setting boundaries, applying number, weight, and measure. The Sefer Yetzirah, then, becomes a kind of **cosmic architect's manual**.

Tradition attributes this mysterious book to Abraham, the patriarch himself, who is said to have **received it by direct revelation** from the Divine. Some sources claim that **Rabbi Akiva**, one of the most revered sages of the Talmudic era, merely edited or preserved it in its current form. Other strands of Jewish lore offer an even more **mythic lineage**: that the wisdom of the Sefer Yetzirah originated with **Adam**, passed to **Noah**, and eventually entrusted to Abraham, who earned the title *"friend of God."* One medieval manuscript stored in the **British Museum** even refers to it as **Kilkot Yetzirah**, a title that suggests the text is only accessible to the truly righteous and spiritually pure — a **manual for initiates**, not the general public.

This emphasis on secrecy and initiation is not merely poetic; it is a profound aspect of the tradition. The **Sefer Yetzirah describes a process of divine construction** that is both **mathematical** and **linguistic in nature**. At the heart of this process are the **"32 mysterious paths of wisdom,"** through which God is said to have fashioned all of reality. These include the **10 Sefirot** — not in the later Kabbalistic sense, but as abstract principles or *emanations* — and the **22 letters of the Hebrew alphabet**, which are regarded not simply as letters but as **living energies, creative tools,** and **spiritual forces**.

The text draws attention to the word **Sefer**, which intriguingly shares a root with several other Hebrew terms that highlight the layered nature of divine creation:

- **Sefer** – a *book*, the written form of knowledge.

- **Sefar** – a *number* or *count*, emphasizing measure, order, and proportion.

- **Sippur** – a *story*, invoking the power of narrative to give meaning to form.

This triad — book, number, story — reveals that the universe is structured like a sacred language, simultaneously mathematical and mythological. It is as if the cosmos is God's text, inscribed with pattern, intention, and purpose.

A central element of the Sefer Yetzirah is its **division of the 22 Hebrew letters** into three categories: **three "mother letters"** (Alef, Mem, Shin), **seven "doubles"** (letters with two pronunciations), and **twelve "elementals"**, each associated with **months, zodiac signs, and human organs**. This system of classification bears remarkable parallels to **Hellenistic cosmological thought**, particularly **Greek theories of harmony, astrology, and sacred geometry** — a fact that has led some historians to hypothesize **cross-cultural influences** between Jewish mysticism and the **Greco-Egyptian mystery schools**.

There is a fascinating story found in the **Babylonian Talmud**, which illustrates the **practical magical power** the Sefer Yetzirah was believed to contain. It is said that on the day before the Sabbath, **Rav Hoshaiah and Rav Hanina** would sit together, **study the Sefer Yetzirah**, and use its knowledge to **create a calf**, which they would then cook and eat. This act is not merely allegorical. In Kabbalistic circles, it is understood as a demonstration of **theurgy** — the capacity to manipulate **divine laws through spiritual understanding**. *The implication is bold: that those who master the Sefer Yetzirah can partake in the act of creation itself.* A mystical reading of **Genesis 18:7** suggests that **Abraham** did something similar when he prepared food for the visiting angels, hinting that his hospitality was not mundane but **miraculously generated** through divine knowledge.

In the **appendix to the Sefer Yetzirah**, it is explained that **Abraham's mastery of this text** came through **divine revelation**, and that his spiritual legacy was encoded not only in his bloodline but also in mystical literacy. This is why **Rabbi Saadia Gaon**, **Judah HaLevi**, and **Shabbethai Donnolo** — leading philosophical and rabbinic authorities — were firm in their conviction that the **Sefer Yetzirah is an authentic document of sacred origin**, not merely an esoteric curiosity. For them, the book was **not a metaphor**, but a **spiritual technology**, showing how the **Divine Will** became **form**.

However, when we shift from **tradition to academic analysis**, the origin story becomes far more contested. **Modern historians** are in sharp disagreement over the **dating and authorship** of the text. Some place its origin in the **early medieval period**, pointing to linguistic and conceptual structures that seem out of place in the biblical or even Talmudic eras. Others argue that the Sefer Yetzirah contains **concepts and cosmologies that predate medieval Jewish thought**, indicating an **earlier genesis**, possibly in the **Talmudic** or **Mishnaic era**.

According to the **Jewish Encyclopedia**, the basic structure and thematic concerns of the Sefer Yetzirah **resonate with the 3rd or 4th centuries**, which would place it **before the rise of classical Kabbalah** but **after the consolidation of early rabbinic Judaism**. The book's peculiar focus on **letter mysticism, divine mathematics, and cosmic**

correspondences suggests influence from — or at least dialogue with — the broader **Gnostic tradition,** which flourished during that time. Some scholars have proposed that the Sefer Yetzirah was **constructed upon the ruins of Jewish Gnosticism,** just before it vanished or was absorbed into Christian and Islamic esoteric thought.

Not all scholars agree on this. **Richard August Reitzenstein,** a noted scholar of ancient religion, proposed a **2nd century BCE** origin, which would make the Sefer Yetzirah **contemporary with early Hellenistic philosophy,** while **Christopher P. Benton** argued that the **Hebrew grammar and syntax** of the text align more closely with writings from the **Mishnaic period,** around the **2nd century CE.**

Interestingly, the **division of the Hebrew alphabet into three symbolic classes,** a cornerstone of the Sefer Yetzirah's cosmology, also appears in **Greek esoteric texts** of the same period — another tantalizing hint of **cross-cultural fusion** in the Mediterranean world. The boundaries between mysticism, language, and cosmology were far more fluid than later dogmatists would like to believe.

Yet despite all this speculation, **the true origin and authorship of the Sefer Yetzirah remain uncertain.** Like the **mysteries it describes,** it resists definitive classification. **Is it a book of magic? A cosmological treatise? A mystical meditation? A divine code?** Perhaps it is all these things at once.

What is certain, however, is that the **Sefer Yetzirah laid the groundwork for much of what would later become the heart of Kabbalistic cosmology.** Its ideas about **language as creation, numbers as divine blueprints,** and **letters as vessels of power** have reverberated through the centuries, influencing not only Jewish mysticism but also **Christian Kabbalah, Western occultism,** and even **modern esoteric movements.**

It remains, to this day, a **book of formation** — not just of the world, but of the soul that dares to read it.

The Sefer Yetzirah Manuscripts form a labyrinth of textual variations, mystical reinterpretations, and evolving commentaries — a constellation of versions orbiting around one of the most elusive and revered books in the Jewish esoteric tradition. While **scholars and mystics alike** have long debated the exact meaning and origin of this text, the different **manuscript traditions** offer profound insight into how the **Book of Formation** has been preserved, interpreted, and reshaped over the centuries.

Among the known versions, **four principal redactions** stand out:

- The Long Version,
- The Short Version,
- The Gra Version,
- The Saadia Version.

Each of these versions shares a core foundation, yet **subtle distinctions** in structure, vocabulary, and arrangement reflect the **doctrinal or philosophical orientation** of the editors and their respective eras.

The **Short Version**, which consists of approximately **1,300 words**, is concise, cryptic, and densely packed with symbolic content. It presents the raw mystical structure of the Sefer Yetzirah — **32 paths of wisdom, 10 Sefirot**, and the **22 letters of the Hebrew alphabet** — with little commentary or elaboration. It is more of a **bare-bones code**, ideal for initiates and meditative contemplation, rather than a didactic or expository work.

In contrast, the **Long Version** roughly **doubles the length** of the Short Version. It includes **additional phrases, clarifications, and sometimes more expansive cosmological reflections**, though it remains **enigmatic** and **highly symbolic**. Its language retains a rhythm of sacred cadence, meant to be **recited or chanted**, not merely studied as one would a modern philosophical tract.

In the **10th century, Saadia Gaon**, one of the preeminent Jewish thinkers of his age, composed a **commentary** on a manuscript that appeared to him as a **more systematized version** of the longer recension. This version — now known as the **Saadia Version** — reflects a more **rationalist and philosophical approach**, consistent with Saadia's background in Jewish Kalam (Jewish-Arabic rational theology). His adaptation attempts to harmonize the **metaphysical speculation** of the Sefer Yetzirah with **logical structure**, making it more accessible to those seeking coherence over mystic abstraction.

Fast forward to the **16th century**, when the revolutionary teachings of **Isaac Luria**, the **Ari**, began to reshape the entire landscape of Kabbalah. Luria **redacted the Short Version** of the Sefer Yetzirah to **align it with the Zoharic and Lurianic cosmology**, infusing it with ideas of **divine contraction (Tzimtzum), shattering of vessels (Shevirat haKelim), and rectification (Tikkun)**. A few centuries later, **the Vilna Gaon** (known as **Gra**) — the Lithuanian genius of the 18th century — made further refinements, producing the **Gra Version**, which blends mystical interpretation with grammatical precision and a return to the **original Hebrew syntax and symbolism**.

Aside from these four major versions, **numerous other redactions** and **manuscript fragments** exist, many of them **slightly altered**, restructured, or glossed by unknown scribes. Despite their differences, the **variations are subtle**, and the essential teachings remain consistent across all versions — a testament to the **sacred integrity** with which the Sefer Yetzirah has been transmitted over millennia.

The **influence of the Sefer Yetzirah** cannot be overstated. It has served as a **touchstone for mystical speculation on creation, language, cosmic order**, and the **divine architecture of the universe**. Its association with **Abraham**, the **first patriarch**, elevates its authority to near-canonical status. To say this book has shaped Jewish mystical consciousness is an understatement — **only the Talmud rivals its long-term spiritual impact**.

Yet, reading the Sefer Yetzirah is no simple task. It is **deliberately obscure**, both in language and structure. Unlike most scriptural or rabbinic texts, it lacks narrative or legal argumentation. Instead, it offers **dense metaphysical statements**, terse as oracles and often **couched in arcane grammatical forms**. Complicating matters further, **no universally accepted critical edition** exists. Every manuscript bears signs of **interpolation, redaction, and mystical tampering**. As a result, **scholars, mystics, and theologians have interpreted the same passage**

in radically different ways, leading to **a multiplicity of meanings** rather than a singular, coherent doctrine.

Even so, the Sefer Yetzirah has become a **central pillar** in the **development of Kabbalistic thought**. Despite some notable differences from later Kabbalah — particularly in its conception of the **Sefirot**, which in Sefer Yetzirah seem to function more like **cosmic dimensions or modalities** rather than **mystical emanations** — the text nonetheless lays the **intellectual and symbolic groundwork** for what would later become **mainstream Kabbalistic metaphysics**.

For example, both the Sefer Yetzirah and later Kabbalah reject the idea of **creation ex nihilo** in favor of a system of **emanations** — gradations of being that unfold between the **Infinite (Ein Sof)** and the **finite world**. In both models, **God is not merely the efficient cause** of the universe, but the **first cause**, the origin point from which all subsequent layers of existence **flow**, **spiral**, or **resonate**.

Between the 11th and 13th centuries, among the **Ashkenazi Hasidim**, a mystical sect in medieval Europe, a derivative version of the Sefer Yetzirah began circulating. This **expanded interpretation** of the original text became one of the earliest sources for what would later be known as Practical Kabbalah—a form of spiritual practice centered on **rituals, incantations, and mystical operations**. This variant explored **the six days of Creation** in depth, mapping them to **internal psychological states, spiritual archetypes, and cosmic cycles**. Some parts of this mystical tradition correspond to **Seder Rabbah de-Bereshit**. This small midrashic text also speculates on the **pre-cosmic conditions and the divine mind before the creation of Genesis**.

Ultimately, the Sefer Yetzirah is a **threshold text** — a liminal portal between the **rational** and the **mystical**, the **linguistic** and the **theurgical**, the **concealed** and the **revealed**. It defies easy categorization because it was never meant to conform. It was meant to be **unlocked, meditated upon**, and **embodied**. It speaks in **codes**, in **numbers**, in **shifting letters** — in the **primordial alphabet of creation itself**.

Those who dare to walk its **narrow paths of wisdom** must leave behind **conventional logic** and enter a space where **language creates reality**, **numbers become prayers**, and **letters sing the structure of the world into being**.

The **Sefer Yetzirah** unfolds a vision of creation as a **symphony of language, number, and spirit**, orchestrated by the singular will of the **Ein Sof**, the Infinite. Rather than a linear narrative, it presents a **sacred structure** — a framework of divine emanation that reverberates through every layer of existence, from the highest realm of spiritual potential to the very atoms of the material world. At the heart of this cosmic architecture are the **"32 wondrous paths of wisdom"**, which comprise **10 Sephirot** and **22 Hebrew letters**, each a key to unlock dimensions of divine expression.

These 32 paths are not abstract ideas. They are **active channels**, vibrating with the force of divine intent. The **10 Sephirot** represent the **ideal, metaphysical vessels** through which sacred light flows. They are not "things" but **modalities of divine will**, stages in the descent from pure unity into multiplicity. The **Sephirot**, beginning with **Keter (Crown)** and moving through **Chokhmah (Wisdom)**, **Binah (Understanding)**, and so forth, are reflections of God's will shaping itself into form — not directly creating matter, but *making creation possible*.

Then come the **22 letters of the Hebrew alphabet**, which are the **real**, the tools through which the ideal manifests. **Aleph, Mem, and Shin** — the **three mother letters** — symbolize the **primordial elements**: *air, water, and fire*. They are the **womb of existence**, out of which everything else is born. These three are followed by **seven doubles** (Bet, Gimel, Dalet, Kaf, Pe, Resh, Tav), linked to **duality**: *life and death, peace and war, beauty and ugliness*. Finally, the **twelve simples** complete the structure, resonating with **the months, the tribes, the constellations**, and **human faculties**. *He, Vav, Zayin…* — each letter holds within it an **archetypal essence**.

This alphabetic framework is **mirrored in the human body** and **cosmic order**. The **three mother letters** correspond to the **three main sections of the body**: *head, torso, and lower limbs*. The **seven doubles** map onto the **seven orifices of the head**: two eyes, two ears, two nostrils, and the mouth — *our gates to the outer world*. These gates, just like the **seven planets**, mediate between inner and outer, above and below. The **twelve simples** align with the **twelve inner organs** and **twelve astrological signs**, forming a mystical anatomy that binds **man, time, and cosmos** into a single, breathing organism.

In this cosmology, **creation is double**: one layer **ideal**, composed of the Sephirot; one layer **real**, shaped by the letters. The real emerges when the **invisible potential** of divine intention is **etched into linguistic reality**. *Each letter is a chisel in the hands of the Creator.* The text reveals that **God did not "say" the world into existence**, but rather **engraved it**, forming reality through precise combinations of letters and numbers. In this sense, *the Torah itself becomes the blueprint of the universe*, and **speech is a sacred form of architecture**.

The **two covenants** revealed to Abraham — the **covenant of circumcision** (milah) and the **covenant of the tongue** (lashon) — symbolize this interplay between **the body and the word**, between **action and speech. Ten fingers and ten toes** correspond to the **Ten Sephirot**, while the **tongue** articulates the **22 letters**. Thus, *man himself is the altar*, and his speech *a creative fire*. The Sefer Yetzirah teaches that it was precisely by mastering this divine alphabet that **Abraham attained gnosis**, receiving the hidden knowledge not through vision, but through *sound and form*.

The **themes of contrast and balance** run deep. The Sefer Yetzirah invokes **syzygies**, pairs of opposing forces — *such as fire and water, light and dark, or good and evil*. These are not moral oppositions, but **creative tensions**. Good and evil are not seen as absolute categories, but as **results of imbalance**. *Fire can purify or destroy. Water can give life or drown.* All is relative to its **intention and effect**. And in the center stands **Aleph**, the balancing principle. It is neither fire nor water, but **spirit** — the harmonizer.

This triadic balance is embedded even in the **vocalization system**. The **five articulatory groups** — **throat, palate, tongue, teeth, and lips** — shape the **22 letters**, much like **the five levels of the soul** mold human consciousness. Each group corresponds not just to a **mode of** pronunciation, but to a **dimension of being**. The **mutes**, like **Mem**, symbolize silence, mystery, potential. The **sibilants**, like **Shin**, are *expressive*, *hissing*, sharp — the fire of speech. And then there is **Aleph**, the breath without sound, the pause between being and becoming, the **equilibrium of opposites**.

The Sefer Yetzirah also resonates with **Gnostic systems**, particularly in the **division of letters, focus on emanations**, and the **emphasis on hidden knowledge**. Like the Gnostic Marcus, the Sefer divides the alphabet into three archetypal classes, linking them to **the elemental structure of the world**. Its teaching that the **spirit becomes air, then water, fire** reflects the **Clementine doctrine**: God emanates **Spirit**, then matter, then form — always descending, never ceasing.

Even **astrology** enters the picture, with the mention of the **dragon** — the *Draco constellation*, curling around the **celestial pole**, forming the **cosmic axis mundi**. This dragon is not evil; it is **direction, structure, bound** — the spine of the heavens around which the stars revolve. *It is the serpent that guards the gate, but also the serpent that leads you home.*

Through all of this, the message is clear: the **universe is language**, and you, too, are a **letter in the mouth of God**. The more you align with the **primordial speech**, the more your being resonates with the **divine architecture**. Every breath, every word, every gesture becomes a **ritual of return**, a **step back to the Ein Sof**, the infinite.

The Sefer Yetzirah does not offer theology. It offers **blueprints**. It invites you not to believe, but to **build**. Not to submit, but to **speak**. It is a call to **align yourself with the deep grammar of creation**, to see yourself not as a passive creation, but as an **active co-creator**, engraving your existence into the Book of Life, letter by letter.

chapter 11

SEFER HA BAHIR

The **Sefer ha-Bahir**, also known as the **Book of Illumination** or **Book of Brightness**, is one of the **foundational mystical texts** of Jewish esotericism. Its origins are **obscure**, its structure **fragmented**, and its influence **profound**. Though traditionally attributed to the **first-century rabbinic sage Nehunya ben HaKanah**, the actual authorship and historical context are far more complex. The attribution stems primarily from the very first sentence of the text: *"Rabbi Nehunya ben HaKanah said..."* — a literary device that imbues the work with ancient authority but does not necessarily reflect its true origin.

Indeed, **Kabbalists of the Middle Ages** considered the Bahir to be **a vessel of secret oral tradition**, transmitted from the early centuries of the Common Era. These mystics did not view it as a singular, coherent book but rather as **a compilation of esoteric fragments**, scattered across scrolls and obscure manuscripts, **later assembled into a loosely connected body of teachings**. The abrupt shifts in theme, mid-sentence transitions, and lack of narrative continuity all suggest that it was stitched together over time from a variety of **literary strata**.

While medieval scholars such as **Moses ben Nahman** (Nachmanides, or Ramban) were among the first to cite the Bahir under the name *Midrash R. Nehunya ben HaKanah*, modern historical research has placed its **actual composition** far later than the 1st century. Some early academic theories proposed **Isaac the Blind**, the 13th-century Provençal Kabbalist, as the possible author, or at least as the leader of the school from which the text emerged. This theory partly arose from a symbolic reading of the phrase *"And now men see not the light which is* *bright in the skies"* (Job 27:21), interpreted as a cryptic reference to **Isaac's blindness**. But this remains speculative.

Scholars such as **Ronit Meroz** have since advanced a more nuanced view. According to Meroz and others, elements of the Bahir go back to **Babylon in the 10th century**, where they were **composed or transmitted** using the **Babylonian system of vocalization**. This now-defunct Hebrew phonetic notation placed diacritical marks *above* the letters. This system was eventually replaced by the **Tiberian vocalization**, which put the vowel signs below the letters and became the standard. The **presence of Babylonian linguistic features** in the Bahir gives us a valuable clue to its dating: it likely originated in an environment still actively using these features, sometime **before the Tiberian system became dominant**.

This linguistic detail is more than technical. It serves as a **key to understanding the spiritual symbology** within the text. For example, in a passage describing **divine vocalization**, the idea that God places a *patah* above a letter and a *segol* below it becomes more **potent and symbolically charged** when read through the lens of the Babylonian vocalization, where such an arrangement would have had **phonetic significance**. In the Tiberian system, that symbolism becomes less coherent. Therefore, the **use of Babylonian phonetics** is not a random artifact but a signpost of the text's **origin in a now-lost Eastern Jewish mystical tradition**.

By the 12th century, the **Provençal school of Kabbalists** — particularly active in the region of southern France — began to circulate the Sefer ha-Bahir among a tiny circle of initiates. The manuscript **first emerged publicly in 1174**, and by **1298**, we have surviving textual evidence from the end of the thirteenth century. As the text spread, **commentaries followed**. The earliest known commentary was written in **1331** by **Rabbi Meir ben Shalom Abi-Sahula**, a student of the renowned **Rashba** (Shlomo ben Aderet). Abi-Sahula's commentary not only attempted to **decode the metaphysical riddles** of the Bahir but also elevated its prestige as a sacred and *inspired revelation*.

In the following centuries, the Bahir would be published repeatedly under various titles. One edition, *Or HaGanuz* ("The Hidden Light"), veiled its identity while continuing to circulate among mystical circles. By the end of the **15th century**, the Bahir had even crossed into the Latin world. Flavius Mithridates translated it, though this version was deemed **overly verbose and nearly unusable,** lacking the clarity and precision necessary for scholarly or mystical practice.

The **first printed edition** of the Bahir appeared in **Amsterdam in 1611,** alongside *Mayan ha-Chokhmah*—subsequent publications followed in **Berlin (1706), Koretz, Lvov, Vilna,** and **Jerusalem**. In modern times, the most influential academic edition was the **German translation by Gershom Scholem,** released in **1923**. This was followed in **1979** by **Rabbi Aryeh Kaplan's English translation,** a milestone in Kabbalistic studies that made the text accessible to a new generation of seekers. A year later, François Secret published a **Latin edition,** and in 2005, **Saverio Campanini** produced a new, improved edition based on Flavius Mithridates' translation.

Despite all these efforts, **the Bahir remains a mysterious book**. It lacks a consistent narrative, with no clear beginning or end. Instead, it is a series of **esoteric sayings, parables, and metaphysical speculations,** all aiming to **illuminate the hidden structure of reality**. Its teachings are cryptic, filled with symbols — numbers, letters, divine names, mystical trees, angelic hierarchies, and cosmic geometries. In many places, it reads more like **a collection of riddles** than a systematic theology. And yet, it is precisely this fragmented, **almost oracular style** that gives the Bahir its power. It speaks not to the rational mind, but to the **intuition,** to the **subconscious longing for light**.

Some modern scholars argue that the Bahir contains **Gnostic elements,** inherited either through direct transmission or indirect cultural overlap with early Christian and dualistic sects. The focus on **light versus darkness, hidden knowledge, emanations,** and the **mystical ladder of divine worlds** closely parallels **Gnostic cosmology**. The influence of **Raza Rabba,** a lost mystical work quoted in several medieval sources, is also suspected. While we lack a full version of Raza Rabba, **quotations found in older mystical texts** suggest strong thematic resonance with the Bahir.

The text's **legacy**, however, cannot be overstated. It **laid the foundation** for later Kabbalistic works, including the **Zohar**, and influenced generations of mystics across **Provence, Spain, Ashkenaz, and beyond**. Rabbi **Isaac HaKohen**, writing in the 13th century, described the Bahir as a **sacred flame**, passed from the sages of **the Land of Israel**, through the **Hasidim of Ashkenaz**, to the **wise men of Provence** — who, unfortunately, only saw part of it. *They glimpsed the light but not the full blaze.*

In its **fractured brilliance**, the Sefer ha-Bahir teaches that **true wisdom is not linear**. It is not always written in the form of treatises or systems. Sometimes, it hides in **shadows**, in **interrupted thoughts**, in **questions that seem to answer nothing but burn inside the soul**. It asks you not just to read it, but to be **changed by it**, to allow its **light to penetrate the dark recesses of your understanding**.

In this way, the Bahir remains what its name implies: not a light for the eyes, but **a brightness for the inner vision** — a glow that cannot be grasped with the intellect alone, but must be **felt**, like a secret whispered by God in the silence between words.

The *Sefer ha-Bahir,* unfolds as a **mystical midrashic tapestry** woven upon the early chapters of Genesis. Structured as a series of short, enigmatic passages—sometimes 60 in form, sometimes 140 depending on the edition—it adopts the form of a **dialogue**, a sacred conversation between master and disciples, echoing the transmission of hidden truths from teacher to seeker across the generations. Among the principal voices are **Rabbi Rahamai** (also spelled Rehumai) and **Rabbi Amora** (or Amorai), whose dialogues serve as the central axis of this esoteric teaching. Interspersed within are insights attributed to **Rabbi Johanan, Rabbi Berechiah, and Rabbi Bun**, names that reappear throughout Midrashic literature, lending a continuity between this mystical text and rabbinic tradition.

The teachings of the *Bahir* are dense, elusive, and pregnant with layered meaning. They mirror the **kabbalistic tradition's love for ambiguity, symbol, and metaphor**, never speaking plainly, constantly invoking mystery. These passages often resemble aphorisms, concise and sharp like blades that cut open the surface of reality to reveal the divine structures underneath. Each utterance echoes the Torah itself, not merely quoting but **penetrating its inner core**, suggesting that Scripture holds within it multiple veils of interpretation—*pshat* (simple), *remez* (hint), *drash* (homiletic), and *sod* (secret). The *Bahir* moves swiftly and unrelentingly toward the *sod*.

A central and recurring metaphor throughout the *Bahir* is that of **a king, his daughter, his gardens, and his servants**. The king, symbolizing the **Divine Source**, interacts with the world through these intermediaries. The daughter, often identified with the Shekhinah or lower aspect of divinity, is exiled, concealed, or sought after. The gardens are the realms of creation, the servants are the celestial forces and human souls who serve as channels of divine light. *Imagine a king hiding a pearl deep within a garden, and sending his loyal ones to search for it without telling them its shape or color — only those who know the fragrance of divine light will find it.*

Though Aryeh Kaplan famously delineated five thematic sections in his translation, the *Bahir* resists being neatly compartmentalized. It defies linear logic in favor of a **spiralic structure**, where ideas are repeated, inverted, expanded, and contradicted—just like the **sefirotic tree** it describes. The early verses explore the mysteries of *Creation*, but not in a literal sense. Instead, they seek to answer what existed *before* existence, what stirred in the mind of God before the world was born.

According to the *Bahir*, **Creation is not a beginning but an unveiling**. The cosmos is not manufactured but disclosed—what we call existence is the appearance of what was eternally latent within **HaGanuz**, the Hidden Light, the first Sephirah, **Keter Elyon**. From this primordial point—**not a point in space, but a point in consciousness**—emerges *Hokhmah* (Wisdom), and from Hokhmah comes *Binah* (Understanding). These are the **three highest Sefirot**, often called the "supernal triad," and from them emanate the **seven lower Sefirot**, which correspond to the qualities that shape our world: Chesed (Lovingkindness), Gevurah (Judgment), Tiferet (Beauty), Netzach (Endurance), Hod (Glory), Yesod (Foundation), and Malkhut (Kingdom).

Each Sefirah is both a **vessel and a channel**, a **receptacle and a transmitter**. The *Bahir* illustrates this beautifully with the Hebrew letter

Gimel, described as a pipe open at both ends—receiving force from one side, giving on the other. This notion transforms the Hebrew alphabet into a **living architecture of divine energy**, with each letter serving as a blueprint for spiritual structure. The Aleph-Bet is not a tool for language but a **cosmic technology**.

Among the most haunting themes explored by the *Sefer ha-Bahir* is **gilgul**, the doctrine of reincarnation. In this vision, the soul is not a static essence but a **migrating flame**, moving through bodies, times, and lifetimes to fulfill its purpose and reach rectification. The text dares to propose that what we call injustice—*the suffering of the righteous, the triumph of the wicked*—might be the unfolding of consequences from **former incarnations**. *A kind and generous man today may be paying the price for cruelty in another life; a tyrant may be reaping the rewards of previous virtue.*

While **mainstream Jewish philosophy** rejected reincarnation, dismissing it as incompatible with rational theology, **Kabbalah embraced it**. For the mystic, the soul is not confined to a single span of years. It is woven into a greater story, a cycle, a wheel—**gilgul** in Hebrew means "cycle" or "roll." The *Bahir* does not present gilgul as a hypothesis, nor does it defend it. It speaks of it **as a given**, as if this teaching belonged to the primordial tradition passed in whispers.

The Talmud's parables and aggadot are reinterpreted through the lens of transmigration. Ecclesiastes 1:4—"One generation passes, and another comes"—is read not as a mere observation but a revelation: the generation that comes *is* the one that passed, *only wearing different garments*. Some Kabbalists believed that the souls of those who perished in the Flood, or even the murdered Abel, began the cycle of gilgul, and that this cycle will end only at **the resurrection of the dead**, when all bodies that ever held a soul will rise again. The **sparks of identity** hidden in them will be made whole.

The *Bahir* also lays the foundation for the deeply controversial idea that even the **death of infants** may be part of this spiritual economy, *not as cruelty, but as a path to purification*. According to Spanish Kabbalists, a soul must incarnate **three times** to atone for its sins, based on the verse in Job 33:29, "God does all these things, twice, three times, with a man." But for the **righteous**, the soul may return again and again—not for its benefit, but for the **rectification of others**.

This spiritual recycling is not without suffering. **Gilgul is both judgment and mercy**. It is punishment, for the soul cannot rest until it repairs what was broken. But it is also mercy, for no soul is discarded; none are eternally lost. *Even those whose crimes deserve annihilation – keritut, the cutting off of the soul – are given one more chance, and another, and another.* Various Kabbalists began mapping commandments to reincarnation, also known as gilgul. Ritual slaughter (*shechita*) was once seen by certain sects as a proof of soul-transference into animals, though the *Bahir* does not support that view. Instead, **levirate marriage** was cited as a mystical mechanism for the soul of the deceased to continue its mission. *Imagine a man who dies childless – his brother marries the widow, and the child born is the vessel for the departed brother's soul. Life recycles life.*

The literature becomes even more nuanced when it discusses **ibbūr**, the impregnation of a living person's soul with an additional one, which is not the same as reincarnation but exists beside it. From the time of the **Zohar**, the term *gilgul* became widely used, while *ibbūr* was reserved for specific moments of possession, guidance, or mission.

Some Kabbalists embraced the idea of **transmigration into gentile bodies, or even into women**, considering them temporary vessels for Jewish souls who had strayed. Others, like those from the **Safed school**, rejected this as dangerously close to heresy. The *Sefer Peli'ah*, on the other hand, considered every convert to Judaism as a **Jewish soul trapped in a foreign body**, finally returning home.

The debate deepened with the relationship between **hell and gilgul**. Some, like **Bahya ben Asher**, argued that the soul only transmigrates after enduring punishment in Gehinnom. Others, including the **Ra'aya Mehemna** in the *Zohar*, saw gilgul and hell as mutually exclusive. For **Joseph of Hamadan**, hell *was* reincarnation—specifically into the bodies of beasts. Eventually, the doctrine evolved further. It began to include transmigration not only into animals but also into **plants and inanimate objects**. This extension met fierce resistance from many Kabbalists, yet it found its way into texts like the *Sefer ha-Temunah*, where every stone and tree was potentially a **soul in exile**. The *Tikkunei Zohar* hints at this, though it stops short of full endorsement.

One anonymous text from 1290, *Ta'amei ha-Mitzvot*, elaborates extensively on human souls entering animals, often as punishment for **sexual transgressions**. This teaching became foundational to later mystical ethics — **every sin creates a karmic echo**, a movement of the soul not toward oblivion but toward rectification through descent.

A more metaphysical take was proposed by Joseph bar Shalom Ashkenazi and his circle. For them, **everything in creation undergoes transformation**, which they called *din benei halof*, the law of exchange. The soul is not merely a human essence but a **divine particle caught in a spiral of matter**, always seeking to return to its origin.

In this view, even the **Sephirot**, the **angels**, and **stones** participate in this metamorphosis. The idea of gilgul thus evolves into a **universal law of metamorphosis**, blurring the boundary between soul and substance, between creation and Creator. It is less a linear chain of reincarnations and more a **cosmic rhythm** — a breathing, a pulsing, a circling.

The most refined manuscript of the *Sefer ha-Bahir* is attributed to **Meir ben Solomon Abi-Sahula**, written in 1331. His anonymous commentary, *Or HaGanuz* — "The Hidden Light" — offered a profound exegesis that would ripple through centuries. The text was later made accessible through **Gershom Scholem's** German translation and **Aryeh Kaplan's** English version, both milestones in the modern study of Kabbalah. In more recent years, **Saverio Campanini** has undertaken a critical edition that restores much of the original intent, language, and mystical nuance. What began as whispers between sages in candlelit rooms now stretches across centuries, cultures, and continents. The *Sefer ha-Bahir* is not merely a book. It is **a key to the invisible**, a doorway to the world behind the world — a world in which letters burn with light, and souls never die, only turn.

chapter 12

KABBALAH IN PRACTICE

Many who approach **Kabbalah** or **Hermeticism** for the first time come with a certain arrogance—an unconscious presumption that they can, without preparation, begin crafting **magical sigils**, engaging in **advanced pathworking**, or producing **Qabalistic interpretations** of sacred texts. This mindset is not just naïve. It is **deeply foolish**—and worse, it is **profoundly dangerous**.

To believe one can create sacred configurations of energy—because that is what a sigil truly is—without first purifying the vessel that will contain and direct that energy, is like handing explosives to a child and expecting fireworks instead of fire. These forces do not care about your enthusiasm or curiosity. **They respond to structure, to purity, and the depth of your inner alignment.**

Imagine an untrained man deciding one morning to run a marathon simply because he feels inspired. He straps on his shoes, breathes in the morning air, and sets off with joy. **He dies before reaching the finish line**, just like the soldier at the Battle of Marathon, who collapsed after delivering the message of victory. Not out of weakness, but because **his body had not been prepared for the task**. No matter how noble the intention, the outcome was fatal.

The same principle holds in Kabbalah, Hermeticism, and esotericism in general. These are not hobbies or spiritual entertainment. They are disciplines of transformation that work directly on your **psyche**, your **nervous system**, and your **soul**. Mishandled, they don't just fail. They corrupt. They unbalance. They shatter what you are not ready to see within yourself. They can drive a person into **madness**, into **spiritual delusion**, or **self-annihilation** cloaked as divine insight.

The Tree of Life is not a ladder of ascent to be climbed on a whim. It is a mirror that reflects what you are and what you are not. Every Sephirah must be earned—not by desire, but by transformation. You don't interpret Qabalistic numerology because you find it fascinating. You interpret it because it burns within you like a second language, learned through **practice, humility, and discipline.**

You wouldn't try to summon fire without knowing how to contain it. Why would you dare touch the language of the Divine without first sanctifying your tongue?

Being a Kabbalist is not something you do in your free time. It is a way of existence that permeates **every word you speak, every intention you carry, every act of will you express**, and even **the thoughts that rise unspoken in your mind**. There is no on and off switch. If you are in, you are *in*. If you are not, then stop pretending.

Three things must shape your life every day—**without exception, without excuse, without delay**:

Study. Not passive reading. Not the consumption of information. Study as a sacrament. You must learn the letters, the correspondences, the cosmology, the metaphors, the paradoxes, and the hidden bones of the Torah and sacred texts. *The alphabet is not a list of sounds – it is a map of the universe.* You must return to it daily, with reverence, hunger, and awe.

Prayer. Not recited from obligation, but breathed like oxygen. Prayer that is more than words. Prayer that reorganizes your body and soul. Prayer that aligns you with the Sefirot—not as concepts, but as realities within you. *Every word must be a chisel reshaping your inner temple.*

Kindness. Not as a performance. Not as virtue signaling. But as the natural overflow of a heart in alignment. Genuine kindness in Kabbalah is not about being nice. It is about becoming a channel through which **Chesed**, the lovingkindness of God, flows into the world. *Not to be kind is to close the vessel. And when the ship closes, the light burns instead of illuminating.*

You may think these three practices are simple. That's because you don't yet understand what they are. They are not steps to get somewhere. **They are the path itself.** Without them, you are not climbing the Tree—you are digging your own spiritual grave, one shallow practice at a time.

Every serious Kabbalist knows that before you can command a name, **you must become worthy of uttering it**. Before you trace a sigil, **you must purify the hand that holds the pen**. Before you interpret the cosmos, **you must interpret your own shadow**.

This path is not for the impatient. It is not for the curious. It is not for the dabbler. It is for those who are willing to burn for the truth—**to be dissolved and reassembled by divine fire**, day after day, year after year.

If you came to Kabbalah looking for shortcuts, leave now. If you came looking for power, ask yourself: *Can you even control your desires, your ego, your breath?* Because if you cannot, what makes you think you are ready to shape divine light?

This is the beginning of the Work. You will not advance unless you live it. And if you try, the damage will not be physical. **It will be spiritual—and permanent.**

The Daily Rite

You do not need to disappear into a cave for thirteen years, nor must you wander alone into an orchard of visions and divine fire. Kabbalistic study doesn't demand exile from the world, but it does require **discipline, humility, and constancy.** The spiritual path is not a weekend retreat. It is a relentless daily work of the soul, and even if your beginning is modest, it is your consistency that will crown you.

You can begin with **just five minutes a day**. That's all. *If you have time to watch a Netflix series, you have time for the Divine.* It is better to return **daily** for five minutes than to immerse yourself in fifty hours of mystical ecstasy and then never open the book again. The soul doesn't need grand gestures. It needs presence.

Study what calls you. The **Pirkei Avot**, the **Bible**, the **Torah**, the **Zohar** — even a single line from these is enough to shake the foundations of your ego. *Don't obsess over chronology or order.* In Kabbalistic thought, **"Ein mukdam u'meuchar baTorah"** — there is no "before" and "after" in Torah. Sacred time is circular. Every page you turn is the first page. Every word is a gateway.

If it helps, study with a **partner**, as the sages did. Sparks fly where two souls collide in search of the Infinite. Use modern commentaries if necessary. Use translations. Don't be ashamed of being a beginner. **The most dangerous thing in Kabbalah is the arrogance of someone who thinks they are not.**

And yes, you must **pray**, not like a robot, not like a priest for show. Pray like a starving man drinks water. **Pray with your voice, your hands, your breath, your pain, your gratitude, your silence.** There is no need to wait for a holiday, nor is there a need for a synagogue. **God does not live in buildings.** The Divine is in your heartbeat, in your kitchen, in your exhaustion, in the moment your pride breaks open.

You can whisper a blessing before sleep, after a meal, while walking, before making love, after breaking down in tears. There are prayers for every moment in Kabbalah, because **every moment is holy.** Even entering and exiting the bathroom can become sacred, not because God cares about plumbing, but because **you are never outside the Divine presence.**

You don't need Hebrew. You don't need Latin. You need **sincerity**. You don't need to know what to say. Just begin with, *"Thank you."* Or with *"I'm lost."* Or with *"Are you there?"* You will be heard. Not always in the way you expect, but always **exactly as your soul needs.**

But study and prayer mean nothing without **kindness**. This is not theoretical. It's not about smiling at strangers or posting quotes online. **Real kindness costs.** In Kabbalah, it is called **Gemilut Chasadim**, the acts of *genuine loving-kindness*. These are not suggestions — they are the proof that your learning has touched your heart.

Visit the sick. Bury the dead. Feed the hungry. **Honor your parents.** Welcome strangers into your home. Even if the world is cold and everyone around you is selfish, **you do not get to become like them.** You are commanded to rise.

Give charity every day, even if it's a coin, even if the beggar looks like a liar, even if you doubt their intentions. In Kabbalah, **you are not judged by the worthiness of the one asking — the generosity of your soul judges you.** You are the one being tested, not them.

And then there is **meditation**, the path inward, the descent into yourself. You don't need a mountain. You need only the will to sit, breathe, and pierce the veil of your chaos. Every day, if possible. But especially in the forty-nine days between **Passover** and **Shavuot**, the counting of the **Omer**.

These are the **days of refinement**, the days to purify the soul through the contemplation of the **Sephirot**, the ten emanations of the Divine. Each of the seven weeks corresponds to one of the lower Sephirot: **Chesed, Gevurah, Tiferet, Netzach, Hod, Yesod, Malchut**. And within each week, every day is a fusion — the attribute of the day, within the attribute of the week.

So on the first day of the first week, contemplate **Chesed within Chesed** — loving-kindness expressed through more loving-kindness. *What does it mean to love gently, without pride or demand?* On the second day, **Gevurah within Chesed** — discipline within love. *How do you set boundaries that protect love instead of destroying it?* On the third day, **Tiferet within Chesed** — harmony in love. *How can your love be not just sincere, but beautiful?*

And so on, day by day. These meditations are not abstract. They are **a mirror for your life.** They will hurt. They will expose your selfishness, your need for control, and your false kindness. And if they don't, then you're doing it wrong.

By the end of forty-nine days, you will not be perfect. But you will no longer be a stranger to your soul.

This is the work. Not symbols. Not mystical diagrams. Not magical names scribbled without understanding. *But daily fire, daily ash, daily surrender.*

You do not get to **create sigils** or **name angels** or **invoke forces** until your ego is crushed and kneaded like dough. **Power without purity is poison.**

So, begin with five minutes. Begin with one act of charity. One true prayer. One honest meditation. And then another. And another. Not because you are holy. But because you are willing.

The spiritual path is not a show. It is a slow death of all that is false. And that death, if embraced, is the beginning of eternal light.

Kabbalah and numerology

Kabbalah is not merely the study of light — it is the discipline of decoding the divine structure behind reality. Among its most ancient and powerful tools is the **numerical interpretation of names**, known as **gematria**. Every Hebrew letter holds a numerical value. Every name, every word, every verse in sacred text, becomes more than language — it becomes a number. And in number, **the hidden architecture of the soul is revealed**.

You begin by taking a name — yours, someone else's, a place, an angel, a phrase from the Torah — and **converting each letter to its numerical value** using the **traditional Kabbalistic letter-number correspondence**, as laid out in previous chapters.

You write out the name in Hebrew letters, then you assign each its numerical value. Once you have all the numbers, you **add them together**. This sum is referred to as the **gematria** of the name.

Take, for instance, the name *Michael* (מיכאל):

- Mem (מ) = 40
- Yod (י) = 10
- Kaf (כ) = 20
- Aleph (א) = 1
- Lamed (ל) = 30

Total: 40 + 10 + 20 + 1 + 30 = **101**

This number — **101** — is not just a total. It's a **key**. It connects this name to **other words and names** in the sacred texts that share the same numerical value. This is where the **magic** begins: *what else in the Torah has the value 101?* What do those words have in common with the person or idea being examined? These parallels are not a coincidence. They are **doorways** into the soul.

But numbers can also be **reduced**. In Kabbalah, many practitioners take the total and continue **reducing it** to its **single-digit essence**, unless the number is one of the **Master Numbers** or **sacred numbers**, such as 10, 22, or 72. Reducing means adding the digits together:

Michael = 101 → 1 + 0 + 1 = **2**

This second number, **2**, points to **duality, balance, receptivity,** and the **Sephirah of Binah**, *Understanding. So, the name Michael not only resonates with the Archangel of protection, but also whispers of wisdom, judgment, and profound feminine insight.*

Names can be interpreted through:

- **Direct number associations** with other words
- **Reduced numbers** and their symbolic meaning
- **Sephirotic correspondences**, linking the numbers to Divine attributes
- **Planetary and angelic associations** in the mystical systems

Interpretation, however, is not about creating meaning — it's about **perceiving** it. You must enter the number with **silence, discipline, and respect**. *Do not bend the number to your desires. Let the number reshape your perception.*

A name that reduces to **1** connects to **Keter**, the Crown, the primal spark, the origin before origin.
A name that reduces to **6** vibrates with **Tiferet**, beauty and harmony, the heart of the Tree of Life.
A name that reduces to **9** may link with **Yesod**, the foundation, the engine of manifestation, and sexual power.

This practice is not a game of cleverness or a tool for ego. **It is a daily fire**, a method to **train your mind to see numbers in words, and words in numbers**.

Each morning, before you open your phone or speak to anyone, sit with one name. Convert it. Interpret it. Compare it to others. Search for it in the **Torah, the Psalms, the Zohar**. What does it teach you today?

What hidden symmetry does it unlock? What unseen connection does it reveal?

Do this **daily**. Build the muscle. Train your perception. Over time, you'll begin to see sacred texts not as stories, but as **maps made of numbers**, designed to awaken your memory of the Divine Code.

You will look at the word "*Bereshit*" — the first word of Genesis — and you will not just see "In the beginning". You will see **913**, and you will also know what else carries that frequency. You will feel it vibrate in your spine.

You will hear a name and feel the corresponding number. You will speak and calculate in the same breath. You will walk through the world as a seer, because **numerical interpretation is not math. It is the language of prophecy.**

But do not run before you can walk. You cannot build a tower of sigils on the foundations of laziness and impulse. **Daily practice** is your discipline. It is your sword and shield. Without it, you will mistake delusion for revelation.

Let every name become a question. Let every number become a gate. And step through — slowly, humbly, with your eyes wide open.

Kabbalah, Chaldean Numerology, and Chaos Magick

Unlike traditional systems like Pythagorean or Chaldean numerology, which follow fixed correspondences and often appeal to symbolic harmony or fate-based mathematics, Kabbalistic numerology — rooted in the esoteric currents of Judaism — does not initially include categories like "Life Path Number," "Karmic Debt," or "Soul Urge." These concepts are **foreign** to classical Jewish mysticism. They emerged much later, shaped by modern occultism and, in particular, by **New Age spirituality**. While parallels *can* be drawn, and while **numbers do carry archetypal significance across traditions, mixing these systems without discipline leads to confusion rather than revelation.**

That said, **chaotes — practitioners of Chaos Magick — have long flirted with heresy for the sake of power**. Rather than adhering to one closed tradition, **they construct hybrid systems** from fragments of Kabbalah, Thelema, Enochian, planetary magic, and even pop culture. *Some of these attempts are absurd or diluted, others have proven strangely effective.* The reason? Because **Kabbalah is not a dead dogma. It is a living current**, and when engaged with respect, even when pulled into new forms, **it responds**.

So, how can Kabbalistic numerology be meaningfully applied to structures like **the Destiny Number, the Karmic Number, or the Birth Path**?

The **first rule** is this: **do not interpret the numbers arbitrarily**. Kabbalah does not grant meaning from aesthetic impressions or "vibes." It requires **sourcing your interpretation from sacred text**. The *Torah*, the *Tanakh*, the *Zohar*, and even apocryphal Jewish mystical texts, such as Sefer Yetzirah and Bahir, become your reference dictionaries. **Every number must be traced back to its sacred echo.**

Let's take an example. Suppose someone's **date of birth** reduces (in the classical way) to **36**, then 3 + 6 = **9**.

In New Age numerology, nine is associated with completion, humanitarianism, and endings. But a **Kabbalist would immediately think of**:

- **Yesod**, the ninth Sephirah, *the Foundation*
- **Tikkunei Zohar, section 9**, to see what mystery is unlocked there
- **Psalm 9**, to study the hidden resonance of that vibration
- **Words in the Torah whose gematria equals 9** (like the Hebrew word טוב / *tov* = "good")

By **weaving these layers**, you don't just describe what the number means. You **experience it** through sacred language, and that is what makes it potent.

Now, imagine taking a name and calculating its **Kabbalistic gematria**. You find that it equals **148**. Instead of reducing it unthinkingly, you look up other Hebrew words that sum to 148. You search the Torah. You look into **Midrash**, and ask: *where does this vibration appear in the Divine narrative?* Only **then** do you reduce it, if appropriate, and relate it to a Sephirah.

If you're working with the **Destiny Number**, as often done in Chaos Magick systems—calculated from the full birth name—you still begin with **the Hebrew transliteration** of that name. You do **not** use the Latin letter values of modern numerology. You **translate the name into Hebrew**, letter by letter, and then assign it its numerical value, or gematria. Once you have the numerical essence, you dive into Torah references, Zoharic visions, or Kabbalistic symbolism **connected to that number**.

Karmic Numbers, too, should be interpreted not as abstract "debts" but as **echoes of prior misalignments with cosmic structure**, which, in Kabbalistic thought, are better understood through **gilgul** (reincarnation) and **tikun** (correction). If your name or birthdate links you to a number historically tied to *judgment, harshness, severance*—like **216**, often associated with **Gevurah**—you must explore what the Torah says about **Din** (judgment), about the **left-hand pillar**, about the *angelic hosts that operate in that vibration*, like **Samael**.

This is not entertainment. This is a **soul diagnosis**.

Chaos magicians have taken this seriously, developing personal grimoires where they **track their gematria-based correspondences** alongside **sigil work**, planetary rituals, and dream journaling. But the **Kabbalistic layer is always the anchor**. Without it, the numbers become noise.

In this way, even hybrid systems gain legitimacy. The problem is not syncretism—it's **ignorance**. You must **train yourself to think kabbalistically**, even when adapting to new situations. That means **daily engagement with scripture, sacred language, angelic hierarchies, and the metaphysics of the Tree of Life**. Only then will your numerology cease to be decoration and become **a map of the Divine blueprint etched in your flesh**.

art of Kabbalistic sigilization

The art of Kabbalistic sigilization is not child's play. It is not a Pinterest symbol-making ritual, nor a game of blending random letters into a pretty logo. It is a **sacred operation**, one that combines **divine language, numerical precision**, and **cosmic intent**. To create a sigil using Kabbalah is to **invoke**, to **bind**, to **open a gateway** between the metaphysical and the physical. A sigil, in its true essence, is not a desire made graphic—it is a **contract written in flame**, etched into the fabric of spiritual law.

Kabbalistic sigils are called **tzurot** or **charutim**, and they are born from the **interplay of letters and numbers**, woven together with intentionality, breath, and sacred discipline. The **Hebrew alphabet is not merely symbolic—it is vibrational**. Each letter is a vessel of divine energy. Each combination of letters forms a structure of reality. When these letters are arranged into a sigil, you are not simply writing: **you are architecting power.**

The process begins with **clarity of purpose**, but unlike modern chaos magick, where the statement of intent is often reduced to a vague desire ("*I want to be rich*"), Kabbalistic intent must be purified through **spiritual alignment**. You must first ask: *Does my will align with the Will of the Divine?* Because if it does not, **your sigil will not bear light—it will rot with darkness**, and bring upon you dissonance, confusion, and sometimes, spiritual consequences far more dangerous than you imagined.

Once your intention is *clear, refined, and purified*, you begin by **translating it into Hebrew**, the holy language. This is not optional. The power of the sigil **resides in the letters** of the sacred tongue. Hebrew is not ornamental—it is the **blueprint of Creation**. When you turn your intention into Hebrew, you begin to **enter the current of Divine Speech**.

From there, each letter is translated into its **gematria**, its numerical value. The numbers are then **added together**, but not to be reduced in the simplistic way of modern numerology. Instead, **you seek** corresponding words, names of angels, divine names, psalms, or verses in Torah that share the same numerical structure. These are your **anchors**. Without them, your sigil floats in nothingness. But when it is grounded in scripture, it becomes a **bridge between worlds**.

Now comes the visual construction. You may choose to **trace the letters on sacred geometric forms**: the **Tree of Life**, the **Star of David**, or a **magic square** formed by numerological resonance. Some Kabbalists use the **Kameas**, ancient number grids that align with specific planets and angelic hierarchies. For instance, if your intention relates to **healing**, you might work with the **Kamea of the Sun**, connecting your Hebrew letters to their numerical points, then drawing the sigil by linking those points across the grid.

But beware: **misplacing even one number, inverting one letter, or misinterpreting the root meaning of a Divine Name can create imbalance**. You may think you're invoking Raphael, the healing force of Hod, and instead awaken **a fragment of severity from the left-hand path**, drawing energy from a shadow current that does not forgive sloppiness. *And if you don't recognize the error – if you don't even know what current you've called – you won't see the curse until it has eaten your confidence, your health, or your clarity.*

This is not fear-mongering. This is spiritual mechanics. You would not wire your home's electricity without knowing amperage and polarity. So why would you wire your soul without understanding which letters conduct divine power, and which ones burn it?

Every authentic Kabbalist knows that before even daring to draw a sigil, one must be **initiated into the mysteries of the Sefirot**, understand **angelic orders, the 231 gates of letter combinations**, and the **paths of the Alef-Bet through the Tree of Life**. The sigil is never just a symbol. It is a **compression of divine architecture** into a single, visual vessel – the more precise your calculation, the more powerful the transmission.

And once the sigil is complete, it must be **activated**, not by mindless chanting or theatrical ritual, but by **meditation, devotion**, and **intense inner stillness**. You must meditate on the name, speak it in purity, perhaps vibrate it with breath, and focus your heart into its core. A Kabbalistic sigil does not "work" in the way of superstition—it *unfolds, unveils,* and *aligns your inner pattern to divine order.*

This practice is advanced, and rightly so. To engage with it casually is like **building a nuclear device when you haven't mastered a candle.** Respect is not enough. **Preparation, humility, and rigorous study are required.** Without them, the letters become poison. But with them— *with reverence, clarity, and sacred alignment-a* Kabbalistic sigil becomes **a ladder of light, reaching from your soul to the Infinite.**

The golem sigil

The tale of the **Golem of Prague** is not merely a myth of clay and miracle—it is a warning disguised as a legend, a Kabbalistic cipher encoded in narrative. It teaches what happens when **words are carved without wisdom,** when **divine letters are placed on flesh not ready to hold them,** and when the **power of sigils escapes the bounds of holy intent.**

According to tradition, the great **Rabbi Judah Loew ben Bezalel**, the Maharal of Prague, fashioned a golem from the clay of the **Moldau River**. This golem was not alive in the way humans are, but was animated through **sacred letters**—through **Kabbalistic invocations** and the secret knowledge of **Sefer Yetzirah**, the Book of Formation.

To awaken the golem, the Rabbi **etched upon its forehead the Hebrew word** אֱמֶת (*Emet*), which means **"Truth."** This word is composed of three letters:
Aleph (א) – the first letter of the Hebrew alphabet, symbol of the Divine, of oneness, the breath of the ineffable.
Mem (מ) – the middle letter, symbol of water, womb, and the hidden mysteries of the Torah.
Tav (ת) – the final letter of the alphabet, symbolizing completion, the material world, and the mark of life or death.

Together, **Aleph-Mem-Tav** form **Emet**, the whole cycle of life, the beginning, middle, and end—**the divine spark within creation.**

But the same word that gives life also holds its undoing.

When the golem grew too violent or too powerful—when its service threatened to become destruction—the Rabbi erased a single letter. He **removed the Aleph (א)** from **Emet**, leaving behind only **Mem-Tav (מת)**, which spells **"Met"**, the Hebrew word for **"Death."**

With the breath of God—the Aleph—removed, **the clay returned to clay**. The form fell lifeless. The spark was gone.

This is the true heart of the story.

A single letter, when aligned with the will of the Creator, **breathes life into matter**. That same letter, when removed or misused, **returns the form to dust. This is Kabbalah.** This is **the danger of working with sigils without mastery**. You do not need to shatter an entire formula to destroy it—**one glyph misplaced, one intention unclean, one sacred name misused**, and **the golem within you turns monstrous**, or collapses altogether.

So remember: the golem is not just a figure of clay—it is **a mirror of the practitioner**. You are the vessel. The letters you place on your mind, your heart, your soul—**they shape what lives inside you**. But if your Aleph is not grounded in divine truth, you will end up with a shell that breathes chaos.

The Maharal's story is not just folklore. It is a Kabbalistic parable. It whispers, in the silence between letters:
"He who inscribes without wisdom shall awaken what he cannot command."

Forging kabbalistic amulets

Suppose the creation of sigils is already a delicate and perilous craft. In that case, the art of forging **amulets in the Kabbalistic tradition** rises to an entirely different level—**a sacred science requiring not only precision but deep alignment with cosmic and spiritual forces**. It is not something that can be improvised. It is not a drawing on parchment or the whimsical inscription of symbols. It is a **ritual act**, a moment in which **Heaven and Earth are drawn together**, and **the practitioner stands between them,** *as priest, scribe, and vessel*.

To craft an authentic amulet—**not a superstitious trinket, but a talismanic object aligned with Divine law and angelic order**—one must possess knowledge **not only of sigils**, but of **the names of angels**, of **planetary dominions**, and the **72-fold Name of God**, the **Shem HaMephorash**. This Name, derived from three verses in Exodus (14:19-21), conceals **seventy-two three-letter permutations**, each linked to **an angelic intelligence**, a **specific spiritual function**, and a **corresponding hour and element**. Without mastery of the **heavenly hierarchy**, without knowledge of which angel governs which sphere of influence—*whether healing, protection, revelation, wealth, fertility, or justice*—one cannot safely or effectively inscribe their name into matter. **Misalignment opens the door not to light, but to corruption**.

Even with correct identification of the angelic name, the **timing of the ritual** must be impeccable. The stars must be favorable. The planetary hour must resonate with the intended power. The practitioner must fast, purify, and prepare. The **material** of the amulet—*parchment, metal, clay, crystal*—must be chosen not arbitrarily but based on the nature of the desired influence. **Gold for solar radiance and glory, silver for lunar receptivity and intuition, iron for Mars and judgment, copper for Venus and desire.**

Each **elemental alignment**, each **Hebrew letter**, must be placed with intention. The **sigil** is not drawn—it is **invoked**. The object is not made—it is **born**.

And if you ask where such sacred work should occur, do not imagine your kitchen table or some random desk will suffice. The **laboratory of sigillation**, the space where the amulet is to be forged, **must itself reflect the architecture of Heaven**. The ancients knew this. They modeled the sacred space for divine operations after the **Temple of Solomon**, whose **geometric proportions mirrored the arrangement of the cosmos**. The inner sanctum (Kodesh haKodashim) served as the axis mundi, connecting the upper worlds and the human realm.

To create an amulet that carries true power, the practitioner must symbolically **rebuild the Temple within their working space**. The altar, the tools, the position of the elements, the ritual garments—even the incense—must mirror the **ritual purity and geometric order of the original Mikdash**. You are not drawing a sigil—you are **replaying Genesis**. Because every truly effective amulet **repeats the act of creation**. First, there is **Tohu vaVohu**—formless void, *the empty altar, the blank parchment, the silent copper plate*. Then, there is **light**: the practitioner speaks the name, breathes the intention, arranges the signs. Then comes **division**—of light and darkness, of pure and impure, of sacred and profane. Then **firmament**, as the name is inscribed into the material. Then **life**, as the sigil is sealed with prayer, breath, and invocation. Only then does the amulet live.

And beware—**if the Genesis is flawed**, if the **day of creation is rushed**, if the **angel's name is misspelled**, if the **ritual vessel is impure**, you are not creating an amulet. You are **unleashing confusion**. You are giving voice to spirits **that do not answer to God**.

This is why **most people should never attempt to make amulets**. It is not a matter of belief—it is a matter of order. **The same alphabet that creates also destroys**, and **the angel who guards can also accuse**, if called without reverence.

But for those few who are trained, disciplined, and pure in intention, the amulet becomes more than a tool—it becomes a **radiant shard of the Divine**, a **portable Temple**, a **voice of the Ineffable sealed in matter**. And through it, the practitioner does not command the world—they **harmonize with its sacred architecture**.

Temple

The **Temple of Solomon**, known in Hebrew as *Beit HaMikdash*, is not merely a building that once stood in Jerusalem—it is a **geometric crystallization of cosmic order**, a **mirror of the Divine Blueprint**, and the **ritual body of Adam Kadmon**, the primordial being. When you seek to recreate a sacred space for the creation of **Kabbalistic amulets**, you are not simply arranging furniture or choosing a quiet room—you are **restaging the structure of the universe**, compressing the **Tree of Life** into stone, wood, and intention.

The architecture of the Temple was never arbitrary. Every measurement, every orientation, every separation of space was a reflection of **higher worlds**, encoded in proportion and geometry. The outer courtyard, the inner court, the Holy, and the **Holy of Holies (Kodesh HaKodashim)**—these correspond to the **four Kabbalistic worlds**: *Assiyah*, *Yetzirah*, *Beriah*, and *Atzilut*, each one a rung of spiritual refinement. **To recreate a sacred altar**, you must walk backward through these worlds, returning from matter to spirit, *from shell to light*.

Your **ritual space**—whether in a dedicated room, a private chamber, or an outdoor sanctuary—must reflect this **quadripartite design**. At the outermost level, there should be a **boundary**—physical or symbolic—that marks the separation between mundane space and sacred interior. *This may be a curtain, a circle of stones, a frame of candles, or even a square drawn in chalk or salt.* Within this perimeter lies the **first court**, the space of preparation, where tools are purified, intentions declared, and the self is separated from impurity. It corresponds to **Assiyah**, the world of action.

Moving inward, your **working altar** must be placed at the center, but slightly towards the **east**. The **east** was the direction of the entrance to the Temple, the place of rising light, and it represents **Chesed**, the sefirah of mercy. The **west**, where the Holy of Holies was concealed, represents **Gevurah**, the hidden and awe-inspiring power of restriction and containment. As such, your orientation during the ritual must be towards the **west**, as if approaching the innermost chamber, the **face of the Shekhinah**.

The **altar** itself must be shaped to reflect the **sefirotic structure**. Ideally, it should be a **rectangle**, not a square—its proportions echo the *Golden Ratio*, and recall the **dimensions of the Ark of the Covenant**. The surface of the altar should be inscribed—*not necessarily visibly, but always consciously*—with the **Tree of Life**, the ten sefirot arranged in their three vertical pillars: the **Right Pillar of Mercy**, the **Left Pillar of Severity**, and the **Middle Pillar of Balance**. Each tool, each amulet component, each symbol or sigil should be **placed on the altar corresponding to its sefirah**.

For example:

- A **golden plate** inscribed with angelic names for healing might rest in the **Netzach** position (Victory, enduring power).

- A **silver chalice** for collecting ritual waters may be positioned in **Yesod** (Foundation, channel).

- Incense burners may stand in **Tiferet** (Beauty, harmony), rising to unify the higher and lower worlds.

Behind the altar, as in the Temple, there should be a **curtain or veil**—this is the **Parochet**, separating the Holy from the Holy of Holies. If you work alone, this can be symbolic: a fabric behind your altar, or even a shadow cast by candlelight. But always let it serve as a reminder that **behind the visible, the invisible waits**.

The **Holy of Holies**, in your recreated space, is the point at which **Divine Intelligence** touches matter. It may be a space behind the altar, or a sealed vessel containing the **Shem HaMephorash**, or the Name YHVH written only once and never spoken. No one, not even the High Priest, entered this place except once a year—so too in your practice, this space should remain untouched except during **the moment of sigillation**, where intention, name, geometry, and Divine Will meet.

The **geometry of the Temple**, much like the **skeleton of Adam Kadmon**, follows sacred proportion. The **pillar layout of the sefirot** mirrors the human form: *Keter as the crown of the head, Chokhmah and Binah as the hemispheres of the brain, Chesed and Gevurah as the right and left arms, Tiferet as the heart and spine, Netzach and Hod as the legs, Yesod as* *the reproductive center, and Malkhut as the feet or Earth.* When you **walk into your sacred space**, you are entering **the body of the Divine**, and when you perform ritual within it, you are **moving through the limbs and organs of a cosmic intelligence**.

Every **opening**, every **window**, every **threshold** should follow this order. If possible, place an entrance on the **east** and an exit or symbolic veil to the **west**. Light should come from above, *as in the Temple, where the windows were narrower on the inside than outside, allowing light to radiate outward rather than in.* This design reflects the Kabbalistic truth that **light is meant to be given, not hoarded**.

And as you stand in the center of this micro-Temple, this **compressed diagram of Heaven**, know this: you are not performing a spell. You are **replicating creation**, whispering the Names that once shaped galaxies, and breathing **Divine fire into form**. Every gesture, every placement, every breath must follow this invisible architecture. *If you forget the Tree, the ritual dies. But if you remember the Tree, it will live through your hands.*

Sacred robes

When one steps into the sacred act of **creating Kabbalistic amulets**, they are not merely crafting an object—they are **channeling Divine Names into matter**, fusing celestial archetypes with earthly vessels. This process, by its very nature, demands **ritual purity, discipline, and sacred attire**. One does not approach the altar in everyday garments. Just as the High Priest in the Temple wore distinct and holy vestments when entering the Holy of Holies, so too must the practitioner cloak themselves in symbols that resonate with the **higher sefirotic energies** and the **power of the tribes of Israel**.

Foremost among these vestments is the **Choshen**, the sacred **breastplate**, worn over the heart. This garment is not decorative; it is a **magical interface** between the human soul and the Divine Will. It is designed to awaken the inner archetype of the **Urim and Thummim**, the lights and perfections, through which revelation once flowed. Each **stone on the Choshen** corresponds to one of the **twelve tribes of Israel**, one of the **months of the sacred calendar**, one of the **signs of the Zodiac**, and more deeply, one of the **paths between the sefirot**. To wear this breastplate consciously is to bind the **power of the entire Tree of Life** onto your chest.

The **Choshen** is traditionally a square, folded double, with **twelve stones set in four rows** of three. The materials of the garment are no less critical: blue, purple, and scarlet threads woven into fine linen, mirroring the fabric of the **Parochet**, the Temple veil. On this square rest the twelve stones, each engraved with the name of a tribe. The order of stones varies depending on the tradition, but their **Kabbalistic significance remains fixed**, anchoring Divine forces into the physical plane.

Let us now explore the **Kabbalistic meaning of each stone**, not as lifeless minerals, but as **spiritual matrices**, each a gate of influence:

1. Odem (Ruby / Carnelian) – *Reuben*
The red stone of blood and fire, **Gevurah**, represents **impulse, passion, and repentance**. It carries the **force of Mars**, initiating and dangerous when unrefined. It activates raw will and exposes hidden desires.

2. Pitdah (Topaz) – *Simeon*
A golden glow that channels **Chesed**, yet refines the emotional turbulence of the soul. **Mercurial in nature**, this stone governs eloquence and persuasion, but also warns against envy and jealousy.

3. Bareket (Emerald) – *Levi*
A deep green gem, sacred to **Yesod**, the foundation. It embodies **memory, lineage, and the binding thread of generations**. Levi, the priestly tribe, carries responsibility for spiritual continuity. This stone is tied to dreamwork and angelic communication.

4. Nofekh (Turquoise / Carbuncle) – *Judah*
A stone of **kingship, leadership, and confession**. Related to **Tiferet**, it mediates between Chesed and Gevurah. Worn by the lion-hearted, it stabilizes identity and charisma. Judah's stone anchors **divine rulership on Earth**.

5. Sapir (Sapphire) – *Issachar*
Linked with **Chokhmah**, the supernal wisdom, and the clarity of the sky. This blue gem symbolizes **study, learning, and cosmic order**. The

tribe of Issachar is known for understanding times and seasons. It aligns with **Saturn** and the discipline of thought.

6. Yahalom (Diamond / Onyx) – *Zebulun*
A stone of **commerce, navigation, and divine protection**. It resonates with **Netzach**, the power to endure and succeed. Its complex, unbreakable nature symbolizes **truth and covenant**.

7. Leshem (Opal / Jacinth) – *Dan*
A mutable and iridescent stone, channeling **Hod**, the sefirah of form, structure, and sacred judgment. Dan, the judge of Israel, wears the stone of illusions and clarity, depending on the purity of the wearer.

8. Shevo (Agate) – *Naphtali*
This is the stone of **freedom, movement, and expression**. Naphtali was a swift deer, a messenger. The stone is connected to **Yesod** and serves those who walk between worlds—travelers, seers, and dancers.

9. Ahlamah (Amethyst) – *Gad*
A protective purple stone linked to **Keter**, it aids in **battle, spiritual warfare, and prophetic vision**. Gad was a warrior tribe, and this stone absorbs toxicity while magnifying inner strength.

10. Tarshish (Beryl / Aquamarine) – *Asher*
The shining of the sea and the abundance. This stone aligns with **Binah**, the great mother. Asher was a tribe of prosperity and taste. It carries the joy of **blessings and fertility**, a gateway to the feminine divine.

11. Shoham (Onyx / Lapis) – *Joseph*
The dreamer's stone is associated with **Yesod** and **Da'at**, the invisible sefirah of mystical knowledge. Joseph's stone is one of mystery, concealment, and revelation. It governs dreams, visions, and the transformation of pain into light.

12. Yashfeh (Jasper) – *Benjamin*
A stone of innocence, protection, and war. Benjamin, the youngest, carried both the sweetness of childhood and the ferocity of a wolf. This stone governs transitions and spiritual resurrection. It is often tied to **Malkhut**, the earthly sefirah.

Each of these stones must be **set in gold**, the symbol of **refined consciousness and divine light**, and inscribed with intention and sacred names. When you wear the Choshen during your amulet rituals, you are not merely donning jewelry—you are becoming **a conduit of the Twelve Tribes, the Twelve Constellations, the Twelve Portals of the Year**.

One must wear this vestment over the heart, the throne of **Tiferet**, and approach the altar with awe. The stones, activated through **sacred names, meditative focus**, and **proper timing**, vibrate at frequencies that open inner gates. But remember: *the rocks do not serve you—you serve the light that flows through them*. Without spiritual discipline and alignment with the **sefirotic energies**, the stones will remain mute. But with proper alignment, they will speak. And they will **illuminate the amulet**, the space, and the soul of the one who dares to create it.

The act of creation

In the sacred tradition of Kabbalah, the act of magical creation is not merely an echo of Divine Will—it is its mirror. The creation of an amulet, when done correctly, is not the assembly of materials or the carving of names, but a profound reenactment of the **Sefer Bereshit**, the Book of Genesis. Each phase of the process must align with the **seven days of Creation**, not just symbolically but **energetically, intellectually**, and **spiritually**. To bypass this pattern is to build a vessel without soul, a form without light.

"Bereshit bara Elohim et haShamayim ve'et haAretz" — "In the beginning, God created the heavens and the earth." This is not just the start of the world. It is the eternal blueprint for all acts of actual creation. To form an amulet is to **imitate the Elohim**, to divide chaos, name the forces, arrange the Sephirot, and breathe life into clay.

Day One – Light from Darkness

"Let there be light." *Yehi or*. This is the first spark, the **Keter**, the undifferentiated will to create. In amulet work, this corresponds to the **intent**—the raw, silent, and formless force that initiates the act. The practitioner must sit in **meditative darkness** before the act begins, until the purpose becomes luminous. The **light** here is not physical. It is

conscious awareness. *What are you creating? Why? For whom?* Until you see that light, you must not act.

Day Two – Division of Waters
God divides the waters above and below. This is the sefirah of **Binah, discernment**. It is the day of separation, of defining boundaries. In magical creation, this is where **you divide the forces**: sacred from profane, useful from dangerous. You **select materials, determine planetary hours**, and **banish distractions**. *Chaos must be parted.* Without this division, the light of Day One floods everything and destroys rather than builds.

Day Three – Dry Land and Vegetation
Here, **structure emerges**. Earth rises. Forms appear. This is **Malkhut**, and also **Tiferet**, where balance begins. In the creation of an amulet, this is the moment when the **base is prepared**: the metal is cut, the parchment chosen, the stone washed, the ink ground. Like the earth bringing forth seed, your materials must now **contain the intent** from Day One and be **ordered** by the separation of Day Two. Each item is chosen **not for beauty, but correspondence**—*What angels govern this stone? What tribes align with this plant?*

Day Four – Lights in the Heavens
Sun, moon, and stars are set to govern time. This is the sefirah of **Netzach** and **Hod**—**timing and form**. *This is the most ignored day by false magicians.* Here you must choose **the precise moment** for engraving or activation. The planetary hour. The astrological condition. The lunar phase. The placement of symbols must follow a cosmic order, not a personal mood. As God placed the greater and lesser lights to rule day and night, you must assign spiritual governors to every aspect of your creation. If Day Four is done incorrectly, the amulet may be beautiful, but it will be powerless.

Day Five – Living Beings in the Waters and Air
Here, the world is animated with movement, spirit, and **voice**. In amulet work, this is the act of **inscription** and **naming**. The letters—*not random, not decorative*—must be placed with **intent, breath, and internal alignment**. This is when the Names of God, angels, or the soul's purpose are written onto the material. One must speak the

names as they are inscribed, as if **calling spirits from the deep**. This is also the stage where the **sigil may be sealed**, if one is used. The breath of the magician becomes the breath of creation.

Day Six – Creation of the Human
This is the culmination: **Adam** is formed from dust and Divine Breath. It is not yet the day of rest. It is the **day of embodiment**. The amulet, like Adam, must now be **anointed, activated,** and **brought into form**. You may breathe over it, immerse it in sacred oils, pass it through fire, or place it beneath the moon. But you must know: *this is the day the soul meets the body*. All the steps before were rehearsal. This is a **manifestation**.

Day Seven – Rest, Sanctification, Separation
Shabbat. Completion. Stillness. This is **the sealing** of the work. No inscription is made. No words are spoken. The amulet must **sit alone**, in darkness or candlelight, in a sacred cloth or upon the altar, and be **left to absorb the Divine silence**. Like the universe on Shabbat, it is no longer being created — it simply **is**. You must step away. You must *cease*.

Each of the seven days is a **spiritual law**, not a suggestion. They govern every successful act of magical creation. To rush them is to **abort the soul** of the amulet. To skip one is to build a house without walls.

Thus, the true Kabbalist builds not only an object, but a world.

Conclusion

BEYOND THE VEIL
— ★ —

We have reached the final words of this book, but in the realm of **Kabbalah**, there is no true ending. What you have discovered here is not a conclusion, but an **initiation**. A beginning. A doorway into a much larger, deeper universe that stretches beyond the seen, beyond the spoken, into the **infinite layers of reality**.

You now hold a foundational understanding of **Kabbalistic wisdom**, but remember: **the Tree of Life continues to unfold** the more you walk its path. The truths you've touched are only the surface of something much greater. **Every sefira, every Hebrew letter, every sacred name** opens a new gate—into the soul, into the cosmos, into the very structure of divine thought made manifest.

Kabbalah is not a philosophy to be read and set aside. It is a **living current**, a way of perceiving and reshaping reality. As you deepen your practice, you will begin to feel the shift—your thoughts, reactions, desires, and even your perception of time and causality will start to change. You will no longer see yourself as a passive observer of a chaotic world. You will recognize yourself as a **participant in Divine orchestration**, a co-creator, a mirror of the Infinite.

Many who follow the Kabbalistic path find that **inner peace, clarity, and purpose** return to them in ways they never imagined. The noise of the world fades into the background, and what remains is the **voice of the Divine**—not as thunder, but as a whisper inside your soul. You begin to notice the signs. The synchronicities. The unseen hand that guides you with subtle precision. *Even when everything seems to fall apart on the outside, you feel something deeper unfolding within. That is the light of Kabbalah taking root.*

By continuing your studies, you will discover how **to harness your desires**, not to destroy them or suppress them, but to **elevate them** — to transform each longing into a **vessel for spiritual light**, in alignment with what is called **"intention to bestow"**. You begin to crave not just for yourself, but for the good of all. You become a channel for divine flow.

In a world driven by confusion and consequence, where so many forget where they came from and where they are going, **Kabbalah offers a map** not just of the stars or the soul, but of the bridge between them. It shows you how to draw from the upper worlds and manifest what is needed below. You will learn to feel the flow of energy through the sefirot, to interpret the patterns that once felt like chaos, and to stand aligned with the **Divine Will**.

Most importantly, you will come to understand that **you are never alone**. Though the illusion of separation dominates our reality, causing conflict, fear, loneliness, and endless pursuit, Kabbalah reveals that *all is One*. Every soul, every breath, every spark of consciousness is **part of a greater Unity**. We are all threads in the same cosmic tapestry. Once you integrate this into your daily practice, something radical happens: **you begin to live for others** as if they are part of you — because they are.

You will no longer speak, think, or act without understanding their ripples in the fabric of reality. You will begin to refine your life, not just for your evolution, but for the evolution of all creation. This is the true meaning of **Tikkun Olam** — the restoration of the world, **one soul, one act, one intention at a time**.

The study you have begun here is just the first gate. There are many more sacred texts to unlock, many more **esoteric techniques**, many more divine names to contemplate. Every letter of the Hebrew alphabet, every configuration of the Tree, every hidden verse in Torah contains **infinite revelation**. And this path never ends.

At Templum Dianae, we continue to gather, translate, and share these teachings—**not to preserve them in books**, but to **ignite transformation** in those who are ready. You will find on the website free articles, meditations, and advanced materials to help you take the following steps. But theory is not enough. **Practice is the gate. Discipline is the key.**

Kabbalah is not a hobby. It is not a trend. It is a sacred science, a divine art, and a path of **initiation** that requires your whole being. The secrets will not yield themselves to the casual seeker. But to the committed one? They will pour forth like living water.

This book ends. But your journey does not.
You now stand at the threshold of something vast and eternal.
The only question that remains is: **Will you walk deeper?**

Discover more at Templum Dianae. The path of Kabbalah awaits you.

Another book from Templum Dianae for you

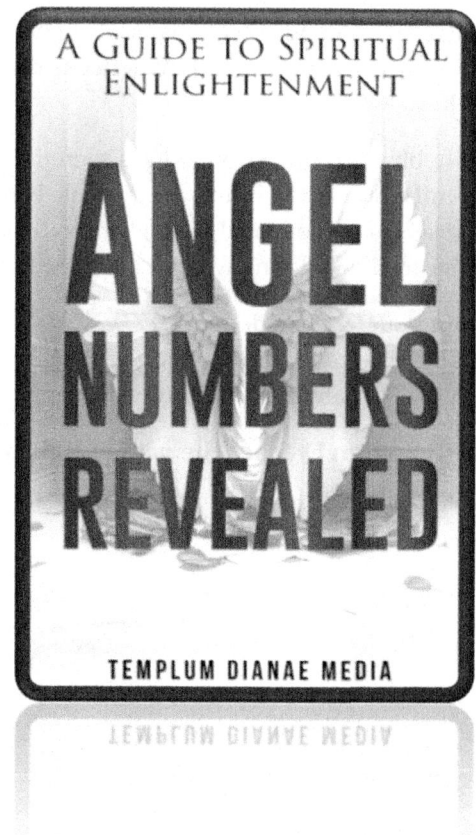

https://www.amazon.com/Angel-Numbers-Revealed-Enlightenment-Numerology/dp/B0CCCPVF27

the book of testimony

What other Seekers saying about Templum Dianae Books.
(in all languages)

 Marruskaa

★★★★★ **Bella scoperta**
Recensito in Italia il 12 agosto 2024

Il testo è scritto in modo chiaro e scorrevole, perfetto per principianti! Quando mi sono avvicinata a questo tipo di mondo all'inizio non avevo ben capito cosa fossero e a cosa servissero. Tuttavia, il loro fascino mi ha spinto a continuare cercare di capire, finché non ho trovato questo libro. Ora tengo questo tomo sempre sul mio comodino e non posso più farne a meno! Davvero consigliato!

 Jamie L.

★★★★★ **Learn about powerful archetypes and how to use them for yourself!**
Reviewed in the United States on October 12, 2024
Verified Purchase

This book gives a comprehensive overview of dark goddesses from different times and regions-- Egyptian, Slavic, Roman, Greek, etc.

It gives enough information about each that you can feel into which one speaks to you at different times in your life.

I've often heard people talk about "working with" goddesses or goddess energies and I had no idea what that meant or how to do it! This book provides different ways to do this--like specific rituals or practices (and there's even a guided meditation with a link to an MP3 file included!) so you can not only learn about the goddesses but also start to incorporate different practices to begin working with them for your own personal transformation.

 Rose Anderson

★★★★★ **Beautifully written and immensely powerful**
Reviewed in the United States on October 8, 2024
Verified Purchase

What a wonderful gift for any modern-day witch or pagan—and everyone else, too.

The first part of "Wicca Lunar Calendar—2025" offers insight for living in these times, self-care, and even wisdom of the cosmos—for a start. It then goes through every month of 2025 in almanac style, with the cycles of the moon, the holidays, and more. There's also a glossary at the end.

It's beautifully written and immensely powerful.

dorawatson96

★★★★★ nützlich für diejenigen, die sich Wicca nähern
Bewertet in Deutschland am 1. Oktober 2024

Ich habe mich dieser Welt im letzten Jahr genähert und habe diesen Kalender in meiner Bibliothek. Ich finde ihn sehr nützlich als Unterstützung auf diesem Weg, den ich eingeschlagen habe

Narnya

★★★★★ Sehr interessant
Bewertet in Deutschland am 12. Oktober 2024
Verifizierter Kauf

Endlich eine gute Beschreibung über Samhain. Zur Erinnerung.
Ich werde das Buch weiter meinen Kindern auch empfehlen.
Vielle Dank ☆

Geneviève

★★★★★ Très intéressant
Avis laissé au Canada le 1 mars 2024
Achat vérifié

Grand calendrier lunaire, très complet et beaucoup d'explications intéressantes. Parfait pour associer au livre de wicca magie blanche.

Steven H.

★★★★★ Una Guía Completa de la Numerología Antigua y los Números Angelicales
Reviewed in the United States on August 1, 2024

"La Numerologia degli Antichi - Numerologia Caldea e Numeri Angelici" es una compilación excepcional para cualquiera fascinado por el mundo místico de los números. Este paquete 3 en 1 cubre los detalles intrincados de la numerología, el significado de los números angelicales y los sistemas de numerología antigua, ofreciendo una exploración completa y atractiva de estos temas.

El autor proporciona tablas, cálculos y explicaciones claras y detalladas, haciendo que los conceptos complejos sean accesibles tanto para principiantes como para entusiastas experimentados de la numerología. Cada sección está bien estructurada, permitiendo a los lectores seguir fácilmente y aplicar el conocimiento a sus propias vidas.

Ana J

★★★★★ La Influencia de la Luna
Reseñado en Estados Unidos el 8 de septiembre de 2024
Compra verificada

Este libro trata de las fases de la luna a la vida moderna, cubriendo todo, desde las rutinas de belleza hasta la jardinería. Al crecer, a menudo escuchaba a los mayores hablar sobre cómo la luna influía en la agricultura y los animales, y este libro refleja esas tradiciones. Las secciones de las fases lunares ofrecen informacion sobre cómo aprovechar la energía lunar para tener resultados óptimos en la jardinería y de belleza. Es una guia interesante para quienes buscan alinear muchas de sus rutinas con la naturaleza.

Sarah Barry

★★★★☆ **Practical exercises**
Reviewed in the United States on September 30, 2024
Verified Purchase

"Twin Flames: Love Yourself and Manifest Ultimate Love" provides practical exercises for healing emotional blocks and attracting love through the Law of Attraction. Worth reading for those seeking self-love and deeper connections.

 Daphne H

★★★★☆ **Muy bueno!**
Reseñado en Australia el 15 de septiembre de 2024
Compra verificada

Cuidar el jardín a través de los movimientos de la luna es una idea genial, ya que en la naturaleza todo está conectado y sin duda los ciclos lunares pueden influir tanto positiva como negativamente. El libro incluye un montón de tips de los cuáles tomé nota.

 Regina Stone

★★★★☆ **Always been curious...**
Recensito negli Stati Uniti il 28 settembre 2024
Acquisto verificato

I'll be honest: I'm not sure I am the intended audience for this book.

I've never been a firm believer in astrology, but my lifelong curiosity drew me to "Moon Calendar 2025."
It was a fascinating read overall, very interesting even if not 100% convincing to my cynical nature.

I would have given it 5 stars but I did find the book a little too sophisticated a launching point for readers new to astrology. However, if this is not an introduction for you - and you are a believer - then I think you will find value in these pages.

contents included

Congratulations on receiving this book!
If you want to attract and manifest more Love and Abundance and discover topics and spirituality, join the Templum Dianae community and receive guided meditation MP3s to awaken your inner self.

This guided meditation is designed to manifest your inner dream in daily life.

templumdianae.com/en/bookmp3/

Bibliographical references
and recommended readings

- **Esoteric Numerology** – *Templum Dianae Media*
- **Revealed Angels and Numbers** – *Templum Dianae Media*
- **Chaldean Numerology** – *Templum Dianae Media*
- **Sefer Yetzirah**
- **Sefer ha-Bahir**
- **Zohar**
- **The Kabbalah Unveiled** – S. L. MacGregor Mathers
- **The Tree of Life** – Israel Regardie
- **Three Books of Occult Philosophy** – Heinrich Cornelius Agrippa
- **Corpus Hermeticum** – translated by G.R.S. Mead
- **The Kybalion** – Three Initiates
- **Magick in Theory and Practice** – Aleister Crowley
- **777 and Other Qabalistic Writings** – Aleister Crowley
- **The Book of Thoth** – Aleister Crowley

All rights reserved. No part of this book may be reproduced in any form without the written permission of the copyright owners. All images in this book have been reproduced with the knowledge and prior consent of the artists concerned, and the producer, publisher, or printer accepts no responsibility for any infringement of copyright or otherwise, resulting from the contents of this publication. Every effort has been made to ensure that the credits accurately conform to the information provided. We apologize for any inaccuracies and will correct inaccurate or missing information in a subsequent reprint of the book.

Text © 2025 Templum Dianae Media

Printed in Dunstable, United Kingdom